QUEEN VICTORIA

QUEEN VICTORIA

BY

LYTTON STRACHEY

NEW YORK

HARCOURT, BRACE AND COMPANY

TO
VIRGINIA WOOLF

CONTENTS

ILLUSTRATIONS

Authority for every important statement of fact in the following pages will be found in the footnotes. The full titles of the works to which reference is made are given in the Bibliography at the end of the volume.

The author is indebted to the Trustees of the British Museum for their permission to make use of certain unpublished passages in the manuscript of the Greville Memoirs.

QUEEN VICTORIA

CHAPTER I

ANTECEDENTS

I

On November 6, 1817, died the Princess Charlotte, only child of the Prince Regent, and heir to the crown of England. Her short life had hardly been a happy one. By nature impulsive, capricious, and vehement, she had always longed for liberty; and she had never possessed it. She had been brought up among violent family quarrels, had been early separated from her disreputable and eccentric mother, and handed over to the care of her disreputable and selfish father. When she was seventeen, he decided to marry her off to the Prince of Orange; she, at first, acquiesced; but, suddenly falling in love with Prince Augustus of Prussia, she determined to break off the engagement. This was not her first love affair, for she had previously carried on a clandestine correspondence with a Captain Hess. Prince

Augustus was already married, morganatically, but she did not know it, and he did not tell her. While she was spinning out the negotiations with the Prince of Orange, the allied sovereigns—it was June, 1814—arrived in London to celebrate their victory. Among them, in the suite of the Emperor of Russia, was the young and handsome Prince Leopold of Saxe-Coburg. He made several attempts to attract the notice of the Princess, but she, with her heart elsewhere, paid very little attention. Next month the Prince Regent, discovering that his daughter was having secret meetings with Prince Augustus, suddenly appeared upon the scene and, after dismissing her household, sentenced her to a strict seclusion in Windsor Park. "God Almighty grant me patience!" she exclaimed, falling on her knees in an agony of agitation: then she jumped up, ran down the backstairs and out into the street, hailed a passing cab, and drove to her mother's house in Bayswater. She was discovered, pursued, and at length, yielding to the persuasions of her uncles, the Dukes of York and Sussex, of Brougham, and of the Bishop of Salisbury, she returned to Carlton House at two o'clock in the morning. She was immured at Windsor, but no more was heard of the Prince of Orange. Prince Augustus, too, disappeared. The way was at last open to Prince Leopold of Saxe-Coburg.[1]

This Prince was clever enough to get round the Regent, to impress the Ministers, and to make friends with another of the Princess's uncles, the Duke of Kent. Through the Duke he was able to communicate privately with the Princess, who now declared that he was necessary to her happiness. When, after Waterloo, he was in Paris, the Duke's aide-de-camp carried letters backwards and forwards across the Channel. In January 1816 he was invited to England, and in May the marriage took place.[2]

The character of Prince Leopold contrasted strangely with that of his wife. The younger son of a German princeling, he was at this time twenty-six years of age; he had served with distinction in the war against Napoleon; he had shown considerable diplomatic skill at the Congress of Vienna;[3] and he was now to try his hand at the task of taming a tumultuous Princess. Cold and formal in manner, collected in speech, careful in action, he soon dominated the wild, impetuous, generous creature by his side. There

[1] Greville, II, 326–8; Stockmar, chap. i, 86; Knight, I, chaps. xv–xviii and Appendix, and II, chap. i.
[2] Grey, 384, 386–8; *Letters*, II, 40.
[3] Grey. 375–86.

was much in her, he found, of which he could
not approve. She quizzed, she stamped, she
roared with laughter; she had very little of that
self-command which is especially required of
princes; her manners were abominable. Of the
latter he was a good judge, having moved, as
he himself explained to his niece many years
later, in the best society of Europe, being in fact
" what is called in French *de la fleur des pois.*"
There was continual friction, but every scene
ended in the same way. Standing before him
like a rebellious boy in petticoats, her body pushed
forward, her hands behind her back, with flaming
cheeks and sparkling eyes, she would declare at
last that she was ready to do whatever he wanted.
" If you wish it, I will do it," she would say. " I
want nothing for myself," he invariably answered;
" when I press something on you, it is from a
conviction that it is for your interest and for
your good." [1]

Among the members of the household at Claremont, near Esher, where the royal pair were
established, was a young German physician, Christian Friedrich Stockmar. He was the son of
a minor magistrate in Coburg, and, after taking
part as a medical officer in the war, he had settled

---

[1] *Letters,* I, 216, 222–3; II, 39–40; Stockmar, 87–90.

down as a doctor in his native town. Here he
had met Prince Leopold, who had been struck
by his ability, and, on, his marriage, brought him
to England as his personal physician. A curious
fate awaited this young man; many were the gifts
which the future held in store for him—many
and various—influence, power, mystery, unhappi-
ness, a broken heart. At Claremont his position
was a very humble one; but the Princess took
a fancy to him, called him " Stocky," and romped
with him along the corridors. Dyspeptic by constitution, melancholic by temperament, he could
yet be lively on occasion, and was known as a
wit in Coburg. He was virtuous, too, and observed the royal *ménage* with approbation. " My
master," he wrote in his diary, " is the best of all
husbands in all the five quarters of the globe;
and his wife bears him an amount of love, the
greatness of which can only be compared with the
English national debt." Before long he gave
proof of another quality—a quality which was to
colour the whole of his life—cautious sagacity.
When, in the spring of 1817, it was known that
the Princess was expecting a child, the post of
one of her physicians-in-ordinary was offered to
him, and he had the good sense to refuse it. He
perceived that his colleagues would be jealous of

him, that his advice would probably not be taken, but that, if anything were to go wrong, it would be certainly the foreign doctor who would be blamed. Very soon, indeed, he came to the opinion that the low diet and constant bleedings, to which the unfortunate Princess was subjected, were an error; he drew the Prince aside, and begged him to communicate this opinion to the English doctors; but it was useless. The fashionable lowering treatment was continued for months. On November 5, at nine o'clock in the evening, after a labour of over fifty hours, the Princess was delivered of a dead boy. At midnight her exhausted strength gave way. Then, at last, Stockmar consented to see her; he went in, and found her obviously dying, while the doctors were plying her with wine. She seized his hand and pressed it. " They have made me tipsy," she said. After a little he left her, and was already in the next room when he heard her call out in her loud voice: " Stocky! Stocky! " As he ran back the death-rattle was in her throat. She tossed herself violently from side to side; then suddenly drew up her legs, and it was over.

The Prince, after hours of watching, had left the room for a few moments' rest; and Stockmar had now to tell him that his wife was dead.

At first he could not be made to realise what had happened. On their way to her room he sank down on a chair while Stockmar knelt beside him: it was all a dream; it was impossible. At last, by the bed, he, too, knelt down and kissed the cold hands. Then rising and exclaiming, "Now I am quite desolate. Promise me never to leave me," he threw himself into Stockmar's arms.[1]

II

The tragedy at Claremont was of a most upsetting kind. The royal kaleidoscope had suddenly shifted, and nobody could tell how the new pattern would arrange itself. The succession to the throne, which had seemed so satisfactorily settled, now became a matter of urgent doubt.

George III was still living, an aged lunatic, at Windsor, completely impervious to the impressions of the outer world. Of his seven sons, the youngest was of more than middle age, and none had legitimate offspring. The outlook, therefore, was ambiguous. It seemed highly improbable that the Prince Regent, who had lately been obliged to abandon his stays, and presented a preposterous figure of debauched

---

[1] Stockmar, *Biographische Skizze,* and cap. iii.

obesity,[1] could ever again, even on the suppo-
sition that he divorced his wife and re-married,
become the father of a family. Besides the Duke
of Kent, who must be noticed separately, the
other brothers, in order of seniority, were the
Dukes of York, Clarence, Cumberland, Sussex,
and Cambridge; their situations and prospects
require a brief description. The Duke of York,
whose escapades in times past with Mrs. Clarke
and the army had brought him into trouble, now
divided his life between London and a large,
extravagantly ordered and extremely uncomfort-
able country house where he occupied himself
with racing, whist, and improper stories. He was
remarkable among the princes for one reason:
he was the only one of them—so we are informed
by a highly competent observer—who had the
feelings of a gentleman. He had been long
married to the Princess Royal of Prussia, a lady
who rarely went to bed and was perpetually surrounded by vast numbers of dogs, parrots, and
monkeys.[2] They had no children. The Duke
of Clarence had lived for many years in complete
obscurity with Mrs. Jordan, the actress, in Bushey
Park. By her he had had a large family of sons

---

[1] Creevey, I, 264, 272: "Prinny has let loose his belly, which now
reaches his knees; otherwise he is said to be well," 279.
[2] Greville, I, 5–7.

and daughters, and had appeared, in effect, to be married to her, when he suddenly separated from her and offered to marry Miss Wykeham, a crazy woman of large fortune, who, however, would have nothing to say to him. Shortly afterwards Mrs. Jordan died in distressed circumstances in Paris.[1] The Duke of Cumberland was probably the most unpopular man in England. Hideously ugly, with a distorted eye, he was bad-tempered and vindictive in private, a violent reactionary in politics, and was subsequently suspected of murdering his valet and of having carried on an amorous intrigue of an extremely scandalous kind.[2] He had lately married a German Princess, but there were as yet no children by the marriage. The Duke of Sussex had mildly literary tastes and collected books.[3] He had married Lady Augusta Murray, by whom he had two children, but the marriage, under the Royal Marriages Act, was declared void. On Lady Augusta's death, he married Lady Cecilia Buggin; she changed her name to Underwood; but this marriage also was void. Of the Duke of Cambridge, the youngest of the brothers, not very much was known. He lived

[1] Greville, IV, 2.
[2] Stockmar, 95; Creevey, I, 148; Greville, I, 228; Lieven, 183-4.
[3] Crawford, 24.

in Hanover, wore a blonde wig, chattered and fidgeted a great deal, and was unmarried.[1]

Besides his seven sons, George III had five surviving daughters. Of these, two—the Queen of Würtemberg and the Duchess of Gloucester— were married and childless. The three unmarried princesses—Augusta, Elizabeth, and Sophia— were all over forty.

III

The fourth son of George III was Edward, Duke of Kent. He was now fifty years of age— a tall, stout, vigorous man, highly-coloured, with bushy eyebrows, a bald top to his head, and what hair he had carefully dyed a glossy black. His dress was extremely neat, and in his whole appearance there was a rigidity which did not belie his character. He had spent his early life in the army—at Gibraltar, in Canada, in the West Indies—and, under the influence of military training, had become at first a disciplinarian and at last a martinet. In 1802, having been sent to Gibraltar to restore order in a mutinous garrison, he was recalled for undue severity, and his active career had come to an end. Since then he had spent his life regulating his domestic arrange-

[1] Crawford, 80, 118.

ments with great exactitude, busying himself with the affairs of his numerous dependents, designing clocks, and struggling to restore order to his finances, for, in spite of his being, as some one said who knew him well "*reglé comme du papier à musique,*" and in spite of an income of £24,000 a year, he was hopelessly in debt. He had quarrelled with most of his brothers, particularly with the Prince Regent, and it was only natural that he should have joined the political Opposition and become a pillar of the Whigs.

What his political opinions may actually have been is open to doubt; it has often been asserted that he was a Liberal, or even a Radical; and, if we are to believe Robert Owen, he was a necessitarian Socialist. His relations with Owen— the shrewd, gullible, high-minded, wrong-headed, illustrious and preposterous father of Socialism and Co-operation—were curious and characteristic. He talked of visiting the Mills at New Lanark; he did, in fact, preside at one of Owen's public meetings; he corresponded with him on confidential terms, and he even (so Owen assures us) returned, after his death, from "the sphere of spirits" to give encouragement to the Owenites on earth. "In an especial manner," says Owen, "I have to name the very anxious feelings of the

spirit of his Royal Highness the late Duke of
Kent (who early informed me there were no
titles in the spiritual spheres into which he had
entered), to benefit, not a class, a sect, a party,
or any particular country, but the whole of the human race through futurity." "His whole spirit-
proceeding with me has been most beautiful,"
Owen adds, "making his own appointments; and
never in one instance has this spirit not been
punctual to the minute he had named." But Owen
was of a sanguine temperament. He also num-
bered among his proselytes President Jefferson,
Prince Metternich, and Napoleon; so that some
uncertainty must still linger over the Duke of
Kent's views. But there is no uncertainty about
another circumstance: his Royal Highness borrowed from Robert Owen, on various occasions,
various sums of money which were never repaid
and amounted in all to several hundred pounds.[1]

After the death of the Princess Charlotte it
was clearly important, for more than one reason,
that the Duke of Kent should marry. From the
point of view of the nation, the lack of heirs in
the reigning family seemed to make the step
almost obligatory; it was also likely to be highly

[1] Stockmar, 112–3; *Letters,* I, 8; Crawford, 27–30; Owen, 193–4,
197–8, 199, 229.

expedient from the point of view of the Duke.
To marry as a public duty, for the sake of the royal
succession, would surely deserve some recognition
from a grateful country. When the Duke of
York had married he had received a settlement
of £25,000 a year. Why should not the Duke
of Kent look forward to an equal sum? But
the situation was not quite simple. There was
the Duke of Clarence to be considered; he was
the elder brother, and, if *he* married, would clearly
have the prior claim. On the other hand, if the
Duke of Kent married, it was important to
remember that he would be making a serious sacrifice: a lady was involved.

The Duke, reflecting upon all these matters
with careful attention, happened, about a month
after his niece's death, to visit Brussels, and
learnt that Mr. Creevey was staying in the town.
Mr. Creevey was a close friend of the leading
Whigs and an inveterate gossip; and it occurred
to the Duke that there could be no better channel
through which to communicate his views upon
the situation to political circles at home. Apparently it did not occur to him that Mr. Creevey
was malicious and might keep a diary. He
therefore sent for him on some trivial pretext,
and a remarkable conversation ensued.

After referring to the death of the Princess, to the improbability of the Regent's seeking a divorce, to the childlessness of the Duke of York, and to the possibility of the Duke of Clarence marrying, the Duke adverted to his own position. " Should the Duke of Clarence not marry," he said, " the next prince in succession is myself, and although I trust I shall be at all times ready to obey any call my country may make upon me, God only knows the sacrifice it will be to make, whenever I shall think it my duty to become a married man. It is now seven-and twenty years that Madame St. Laurent and I have lived together: we are of the same age, and have been in all climates, and in all difficulties together, and you may well imagine, Mr. Creevey, the pang it will occasion me to part with her. I put it to your own feelings—in the event of any separation between you and Mrs. Creevey. . . . As for Madame St. Laurent herself, I protest I don't know what is to become of her if a marriage is to be forced upon me; her feelings are already so agitated upon the subject." The Duke went on to describe how, one morning, a day or two after the Princess Charlotte's death, a paragraph had appeared in the *Morning Chronicle,* alluding to the possibility of his marriage. He had received the newspaper at breakfast together with his letters, and " I did as is my constant practice, I threw the newspaper across the table to Madame St. Laurent, and began to open and read my letters. I had not done so but a very short time, when my attention was called to an extraordinary noise and a strong convulsive movement in Madame St. Laurent's throat. For a short time I entertained serious apprehensions for her safety; and when, upon her recovery, I enquired into the occasion of this attack, she pointed to the article in the *Morning Chronicle*."

The Duke then returned to the subject of the Duke of Clarence. " My brother the Duke of Clarence is the elder brother, and has certainly the right to marry if he chooses, and I would not interfere with him on any account. If he wishes to be king—to be married and have children, poor man—God help him! let him do so. For myself—I am a man of no ambition, and wish only to remain as I am. . . . Easter, you know, falls very early this year—the 22nd of March. If the Duke of Clarence does not take any step before that time, I must find some pretext to reconcile Madame St. Laurent to my going to England for a short time. When once there, it will be easy for me to consult with my friends as to the proper steps to be taken. Should the Duke of Clarence do nothing before that time as to marrying it will become my duty, no doubt, to take some measures upon the subject myself." Two names, the Duke said, had been mentioned in this connection—those of the Princess of Baden and the Princess of Saxe-Coburg. The latter, he thought, would perhaps be the better of the two, from the circumstance of Prince Leopold being so popular with the nation; but before any other steps were taken, he hoped and expected to see justice done to Madame St. Laurent. "She is," he explained, "of very good family, and has never been an actress, and I am the first and only person who ever lived with her. Her disinterestedness, too, has been equal to her fidelity. When she first came to me it was upon £100 a year. That sum was afterwards raised to £400, and finally to £1000; but when my debts made it necessary for me to sacrifice a great part of my income, Madame St. Laurent insisted upon again returning to her income of £400 a year. If Madame St. Laurent is to return to live amongst her friends, it must be in such a state of independence as to command their respect. I shall not require very much, but a certain number of servants and

a carriage are essentials." As to his own settlement, the Duke observed that he would expect
the Duke of York's marriage to be considered
the precedent. " That," he said, " was a marriage
for the succession, and £25,000 for income was
settled, in addition to all his other income,
purely on that account. I shall be contented
with the same arrangement, without making
any demands grounded on the difference of the
value of money in 1792 and at present. As
for the payment of my debts," the Duke concluded, " I don't call them great. The nation,
on the contrary, is greatly my debtor." Here a
clock struck, and seemed to remind the Duke
that he had an appointment; he rose, and Mr.
Creevey left him.

Who could keep such a communication secret?
Certainly not Mr. Creevey. He hurried off to
tell the Duke of Wellington, who was very
much amused, and he wrote a long account of
it to Lord Sefton, who received the letter "very
apropos," while a surgeon was sounding his
bladder to ascertain whether he had a stone. " I
never saw a fellow more astonished than he was,"
wrote Lord Sefton in his reply, " at seeing me
laugh as soon as the operation was over. Nothing
could be more first-rate than the royal Edward's

ingenuousness.   One does not know which to
admire most—the delicacy of his attachment to
Madame St. Laurent, the refinement of his sentiments towards the Duke of Clarence, or his own
perfect disinterestedness in pecuniary matters."[1]

As it turned out, both the brothers decided to
marry. The Duke of Kent, selecting the Princess
of Saxe-Coburg in preference to the Princess
of Baden, was united to her on May 29, 1818.
On June 11, the Duke of Clarence followed suit
with a daughter of the Duke of Saxe-Meiningen.
But they were disappointed in their financial
expectations; for though the Government brought
forward proposals to increase their allowances,
together with that of the Duke of Cumberland,
the motions were defeated in the House of
Commons. At this the Duke of Wellington was
not surprised. " By God! " he said, " there is a
great deal to be said about that. They are the
damnedest millstones about the necks of any
Government that can be imagined. They have
insulted—*personally* insulted—two-thirds of the
gentlemen of England, and how can it be won-
dered at that they take their revenge upon them
in the House of Commons? It is their only
opportunity, and I think, by God! they are quite

1 Creevey, I, 267–71.

right to use it." [1] Eventually, however, Parliament increased the Duke of Kent's annuity by £6000.

The subsequent history of Madame St. Laurent has not transpired.

IV

The new Duchess of Kent, Victoria Mary Louisa, was a daughter of Francis, Duke of Saxe-Coburg-Saalfeld, and a sister of Prince Leopold. The family was an ancient one, being a branch of the great House of Wettin, which since the eleventh century had ruled over the March of Meissen on the Elbe. In the fifteenth century the whole possessions of the House had been divided between the Albertine and Ernestine branches: from the former descended the electors and kings of Saxony; the latter, ruling over Thuringia, became further subdivided into five branches, of which the duchy of Saxe-Coburg was one. This principality was very small, containing about 60,000 inhabitants, but it enjoyed independent and sovereign rights. During the disturbed years which followed the French Revolution, its affairs became terribly involved. The Duke was extravagant, and kept open house for the swarms of refugees, who fled eastward

[1] Creevey, I, 276-7.

over Germany as the French power advanced.
Among these was the Prince of Leiningen, an
elderly beau, whose domains on the Moselle
had been seized by the French, but who was
granted in compensation the territory of Amorbach in Lower Franconia. In 1803 he married
the Princess Victoria, at that time seventeen
years of age. Three years later Duke Francis
died a ruined man. The Napoleonic harrow
passed over Saxe-Coburg. The duchy was seized
by the French, and the ducal family were
reduced to beggary, almost to starvation. At
the same time the little principality of Amorbach
was devastated by the French, Russian, and
Austrian armies, marching and counter-marching
across it. For years there was hardly a cow in
the country, nor enough grass to feed a flock
of geese. Such was the desperate plight of
the family which, a generation later, was to
have gained a foothold in half the reigning
Houses of Europe. The Napoleonic harrow had
indeed done its work; the seed was planted; and
the crop would have surprised Napoleon. Prince
Leopold, thrown upon his own resources at fifteen,
made a career for himself and married the
heiress of England. The Princess of Leiningen,
struggling at Amorbach with poverty, military

requisitions, and a futile husband, developed an independence of character and a tenacity of purpose which were to prove useful in very different circumstances. In 1814, her husband died, leaving her with two children and the regency of the principality. After her brother's marriage with the Princess Charlotte, it was proposed that she should marry the Duke of Kent; but she declined, on the ground that the guardianship of her children and the management of her domains made other ties undesirable. The Princess Charlotte's death, however, altered the case; and when the Duke of Kent renewed his offer, she accepted it. She was thirty-two years old—short, stout, with brown eyes and hair, and rosy cheeks, cheerful and voluble, and gorgeously attired in rustling silks and bright velvets.[1]

She was certainly fortunate in her contented disposition; for she was fated, all through her life, to have much to put up with. Her second marriage, with its dubious prospects, seemed at first to be chiefly a source of difficulties and discomforts. The Duke, declaring that he was still too poor to live in England, moved about with uneasy precision through Belgium and

[1] *Letters*, I, 1-3; Grey, 378-81, 389; Crawford, 30-4; Stockmar, 113.

Germany, attending parades and inspecting barracks in a neat military cap, while the English notabilities looked askance, and the Duke of Wellington dubbed him the Corporal. " God damme! " he exclaimed to Mr. Creevey, " d'ye know what his sisters call him? By God! they call him Joseph Surface! " At Valenciennes, where there was a review and a great dinner, the Duchess arrived with an old and ugly lady-in-waiting, and the Duke of Wellington found himself in a difficulty. " Who the devil is to take out the maid of honour? " he kept asking; but at last he thought of a solution. " Damme, Freemantle, find out the mayor and let him do it." So the Mayor of Valenciennes was brought up for the purpose, and—so we learn from Mr. Creevey—" a capital figure he was." A few days later, at Brussels, Mr. Creevey himself had an unfortunate experience. A military school was to be inspected—before breakfast. The company assembled; everything was highly satisfactory; but the Duke of Kent continued for so long examining every detail and asking meticulous question after meticulous question, that Mr. Creevey at last could bear it no longer, and whispered to his neighbour that he was damned hungry. The Duke of Wellington heard

him, and was delighted. " I recommend you,"
he said, " whenever you start with the royal
family in a morning, and particularly with *the
Corporal,* always to breakfast first." He and
his staff, it turned out, had taken that precaution,
and the great man amused himself, while the
stream of royal inquiries poured on, by pointing
at Mr. Creevey from time to time with the
remark, " Voilà le monsieur qui n'a pas
déjeuné! "[1]

Settled down at last at Amorbach, the time
hung heavily on the Duke's hands. The establishment was small, the country was impoverished;
even clock-making grew tedious at last. He
brooded—for in spite of his piety the Duke was
not without a vein of superstition—over the
prophecy of a gipsy at Gibraltar who told him
that he was to have many losses and crosses,
that he was to die in happiness, and that his only
child was to be a great queen. Before long
it became clear that a child was to be expected:
the Duke decided that it should be born in
England. Funds were lacking for the journey,
but his determination was not to be set aside.
Come what might, he declared, his child must be
English-born. A carriage was hired, and the

[1] Creevey, I, 282-4.

Duke himself mounted the box. Inside were the
Duchess, her daughter Feodora, a girl of fourteen,
with maids, nurses, lap-dogs, and canaries. Off
they drove—through Germany, through France:
bad roads, cheap inns, were nothing to the
rigorous Duke and the equable, abundant Duchess.
The Channel was crossed, London was reached
in safety. The authorities provided a set of
rooms in Kensington Palace; and there, on May
24, 1819, a female infant was born.[1]

[1] Crawford, 25, 37–8.

CHAPTER II

CHILDHOOD

I

THE child who, in these not very impressive circumstances, appeared in the world, received but scant attention. There was small reason to foresee her destiny. The Duchess of Clarence, two months before, had given birth to a daughter; this infant, indeed, had died almost immediately; but it seemed highly probable that the Duchess would again become a mother; and so it actually fell out. More than this, the Duchess of Kent was young, and the Duke was strong; there was every likelihood that before long a brother would follow, to snatch her faint chance of the succession from the little princess.

Nevertheless, the Duke had other views: there were prophecies. . . . At any rate, he would christen the child Elizabeth, a name of happy augury. In this, however, he reckoned without the Regent, who, seeing a chance of annoying his brother, suddenly announced that he himself

would be present at the baptism, and signified
at the same time that one of the godfathers was
to be the Emperor Alexander of Russia. And
so when the ceremony took place, and the Archbishop of Canterbury asked by what name he
was to baptise the child, the Regent replied
" Alexandria." At this the Duke ventured to
suggest that another name might be added.
" Certainly," said the Regent; " Georgina? " " Or
Elizabeth? " said the Duke. There was a pause,
during which the Archbishop, with the baby in
his lawn sleeves, looked with some uneasiness
from one Prince to the other. " Very well,
then," said the Regent at last, " call her after
her mother. But Alexandrina must come first."
Thus, to the disgust of her father, the child was
christened Alexandrina Victoria.[1]

The Duke had other subjects of disgust. The
meagre grant of the Commons had by no means
put an end to his financial distresses. It was
to be feared that his services were not appreciated by the nation. His debts continued to
grow. For many years he had lived upon £7000
a year; but now his expenses were exactly
doubled; he could make no further reductions;
as it was, there was not a single servant in his

[1] Murray, 62–3; Lee, 11–12.

establishment who was idle for a moment from morning to night. He poured out his griefs in a long letter to Robert Owen, whose sympathy had the great merit of being practical. "I now candidly state," he wrote, "that, after viewing the subject in every possible way, I am satisfied that, to continue to live in England, even in the quiet way in which we are going on, *without splendour,* and *without show, nothing short of doubling the seven thousand pounds will do,* REDUCTION BEING IMPOSSIBLE." It was clear that he would be obliged to sell his house for £51,300: if that failed, he would go and live on the Continent. "If my services are useful to my country, it surely becomes *those who have the power* to support me in substantiating those just claims I have for the very extensive losses and privations I have experienced, during the very long period of my professional servitude in the Colonies; and if this is not attainable, *it is a clear proof to me that they are not appreciated;* and under that impression I shall not scruple, in *due* time, to resume my retirement abroad, when the Duchess and myself shall have fulfilled our duties in establishing the *English* birth of my child, and giving it material nutriment on the soil of Old England; and which we shall certainly repeat, if Providence destines to give us any further increase of family." [1]

In the meantime, he decided to spend the winter at Sidmouth, " in order," he told Owen, " that the Duchess may have the benefit of tepid sea bathing, and our infant that of sea air, on the fine coast of Devonshire, during the months of the year that are so odious in London." [2] In December the move was made. With the new year, the Duke remembered another prophecy. In 1820, a fortune-teller had told him, two members of the Royal Family would die. Who would they be? He speculated on the various possibilities: the King, it was plain, could not live much longer; and the Duchess of York had been attacked by a mortal disease. Probably it would be the King and the Duchess of York; or perhaps the King and the Duke of York; or the King and the Regent. He himself was one of the healthiest men in England. [3] " My brothers," he declared, " are not so strong as I am; I have lived a regular life. I shall outlive them all. The crown will come to me and my children." [4] He went out for a walk, and got his feet wet.

[1] Owen, *Journal*, No. 1, February, 1853, 28–9.
[2] *Ibid.*, 31.
[3] Croker, I, 155.
[4] Stockmar, 113.

On coming home, he neglected to change his stockings. He caught cold, inflammation of the lungs set in, and on January 22 he was a dying man. By a curious chance, young Dr. Stockmar was staying in the house at the time; two years before, he had stood by the death-bed of the Princess Charlotte; and now he was watching the Duke of Kent in his agony. On Stockmar's advice, a will was hastily prepared. The Duke's earthly possessions were of a negative character; but it was important that the guardianship of the unwitting child, whose fortunes were now so strangely changing, should be assured to the Duchess. The Duke was just able to understand the document, and to append his signature. Having inquired whether his writing was perfectly clear, he became unconscious, and breathed his last on the following morning.[1] Six days later came the fulfilment of the second half of the gipsy's prophecy. The long, unhappy, and inglorious life of George the Third of England was ended.

II

Such was the confusion of affairs at Sidmouth, that the Duchess found herself without the means of returning to London. Prince Leopold hurried

[1] Stockmar, 114–5.

down, and himself conducted his sister and her
family, by slow and bitter stages, to Kensington.
The widowed lady, in her voluminous blacks,
needed all her equanimity to support her. Her
prospects were more dubious than ever. She had
£6000 a year of her own; but her husband's debts
loomed before her like a mountain. Soon she
learnt that the Duchess of Clarence was once
more expecting a child. What had she to look
forward to in England? Why should she remain
in a foreign country, among strangers, whose
language she could not speak, whose customs
she could not understand? Surely it would be
best to return to Amorbach, and there, among her
own people, bring up her daughters in economical
obscurity. But she was an inveterate optimist;
she had spent her life in struggles, and would
not be daunted now. And besides, she adored
her baby. " C'est mon bonheur, mes délices, mon
existence," she declared; the darling should be
brought up as an English princess, whatever
lot awaited her. Prince Leopold came forward
nobly with an offer of an additional £3000 a year;
and the Duchess remained at Kensington.[1]

The child herself was extremely fat, and bore
a remarkable resemblance to her grandfather.

[1] *Letters*, I, 15, 257–8; Grey, App. A.

" C'est l'image du feu Roi!" exclaimed the
Duchess. " C'est le Roi Georges en jupons,"
echoed the surrounding ladies, as the little creature waddled with difficulty from one to the
other.[1]

Before long, the world began to be slightly
interested in the nursery at Kensington. When,
early in 1821, the Duchess of Clarence's second
child, the Princess Elizabeth, died within three
months of its birth, the interest increased. Great
forces and fierce antagonisms seemed to be
moving, obscurely, about the royal cradle. It
was a time of faction and anger, of violent
repression and profound discontent. A powerful
movement, which had for long been checked
by adverse circumstances, was now spreading
throughout the country. New passions, new
desires, were abroad; or rather old passions and
old desires, reincarnated with a new potency:
love of freedom, hatred of injustice, hope for
the future of man. The mighty still sat proudly
in their seats, dispensing their ancient tyranny;
but a storm was gathering out of the darkness,
and already there was lightning in the sky. But
the vastest forces must needs operate through
frail human instruments; and it seemed for many

[1] Granville, I, 168–9.

years as if the great cause of English liberalism
hung upon the life of the little girl at Kensington.
She alone stood between the country and her
terrible uncle, the Duke of Cumberland, the
hideous embodiment of reaction. Inevitably, the
Duchess of Kent threw in her lot with her
husband's party; Whig leaders, Radical agitators,
rallied round her; she was intimate with the
bold Lord Durham, she was on friendly terms
with the redoubtable O'Connell himself. She
received Wilberforce—though, to be sure, she
did not ask him to sit down.[1] She declared in
public that she put her faith in " the liberties
of the People." [2] It was certain that the young
Princess would be brought up in the way that
she should go; yet there, close behind the throne,
waiting, sinister, was the Duke of Cumberland.
Brougham, looking forward into the future in
his scurrilous fashion, hinted at dreadful possibilities. " I never prayed so heartily for a Prince
before," he wrote, on hearing that George IV
had been attacked by illness. " If he had gone,
all the troubles of these villains [the Tory
Ministers] went with him, and they had Fred. I
[the Duke of York] their own man for his life.
. . . He [Fred. I] won't live long either; that

1 *Wilberforce, William,* V, 71-2.   2 *Letters,* I, 17.

Prince of Blackguards, 'Brother William,' is as bad a life, so we come in the course of nature to be *assassinated* by King Ernest I or Regent Ernest [the Duke of Cumberland]." [1] Such thoughts were not peculiar to Brougham; in the seething state of public feeling, they constantly leapt to the surface; and, even so late as the year previous to her accession, the Radical newspapers were full of suggestions that the Princess Victoria was in danger from the machinations of her wicked uncle. [2]

But no echo of these conflicts and forebodings reached the little Drina—for so she was called in the family circle—as she played with her dolls, or scampered down the passages, or rode on the donkey her uncle York had given her [3] along the avenues of Kensington Gardens. The fair-haired, blue-eyed child was idolised by her nurses, and her mother's ladies, and her sister Feodora; and for a few years there was danger, in spite of her mother's strictness, of her being spoilt. From time to time, she would fly into a violent passion, stamp her little foot, and set everyone at defiance; whatever they might say, she would not learn her letters—no, she *would not;* after-

---

[1] Creevey, I, 297–8.   [2] Jerrold, *Early Court*, 15–17.
[3] *Letters*, I, 10.

wards, she was very sorry, and burst into tears;
but her letters remained unlearnt. When she
was five years old, however, a change came, with
the appearance of Fräulein Lehzen. This lady,
who was the daughter of a Hanoverian clergyman and had previously been the Princess
Feodora's governess, soon succeeded in instilling
a new spirit into her charge. At first, indeed, she
was appalled by the little Princess's outbursts
of temper; never in her life, she declared, had
she seen such a passionate and naughty child.
Then she observed something else; the child was
extraordinarily truthful; whatever punishment
might follow, she never told a lie.[1] Firm, very
firm, the new governess yet had the sense to
see that all the firmness in the world would be
useless, unless she could win her way into little
Drina's heart. She did so, and there were no
more difficulties. Drina learnt her letters like
an angel; and she learnt other things as well. The
Baroness de Späth taught her how to make little
board boxes and decorate them with tinsel and
painted flowers;[2] her mother taught her religion.
Sitting in the pew every Sunday morning, the
child of six was seen listening in rapt attention to the clergyman's endless sermon, for she

---

[1] *Letters,* I, 14; *Girlhood,* I, 280. [2] Crawford, 6.

was to be examined upon it in the afternoon.[1] The
Duchess was determined that her daughter, from
the earliest possible moment, should be prepared
for her high station in a way that would commend
itself to the most respectable; her good, plain,
thrifty German mind recoiled with horror and
amazement from the shameless junketings at Carlton House; Drina should never be allowed to forget for a moment the virtues of simplicity, regularity, propriety, and devotion. The little girl,
however, was really in small need of such lessons,
for she was naturally simple and orderly, she was
pious without difficulty, and her sense of propriety
was keen. She understood very well the niceties
of her own position. When, a child of six, Lady
Jane Ellice was taken by her grandmother to
Kensington Palace, she was put to play with the
Princess Victoria, who was the same age as herself. The young visitor, ignorant of etiquette, began to make free with the toys on the floor, in a
way which was a little too familiar; but " You
must not touch those," she was quickly told, " they
are mine; and I may call you Jane, but you must
not call me Victoria." [2] The Princess's most constant playmate was Victoire, the daughter of Sir
John Conroy, the Duchess's major-domo. The

[1] Smith, 21-2. [2] *Cornhill Magazine*, LXXV, 730.

two girls were very fond of one another; they
would walk hand in hand together in Kensington
Gardens. But little Drina was perfectly aware
for which of them it was that they were followed,
at a respectful distance, by a gigantic scarlet
flunkey.[1]

Warm-hearted, responsive, she loved her dear
Lehzen, and she loved her dear Feodora, and her
dear Victoire, and her dear Madame de Späth.
And her dear Mamma . . . of course, she loved
her too; it was her duty; and yet—she could not
tell why it was—she was always happier when she
was staying with her Uncle Leopold at Claremont. There old Mrs. Louis, who, years ago, had
waited on her Cousin Charlotte, petted her to her
heart's content; and her uncle himself was wonderfully kind to her, talking to her seriously and
gently, almost as if she were a grown-up person.
She and Feodora invariably wept when the too
short visit was over, and they were obliged to return to the dutiful monotony, and the affectionate
supervision of Kensington. But sometimes when
her mother had to stay at home, she was allowed
to go out driving all alone with her dear Feodora
and her dear Lehzen, and she could talk and look
as she liked, and it was very delightful.[2]

[1] Hunt, II, 257-8.   [2] *Letters*, I, 10, 19.

The visits to Claremont were frequent enough; but one day, on a special occasion, she paid one of a rarer and more exciting kind. When she was seven years old, she and her mother and sister were asked by the King to go down to Windsor. George IV, who had transferred his fraternal ill-temper to his sister-in-law and her family, had at last grown tired of sulking, and decided to be agreeable. The old rip, bewigged and gouty, ornate and enormous, with his jewelled mistress by his side and his flaunting court about him, received the tiny creature who was one day to hold in those same halls a very different state. " Give me your little paw," he said; and two ages touched. Next morning, driving in his phaeton with the Duchess of Gloucester, he met the Duchess of Kent and her child in the Park. " Pop her in," were his orders, which, to the terror of the mother and the delight of the daughter, were immediately obeyed. Off they dashed to Virginia Water, where there was a great barge, full of lords and ladies fishing, and another barge with a band; and the King ogled Feodora, and praised her manners, and then turned to his own small niece. " What is your favourite tune? The band shall play it." " God save the King, sir," was the instant answer. The Princess's reply has been praised as an early example of a tact which was afterwards famous. But she was a very truthful child, and perhaps it was her genuine opinion.[1]

III

In 1827 the Duke of York, who had found some consolation for the loss of his wife in the sympathy of the Duchess of Rutland, died, leaving behind him the unfinished immensity of Stafford House and £200,000 worth of debts. Three years later George IV also disappeared, and the Duke of Clarence reigned in his stead. The new Queen, it was now clear, would in all probability never again be a mother; the Princess Victoria, therefore, was recognised by Parliament as heir-presumptive; and the Duchess of Kent, whose annuity had been doubled five years previously, was now given an additional £10,000 for the maintenance of the Princess, and was appointed regent, in case of the death of the King before the majority of her daughter. At the same time a great convulsion took place in the constitution of the State. The power of the Tories, who had dominated England for more than forty years, suddenly began to crumble. In the tremendous struggle that followed, it seemed for a moment

[1] *Letters*, I, 11–12; Lee, 26.

as if the tradition of generations might be snapped,
as if the blind tenacity of the reactionaries and
the determined fury of their enemies could have
no other issue than revolution. But the forces of
compromise triumphed: the Reform Bill was
passed. The centre of gravity in the constitution
was shifted towards the middle classes; the Whigs
came into power; and the complexion of the Government assumed a Liberal tinge. One of the
results of this new state of affairs was a change in
the position of the Duchess of Kent and her daughter. From being the *protégées* of an opposition
clique, they became assets of the official majority
of the nation. The Princess Victoria was henceforward the living symbol of the victory of the
middle classes.

The Duke of Cumberland, on the other hand,
suffered a corresponding eclipse: his claws had
been pared by the Reform Act. He grew insignificant and almost harmless, though his ugliness
remained; he was the wicked uncle still—but only
of a story.

The Duchess's own liberalism was not very profound. She followed naturally in the footsteps
of her husband, repeating with conviction the
catchwords of her husband's clever friends and
the generalisations of her clever brother Leopold.

She herself had no pretensions to cleverness; she did not understand very much about the Poor Law and the Slave Trade and Political Economy; but she hoped that she did her duty; and she hoped—she ardently hoped—that the same might be said of Victoria. Her educational conceptions were those of Dr. Arnold, whose views were just then beginning to permeate society. Dr. Arnold's object was, first and foremost, to make his pupils " in the highest and truest sense of the words, Christian gentlemen "; intellectual refinements might follow. The Duchess felt convinced that it was her supreme duty in life to make quite sure that her daughter should grow up into a Christian queen. To this task she bent all her energies; and, as the child developed, she flattered herself that her efforts were not unsuccessful. When the Princess was eleven, she desired the Bishops of London and Lincoln to submit her daughter to an examination, and report upon the progress that had been made. " I feel the time to be now come," the Duchess explained, in a letter obviously drawn up by her own hand, " that what has been done should be put to some test, that if anything has been done in error of judgment it may be corrected, and that the plan for the future should be open to consideration and revision. . . . I attend

almost always myself every lesson, or a part; and
as the lady about the Princess is a competent
person, she assists Her in preparing Her lessons,
for the various masters, as I resolved to act in
that manner so as to be Her Governess myself.
. . . When she was at a proper age she commenced
attending Divine Service regularly with me, and I
have every feeling that she has religion at Her
heart, that she is morally impressed with it to that
degree, that she is less liable to error by its application to her feelings as a Child capable of reflection." " The general bent of Her character," added
the Duchess, " is strength of intellect, capable of
receiving with ease, information, and with a peculiar readiness in coming to a very just and benig-
nant decision on any point Her opinion is asked on.
Her adherence to truth is of so marked a character
that I feel no apprehension of that Bulwark being
broken down by any circumstances." The Bishops attended at the Palace, and the result of their
examination was all that could be wished. " In
answering a great variety of questions proposed
to her," they reported, " the Princess displayed an
accurate knowledge of the most important features of Scripture History, and of the leading
truths and precepts of the Christian Religion as
taught by the Church of England, as well as an

acquaintance with the Chronology and principal facts of English History remarkable in so young a person. To questions in Geography, the use of the Globes, Arithmetic, and Latin Grammar, the answers which the Princess returned were equally satisfactory." They did not believe that the Duchess's plan of education was susceptible of any improvement; and the Archbishop of Canterbury, who was also consulted, came to the same gratifying conclusion.[1]

One important step, however, remained to be taken. So far, as the Duchess explained to the Bishops, the Princess had been kept in ignorance of the station that she was likely to fill. " She is aware of its duties, and that a Sovereign should live for others; so that when Her innocent mind receives the impression of Her future fate, she receives it with a mind formed to be sensible of what is to be expected from Her, and it is to be hoped, she will be too well grounded in Her principles to be dazzled with the station she is to look to." [2]   In the following year it was decided that she should be enlightened on this point. The well-known scene followed: the history lesson, the genealogical table of the Kings of England slipped beforehand by the governess into the book, the

[1] *Letters,* I, 14–17.   [2] *Ibid.,* I, 16.

Princess's surprise, her inquiries, her final realisa-
tion of the facts. When the child at last understood, she was silent for a moment, and then she
spoke: " I will be good," she said. The words
were something more than a conventional protes-
tation, something more than the expression of a
superimposed desire; they were, in their limitation
and their intensity, their egotism and their humil-
ity, an instinctive summary of the dominating
qualities of a life. " I cried much on learning it,"
her Majesty noted long afterwards. No doubt,
while the others were present, even her dear Lehzen, the little girl kept up her self-command; and
then crept away somewhere to ease her heart of an
inward, unfamiliar agitation, with a handkerchief,
out of her mother's sight.[1]

But her mother's sight was by no means an easy
thing to escape. Morning and evening, day and
night, there was no relaxation of the maternal
vigilance. The child grew into the girl, the girl
into the young woman; but still she slept in her
mother's bedroom; still she had no place allowed
her where she might sit or work by herself.[2] An
extraordinary watchfulness surrounded her every
step: up to the day of her accession, she never
went downstairs without someone beside her hold-

<hr>

[1] Martin, I, 13.   [2] *Letters*, I, 11.

ing her hand.[1] Plainness and regularity ruled the household. The hours, the days, the years passed slowly and methodically by. The dolls—the innumerable dolls, each one so neatly dressed, each one with its name so punctiliously entered in the catalogue—were laid aside, and a little music and a little dancing took their place. Taglioni came, to give grace and dignity to the figure,[2] and Lablache, to train the piping treble upon his own rich bass. The Dean of Chester, the official preceptor, continued his endless instruction in Scripture history, while the Duchess of Northumberland, the official governess, presided over every lesson with becoming solemnity. Without doubt, the Princess's main achievement during her schooldays was linguistic. German was naturally the first language with which she was familiar; but English and French quickly followed; and she became virtually trilingual, though her mastery of English grammar remained incomplete. At the same time, she acquired a working knowledge of Italian and some smattering of Latin. Nevertheless, she did not read very much. It was not an occupation that she cared for; partly, perhaps, because the books that were given her were all either sermons, which were very dull, or poetry, which was

1 *Girlhood*, I, 42.   2 Crawford, 87.

incomprehensible. Novels were strictly forbidden. Lord Durham persuaded her mother to get her some of Miss Martineau's tales, illustrating the truths of Political Economy, and they delighted her; but it is to be feared that it was the unaccustomed pleasure of the story that filled her mind, and that she never really mastered the theory of exchanges or the nature of rent.[1]

It was her misfortune that the mental atmosphere which surrounded her during these years of adolescence was almost entirely feminine. No father, no brother, was there to break in upon the gentle monotony of the daily round with impetuosity, with rudeness, with careless laughter and wafts of freedom from the outside world. The Princess was never called by a voice that was loud and growling; never felt, as a matter of course, a hard rough cheek on her own soft one; never climbed a wall with a boy. The visits to Claremont —delicious little escapes into male society—came to an end when she was eleven years old and Prince Leopold left England to be King of the Belgians. She loved him still; he was still " il mio secondo padre—or, rather, *solo* padre, for he is indeed like my real father, as I have none "; but his fatherliness now came to her dimly and indi-

[1] Martineau, II, 118–9.

rectly, through the cold channel of correspondence. Henceforward female duty, female elegance, female enthusiasm, hemmed her completely in; and her spirit, amid the enclosing folds, was hardly reached by those two great influences, without which no growing life can truly prosper—humour and imagination. The Baroness Lehzen—for she had been raised to that rank in the Hanoverian nobility by George IV before he died—was the real centre of the Princess's world. When Feodora married, when Uncle Leopold went to Belgium, the Baroness was left without a competitor. The Princess gave her mother her dutiful regards; but Lehzen had her heart. The voluble, shrewd daughter of the pastor in Hanover, lavishing her devotion on her royal charge, had reaped her reward in an unbounded confidence and a passionate adoration. The girl would have gone through fire for her "*precious* Lehzen," the " best and truest friend," she declared, that she had had since her birth. Her journal, begun when she was thirteen, where she registered day by day the small succession of her doings and her sentiments, bears on every page of it the traces of the Baroness and her circumambient influence. The young creature that one sees there, self-depicted in ingenuous clarity, with her sincerity, her simplicity, her quick affec-

tions and pious resolutions, might almost have been
the daughter of a German pastor herself. Her
enjoyments, her admirations, her *engouements*
were of the kind that clothed themselves naturally
in underlinings and exclamation marks. " It was
a *delightful* ride. We cantered a good deal.
SWEET LITTLE ROSY WENT BEAUTIFULLY! ! We
came home at a ¼ past 1. . . . At 20 minutes
to 7 we went out to the Opera. . . . Rubini came
on and sang a song out of ' Anna Boulena ' *quite
beautifully*. We came home at ½ past 11." [1] In
her comments on her readings, the mind of the
Baroness is clearly revealed. One day, by some
mistake, she was allowed to take up a volume of
memoirs by Fanny Kemble. " It is certainly very
pertly and oddly written. One would imagine by
the style that the authoress must be very pert, and
not well bred; for there are so many vulgar expressions in it. It is a great pity that a person
endowed with so much talent, as Mrs. Butler really
is, should turn it to so little account and publish a
book which is so full of trash and nonsense which
can only do her harm. I stayed up till 20 minutes
past 9." Madame de Sévigné's letters, which the
Baroness read aloud, met with more approval.
" How truly elegant and natural her style is! It

---

[1] *Girlhood*, I, 66–7.

is so full of *naïveté,* cleverness, and grace." But
her highest admiration was reserved for the Bishop
of Chester's "Exposition of the Gospel of St.
Matthew." "It is a very fine book indeed. Just
the sort of one I like; which is just plain and
comprehensible and full of truth and good feeling.
It is not one of those learned books in which you
have to cavil at almost every paragraph. Lehzen
gave it me on the Sunday that I took the Sacra-
ment." [1] A few weeks previously she had been
confirmed, and she described the event as follows:
"I felt that my confirmation was one of the most
solemn and important events and acts in my life;
and that I trusted that it might have a salutary
effect on my mind. I felt deeply repentant for
all what I had done which was wrong and trusted
in God Almighty to strengthen my heart and
mind; and to forsake all that is bad and follow all
that is virtuous and right. I went with the firm
determination to become a true Christian, to try
and comfort my dear Mamma in all her griefs,
trials, and anxieties, and to become a dutiful and
affectionate daughter to her. Also to be obedient
to *dear* Lehzen, who has done so much for me. I
was dressed in a white lace dress, with a white
crape bonnet with a wreath of white roses round

[1] *Girlhood,* I, 129.

it. I went in the chariot with my dear Mamma and the others followed in another carriage." [1] One seems to hold in one's hand a small smooth crystal pebble, without a flaw and without a scintillation, and so transparent that one can see through it at a glance.

Yet perhaps, after all, to the discerning eye, the purity would not be absolute. The careful searcher might detect, in the virgin soil, the first faint traces of an unexpected vein. In that conventual existence visits were exciting events; and, as the Duchess had many relatives, they were not infrequent; aunts and uncles would often appear from Germany, and cousins too. When the Princess was fourteen she was delighted by the arrival of a couple of boys from Würtemberg, the Princes Alexander and Ernst, sons of her mother's sister and the reigning duke. " They are both *extremely tall,*" she noted; " Alexander is *very handsome,* and Ernst has a *very kind expression.* They are both extremely *amiable.*" And their departure filled her with corresponding regrets. " We saw them get into the barge, and watched them sailing away for some time on the beach. They were so amiable and so pleasant to have in the house; they were *always satisfied, always good-humoured;*

[1] *Girlhood,* I, 124-5.

Alexander took such care of me in getting out of the boat, and rode next to me; so did Ernst." [1] Two years later, two other cousins arrived, the Princes Ferdinand and Augustus. " Dear Ferdinand," the Princess wrote, " has elicited universal admiration from all parties. . . . He is so very unaffected, and has such a very distinguished appearance and carriage. They are both very dear and charming young men. Augustus is very amiable, too, and, when known, shows much good sense." On another occasion, " Dear Ferdinand came and sat near me and talked so dearly and sensibly. I do *so* love him. Dear Augustus sat near me and talked with me, and he is also a dear good young man, and is very handsome." She could not quite decide which was the handsomer of the two. On the whole, she concluded, " I think Ferdinand handsomer than Augustus, his eyes are so beautiful, and he has such a lively clever expression; *both* have such a sweet expression; Ferdinand has something *quite beautiful* in his expression when he speaks and smiles, and he is *so* good." However, it was perhaps best to say that they were " both very handsome and *very dear*." [2] But shortly afterwards two more cousins arrived, who threw all the rest into the shade. These were the

1 *Girlhood*, I, 78, 82.   2 *Ibid.*, I, 150–3.

Princes Ernest and Albert, sons of her mother's eldest brother, the Duke of Saxe-Coburg. This time the Princess was more particular in her observations. "Ernest," she remarked, "is as tall as Ferdinand and Augustus; he has dark hair, and fine dark eyes and eyebrows, but the nose and mouth are not good; he has a most kind, honest and intelligent expression in his countenance, and has a very good figure. Albert, who is just as tall as Ernest but stouter, is extremely handsome; his hair is about the same colour as mine; his eyes are large and blue, and he has a beautiful nose and a very sweet mouth with fine teeth; but the charm of his countenance is his expression, which is most delightful; *c'est à la fois* full of goodness and sweetness, and very clever and intelligent." "Both my cousins," she added, "are so kind and good; they are much more *formés* and men of the world than Augustus; they speak English very well, and I speak it with them. Ernest will be 18 years old on the 21st of June, and Albert 17 on the 26th of August. Dear Uncle Ernest made me the present of a most delightful *Lory,* which is so tame that it remains on your hand and you may put your finger into its beak, or do anything with it, without its ever attempting to bite. It is larger than Mamma's grey parrot." A little later, "I sat between my dear cousins on the sofa and we looked at drawings. They both draw very well, particularly Albert, and are both exceedingly fond of music; they play very nicely on the piano. The more I see them the more I am delighted with them, and the more I love them. . . . It is delightful to be with them; they are so fond of being occupied too; they are quite an example for any young person." When, after a stay of three weeks, the time came for the young men and their father to return to Germany, the moment of parting was a melancholy one. " It was our last HAPPY HAPPY breakfast, with this dear Uncle and those *dearest* beloved cousins, whom I *do* love so VERY VERY dearly; *much more dearly* than any other cousins in the *world*. Dearly as I love Ferdinand, and also good Augustus, I love Ernest and Albert *more* than them, oh yes, MUCH *more*. . . . They have both learnt a good deal, and are very clever, naturally clever, particularly Albert, who is the most reflecting of the two, and they like very much talking about serious and instructive things and yet are so *very very* merry and gay and happy, like young people ought to be; Albert always used to have some fun and some clever witty answer at breakfast and everywhere; he used to play and fondle Dash so funnily too. . . . Dearest Albert was playing on the piano when I came down. At 11 dear Uncle, my *dearest beloved* cousins, and Charles, left us, accompanied by Count Kolowrat. I embraced both my dearest cousins most warmly, as also my dear Uncle. I cried bitterly, very bitterly."[1] The Princes shared her ecstasies and her italics between them; but it is clear enough where her secret preference lay. " Particularly Albert "! She was just seventeen; and deep was the impression left upon that budding organism by the young man's charm and goodness and accomplishments, and his large blue eyes and beautiful nose, and his sweet mouth and fine teeth.

IV

King William could not away with his sister-in-law, and the Duchess fully returned his antipathy. Without considerable tact and considerable forbearance their relative positions were well calculated to cause ill-feeling; and there was very little tact in the composition of the Duchess, and no forbearance at all in that of his Majesty. A bursting, bubbling old gentleman, with quarter-deck gestures, round rolling eyes, and a head like a pineapple, his sudden elevation to the throne after fifty-six years of utter insignificance had al-

[1] *Girlhood*, I, 157–61.

most sent him crazy. His natural exuberance completely got the best of him; he rushed about doing preposterous things in an extraordinary manner, spreading amusement and terror in every direction, and talking all the time. His tongue was decidedly Hanoverian, with its repetitions, its catchwords—" That's quite another thing! That's quite another thing!"—its rattling indomitability, its loud indiscreetness. His speeches, made repeatedly at the most inopportune junctures, and filled pell-mell with all the fancies and furies that happened at the moment to be whisking about in his head, were the consternation of Ministers. He was one part blackguard, people said, and three parts buffoon; but those who knew him better could not help liking him—he meant well; and he was really good-humoured and kind-hearted, if you took him the right way. If you took him the wrong way, however, you must look out for squalls, as the Duchess of Kent discovered.

She had no notion of how to deal with him—could not understand him in the least. Occupied with her own position, her own responsibilities, her duty, and her daughter, she had no attention to spare for the peppery susceptibilities of a foolish, disreputable old man. She was the mother of the heiress of England; and it was for him to recog-

nise the fact—to put her at once upon a proper
footing—to give her the precedence of a dowager
Princess of Wales, with a large annuity from the
privy purse.[1] It did not occur to her that such
pretensions might be galling to a king who had
no legitimate child of his own, and who yet had
not altogether abandoned the hope of having one.
She pressed on, with bulky vigour, along the
course she had laid out. Sir John Conroy, an
Irishman with no judgment and a great deal of
self-importance, was her intimate counsellor, and
egged her on. It was advisable that Victoria
should become acquainted with the various dis-
tricts of England, and through several summers
a succession of tours—in the West, in the Mid-
lands, in Wales—were arranged for her. The
intention of the plan was excellent, but its execution was unfortunate. The journeys, advertised
in the Press, attracting enthusiastic crowds, and
involving official receptions, took on the air of
royal progresses. Addresses were presented by
loyal citizens; the delighted Duchess, swelling in
sweeping feathers and almost obliterating the
diminutive Princess, read aloud, in her German
accent, gracious replies prepared beforehand by
Sir John, who, bustling and ridiculous, seemed to

[1] Greville, II, 195–6.

be mingling the rôles of major-domo and Prime Minister. Naturally the King fumed over his newspaper at Windsor. "Th*s* woman is a nuisance!" he exclaimed. Po*o*r Queen Adelaide, amiable though disappointed, did her best to smooth things down, changed the subject, and wrote affectionate letters to Victoria; but it was useless. News arrived that the Duchess of Kent, sailing in the Solent, had insisted that whenever her yacht appeared it should be received by royal salutes from all the men-of-war and all the forts. The King declared that these continual poppings must cease; the Premier and the First Lord of the Admiralty were consulted; and they wrote privately to the Duchess, begging her to waive her rights. But she would not hear of it; Sir John Conroy was adamant. "As her Royal Highness's *confidential adviser*," he said, "I cannot recommend her to give way on this point." Eventually the King, in a great state of excitement, issued a special Order in Council, prohibiting the firing of royal salutes to any ships except those which carried the reigning sovereign or his consort on board.[1]

When King William quarrelled with his Whig Ministers the situation grew still more embittered,

[1] Greville, III, 321, 324.

for now the Duchess, in addition to her other short-comings, was the political partisan of his enemies. In 1836 he made an attempt to prepare the ground for a match between the Princess Victoria and one of the sons of the Prince of Orange, and at the same time did his best to prevent the visit of the young Coburg princes to Kensington. He failed in both these objects; and the only result of his efforts was to raise the anger of the King of the Belgians, who, forgetting for a moment his royal reserve, addressed an indignant letter on the subject to his niece. " I am really *astonished,*" he wrote, " at the conduct of your old Uncle the King; this invitation of the Prince of Orange and his sons, this forcing him on others, is very extraordinary. . . . Not later than yesterday I got a half-official communication from England, insinuating that it would be *highly* desirable that the visit of *your* relatives *should not take place this year*—qu'en dites-vous? The relations of the Queen and the King, therefore, to the God-knows-what degree, are to come in shoals and rule the land, when *your relations* are to be *forbidden* the country, and that when, as you know, the whole of your relations have ever been very dutiful and kind to the King. Really and truly I never heard or saw anything like it, and I hope it will a *little rouse your spirit;* now that slavery is even abolished in the British Colonies, I do not comprehend *why your lot alone should be to be kept a white little slavey in England,* for the pleasure of the Court, who never bought you, as I am not aware of their ever having gone to any expense on that head, or the King's ever having *spent a sixpence for your existence.* . . . Oh, consistency and political or *other honesty,* where must one look for you!"[1]

Shortly afterwards King Leopold came to England himself, and his reception was as cold at Windsor as it was warm at Kensington. " To hear dear Uncle speak on any subject," the Princess wrote in her diary, " is like reading a highly instructive book; his conversation is so enlightened, so clear. He is universally admitted to be one of the first politicians now extant. He speaks so mildly, yet firmly and impartially, about politics. Uncle tells me that Belgium is quite a pattern for its organisation, its industry, and prosperity; the finances are in the greatest perfection. Uncle is so beloved and revered by his Belgian subjects, that it must be a great compensation for all his extreme trouble."[2] But her other uncle by no means shared her sentiments. He could not, he

---

[1] *Letters,* I, 47–8.   [2] *Girlhood,* I, 168.

said, put up with a water-drinker; and King Leopold would touch no wine. "What's that you're drinking, sir?" he asked him one day at dinner. "Water, sir." "God damn it, sir!" was the rejoinder. "Why don't you drink wine? I never allow anybody to drink water at my table."[1]

It was clear that before very long there would be a great explosion; and in the hot days of August it came. The Duchess and the Princess had gone down to stay at Windsor for the King's birthday party, and the King himself, who was in London for the day to prorogue Parliament, paid a visit at Kensington Palace in their absence. There he found that the Duchess had just appropriated, against his express orders, a suite of seventeen apartments for her own use. He was extremely angry, and, when he returned to Windsor, after greeting the Princess with affection, he publicly rebuked the Duchess for what she had done. But this was little to what followed. On the next day was the birthday banquet; there were a hundred guests; the Duchess of Kent sat on the King's right hand, and the Princess Victoria opposite. At the end of the dinner, in reply to the toast of the King's health, he rose, and, in a long, loud, passionate speech, poured out the vials of

[1] Greville, III, 377.

his wrath upon the Duchess. She had, he declared, insulted him—grossly and continually; she had kept the Princess away from him in the most improper manner; she was surrounded by evil advisers, and was incompetent to act with propriety in the high station which she filled; but he would bear it no longer; he would have her to know he was King; he was determined that his authority should be respected; henceforward the Princess should attend at every Court function with the utmost regularity; and he hoped to God that his life might be spared for six months longer, so that the calamity of a regency might be avoided, and the functions of the Crown pass directly to the heiress-presumptive instead of into the hands of the "person now near him," upon whose conduct and capacity no reliance whatever could be placed. The flood of vituperation rushed on for what seemed an interminable period, while the Queen blushed scarlet, the Princess burst into tears, and the hundred guests sat aghast. The Duchess said not a word until the tirade was over and the company had retired; then in a tornado of rage and mortification, she called for her carriage and announced her immediate return to Kensington. It was only with the utmost difficulty that some show of a reconciliation was patched up, and the out-

raged lady was prevailed upon to put off her departure till the morrow.[1]

Her troubles, however, were not over when she
had shaken the dust of Windsor from her feet.
In her own household she was pursued by bitterness and vexation of spirit. The apartments at
Kensington were seething with subdued disaffec-
tion, with jealousies and animosities virulently intensified by long years of propinquity and spite.

There was a deadly feud between Sir John
Conroy and Baroness Lehzen. But that was not
all. The Duchess had grown too fond of her
Major-Domo. There were familiarities, and one
day the Princess Victoria discovered the fact. She
confided what she had seen to the Baroness, and
to the Baroness's beloved ally, Madame de Späth.
Unfortunately, Madame de Späth could not hold
her tongue, and was actually foolish enough to
reprove the Duchess; whereupon she was instantly
dismissed. It was not so easy to get rid of the
Baroness. That lady, prudent and reserved,
maintained an irreproachable demeanour. Her
position was strongly entrenched; she had managed to secure the support of the King; and Sir
John found that he could do nothing against her.
But henceforward the household was divided into

1 Greville, III, 374-6.

two camps.[1] The Duchess supported Sir John
with all the abundance of her authority; but the
Baroness, too, had an adherent who could not be
neglected. The Princess Victoria said nothing,
but she had been much attached to Madame de
Späth, and she adored her Lehzen. The Duchess
knew only too well that in this horrid embroilment
her daughter was against her. Chagrin, annoyance, moral reprobation, tossed her to and fro.
She did her best to console herself with Sir John's
affectionate loquacity, or with the sharp remarks
of Lady Flora Hastings, one of her maids of honour, who had no love for the Baroness. The subject lent itself to satire; for the pastor's daughter,
with all her airs of stiff superiority, had habits
which betrayed her origin. Her passion for carra-
way seeds, for instance, was uncontrollable. Little
bags of them came over to her from Hanover, and
she sprinkled them on her bread and butter, her

[1] Greville, IV, 21; and August 15, 1839 (unpublished). "The
cause of the Queen's alienation from the Duchess and hatred of
Conroy, the Duke [of Wellington] said, was unquestionably owing
to her having witnessed some familiarities between them. What
she had seen she repeated to Baroness Spaeth, and Spaeth not
only did not hold her tongue, but (he thinks) remonstrated with
the Duchess herself on the subject. The consequence was that
they got rid of Spaeth, and they would have got rid of Lehzen,
too, if they had been able, but Lehzen, who knew very well what
was going on, was prudent enough not to commit herself, and
she was, besides, powerfully protected by George IV and
William IV, so that they did not dare to attempt to expel her."

cabbage, and even her roast beef. Lady Flora
could not resist a caustic observation; it was repeated to the Baroness, who pursed her lips in
fury; and so the mischief grew.[1]

v

The King had prayed that he might live till his
niece was of age; and a few days before her eighteenth birthday—the date of her legal majority—
a sudden attack of illness very nearly carried him
off. He recovered, however, and the Princess was
able to go through her birthday festivities—a state
ball and a drawing-room—with unperturbed enjoyment. "Count Zichy," she noted in her diary,
" is very good-looking in uniform, but not in plain
clothes. Count Waldstein looks remarkably well
in his pretty Hungarian uniform."[2] With the
latter young gentleman she wished to dance, but
there was an insurmountable difficulty. "He
could not dance quadrilles, and, as in my station I
unfortunately cannot valse and gallop, I could not
dance with him."[3] Her birthday present from the
King was of a pleasing nature, but it led to a
painful domestic scene. In spite of the anger of
her Belgian uncle, she had remained upon good

[1] Greville, IV, 21; Crawford, 128–9.   [2] *Girlhood*, I, 192–3.
[3] *Ibid.*, I, 191.

terms with her English one. He had always been
very kind to her, and the fact that he had quarrelled with her mother did not appear to be a reason for disliking him. He was, she said, "odd,
very odd and singular," but "his intentions were
often ill interpreted."[1] He now wrote her a letter, offering her an allowance of £10,000 a year,
which he proposed should be at her own disposal,
and independent of her mother. Lord Conyngham, the Lord Chamberlain, was instructed to
deliver the letter into the Princess's own hands.
When he arrived at Kensington, he was ushered
into the presence of the Duchess and the Princess,
and, when he produced the letter, the Duchess put
out her hand to take it. Lord Conyngham begged
her Royal Highness's pardon, and repeated the
King's commands. Thereupon the Duchess drew
back, and the Princess took the letter. She immediately wrote to her uncle, accepting his kind proposal. The Duchess was much displeased; £4000
a year, she said, would be quite enough for Victoria; as for the remaining £6000, it would be only
proper that she should have that herself.[2]

King William had thrown off his illness, and
returned to his normal life. Once more the royal
circle at Windsor—their Majesties, the elder Prin-

cesses, and some unfortunate Ambassadress or Minister's wife—might be seen ranged for hours round a mahogany table, while the Queen netted a purse, and the King slept, occasionally waking from his slumbers to observe "Exactly so, ma'am, exactly so!"[1] But this recovery was of short duration. The old man suddenly collapsed; with no specific symptoms besides an extreme weakness, he yet showed no power of rallying; and it was clear to everyone that his death was now close at hand.

All eyes, all thoughts, turned towards the Princess Victoria; but she still remained, shut away in the seclusion of Kensington, a small, unknown figure, lost in the large shadow of her mother's domination. The preceding year had in fact been an important one in her development. The soft tendrils of her mind had for the first time begun to stretch out towards unchildish things. In this King Leopold encouraged her. After his return to Brussels, he had resumed his correspondence in a more serious strain; he discussed the details of foreign politics; he laid down the duties of kingship; he pointed out the iniquitous foolishness of the newspaper press. On the latter subject, indeed, he wrote with some asperity. "If all the editors," he said, "of the papers in the countries

[1] Creevey, II. 262.

where the liberty of the press exists were to be assembled, we should have a *crew* to which you would *not* confide a dog that you would value, still less your honour and reputation." [1] On the functions of a monarch, his views were unexceptionable. " The business of the highest in a State," he wrote, " is certainly, in my opinion, to act with great impartiality and a spirit of justice for the good of all." [2] At the same time the Princess's tastes were opening out. Though she was still passionately devoted to riding and dancing, she now began to have a genuine love of music as well, and to drink in the roulades and arias of the Italian opera with high enthusiasm. She even enjoyed reading poetry—at any rate, the poetry of Sir Walter Scott. [3]

When King Leopold learnt that King William's death was approaching, he wrote several long letters of excellent advice to his niece. " In every letter I shall write to you," he said, " I mean to repeat to you, as a *fundamental rule, to be courageous, firm, and honest, as you have been till now.*" For the rest, in the crisis that was approaching, she was not to be alarmed, but to trust in her " good natural sense and the *truth* " of her character; she was to do nothing in a hurry; to

---

[1] *Letters*, I, 53.   [2] *Letters*, I, 61.   [3] *Girlhood*, I, 175.

hurt no one's *amour-propre,* and to continue her confidence in the Whig administration.[1] Not content with letters, however, King Leopold determined that the Princess should not lack personal guidance, and sent over to her aid the trusted friend whom, twenty years before, he had taken to his heart by the death-bed at Claremont. Thus, once again, as if in accordance with some preordained destiny, the figure of Stockmar is discernible—inevitably present at a momentous hour.

On June 18, the King was visibly sinking. The Archbishop of Canterbury was by his side, with all the comforts of the church. Nor did the holy words fall upon a rebellious spirit; for many years his Majesty had been a devout believer. "When I was a young man," he once explained at a public banquet, "as well as I can remember, I believed in nothing but pleasure and folly—nothing at all. But when I went to sea, got into a gale, and saw the wonders of the mighty deep, then I believed; and I have been a sincere Christian ever since." [1] It was the anniversary of the Battle of Waterloo, and the dying man remembered it. He should be glad to live, he said, over that day; he would never see another sunset. "I hope your Majesty may live to see many," said Dr. Chambers. "Oh! that's

---

[1] *Letters,* I, 79–1.   [2] Torrens, 419.

quite another thing, that's quite another thing," was the answer.[1] One other sunset he did live to see; and he died in the early hours of the following morning. It was on June 20, 1837.

When all was over, the Archbishop and the Lord Chamberlain ordered a carriage, and drove post-haste from Windsor to Kensington. They arrived at the Palace at five o'clock, and it was only with considerable difficulty that they gained admittance.[2] At six the Duchess woke up her daughter, and told her that the Archbishop of Canterbury and Lord Conyngham were there, and wished to see her. She got out of bed, put on her dressing-gown, and went, alone, into the room where the messengers were standing. Lord Conyngham fell on his knees, and officially announced the death of the King; the Archbishop added some personal details. Looking at the bending, murmuring dignitaries before her, she knew that she was Queen of England. " Since it has pleased Providence," she wrote that day in her journal, " to place me in this station, I shall do my utmost to fulfil my duty towards my country; I am very young, and perhaps in many, though not in all things, inexperienced, but I am sure, that very few have more real good will and more real desire

1 Huish, 686.   2 Wynn, 281.

to do what is fit and right than I have." [1] But
there was scant time for resolutions and reflections. At once, affairs were thick upon her.
Stockmar came to breakfast, and gave some good
advice. She wrote a letter to her uncle Leopold,
and a hurried note to her sister Feodora. A letter
came from the Prime Minister, Lord Melbourne,
announcing his approaching arrival. He came at
nine, in full court dress, and kissed her hand. She
saw him alone, and repeated to him the lesson
which, no doubt, the faithful Stockmar had taught
her at breakfast. " It has long been my intention
to retain your Lordship and the rest of the present Ministry at the head of affairs; " whereupon
Lord Melbourne again kissed her hand and shortly
after left her. She then wrote a letter of condolence to Queen Adelaide. At eleven, Lord Melbourne came again; and at half-past eleven she
went downstairs into the red saloon to hold her
first Council. [2] The great assembly of lords and
notables, bishops, generals, and Ministers of State,
saw the doors thrown open and a very short, very
slim girl in deep plain mourning come into the
room alone and move forward to her seat with extraordinary dignity and grace; they saw a countenance, not beautiful, but prepossessing—fair

1 *Girlhood*, I, 195–6.　　　　　　2 *Ibid.*, I, 196–7.

hair, blue prominent eyes, a small curved nose,
an open mouth revealing the upper teeth, a
tiny chin, a clear complexion, and, over all, the
strangely mingled signs of innocence, of gravity,
of youth, and of composure; they heard a high
unwavering voice reading aloud with perfect clarity; and then, the ceremony was over, they saw the
small figure rise and, with the same consummate
grace, the same amazing dignity, pass out from
among them, as she had come in, alone.[1]

[1] Greville, III, 414–6.

CHAPTER III

LORD MELBOURNE

I

THE new queen was almost entirely unknown to her subjects. In her public appearances her mother had invariably dominated the scene. Her private life had been that of a novice in a convent: hardly a human being from the outside world had ever spoken to her; and no human being at all, except her mother and the Baroness Lehzen, had ever been alone with her in a room. Thus it was not only the public at large that was in ignorance of everything concerning her; the inner circles of statesmen and officials and high-born ladies were equally in the dark.[1] When she suddenly emerged from this deep obscurity, the impression that she created was immediate and profound. Her bearing at her first Council filled the whole gathering with astonishment and admiration; the Duke of Wellington, Sir Robert Peel, even the savage Croker, even the cold and caustic Greville—all were completely carried away. Everything that

[1] Greville, III, 411.

was reported of her subsequent proceedings seemed
to be of no less happy augury. Her perceptions
were quick, her decisions were sensible, her language was discreet; she performed her royal duties
with extraordinary facility.[1] Among the outside
public there was a great wave of enthusiasm. Sentiment and romance were coming into fashion; and
the spectacle of the little girl-queen, innocent,
modest, with fair hair and pink cheeks, driving
through her capital, filled the hearts of the behold-
ers with raptures of affectionate loyalty. What,
above all, struck everybody with overwhelming
force was the contrast between Queen Victoria
and her uncles. The nasty old men, debauched
and selfish, pig-headed and ridiculous, with their
perpetual burden of debts, confusions, and disrep-
utabilities—they had vanished like the snows of
winter, and here at last, crowned and radiant, was
the spring. Lord John Russell, in an elaborate
oration, gave voice to the general sentiment. He
hoped that Victoria might prove an Elizabeth
without her tyranny, an Anne without her weakness. He asked England to pray that the illustrious Princess who had just ascended the throne
with the purest intentions and the justest desires
might see slavery abolished, crime diminished, and

[1] Greville, IV, 7, 9, 14–15.

education improved. He trusted that her people
would henceforward derive their strength, their
conduct, and their loyalty from enlightened religious and moral principles, and that, so fortified,
the reign of Victoria might prove celebrated
to posterity and to all the nations of the
earth.[1]

Very soon, however, there were signs that the
future might turn out to be not quite so simple
and roseate as a delighted public dreamed. The
"illustrious Princess" might perhaps, after all,
have something within her which squared ill with
the easy vision of a well-conducted heroine in an
edifying story-book. The purest intentions and
the justest desires? No doubt; but was that all?
To those who watched closely, for instance, there
might be something ominous in the curious con-
tour of that little mouth. When, after her first
Council, she crossed the ante-room and found her
mother waiting for her, she said, "And now, Mamma, am I really and truly Queen?" "You see,
my dear, that it is so." "Then, dear Mamma, I
hope you will grant me the first request I make to
you, as Queen. Let me be by myself for an
hour."[2] For an hour she remained in solitude.
Then she reappeared, and gave a significant order:

[1] Walpole, I, 284.   [2] Crawford, 156–7.

her bed was to be moved out of her mother's room.
It was the doom of the Duchess of Kent. The
long years of waiting were over at last; the moment of a lifetime had come; her daughter was
Queen of England; and that very moment brought
her own annihilation. She found herself, absolutely and irretrievably, shut off from every vestige of influence, of confidence, of power. She
was surrounded, indeed, by all the outward signs
of respect and consideration; but that only made
the inward truth of her position the more intolerable. Through the mingled formalities of Court
etiquette and filial duty, she could never penetrate
to Victoria. She was unable to conceal her disappointment and her rage. " Il n'y a plus d'avenir
pour moi," she exclaimed to Madame de Lieven;
" je ne suis plus rien." For eighteen years, she
said, this child had been the sole object of her existence, of her thoughts, her hopes, and now—no!
she would not be comforted, she had lost everything, she was to the last degree unhappy.[1] Sailing, so gallantly and so pertinaciously, through the
buffeting storms of life, the stately vessel, with
sails still swelling and pennons flying, had put into
harbour at last; to find there nothing—a land of
bleak desolation.

[1] Greville, IV, 16.

Within a month of the accession, the realities of the new situation assumed a visible shape. The whole royal household moved from Kensington to Buckingham Palace, and, in the new abode, the Duchess of Kent was given a suite of apartments entirely separate from the Queen's. By Victoria herself the change was welcomed, though, at the moment of departure, she could afford to be sentimental. "Though I rejoice to *go* into B. P. for many reasons," she wrote in her diary, "it is not without feelings of regret that I shall bid adieu *for ever* to this my birthplace, where I have been born and bred, and to which I am really attached!" Her memory lingered for a moment over visions of the past: her sister's wedding, pleasant balls and *delicious* concerts . . . and there were other recollections. "I have gone through painful and disagreeable scenes here, 'tis true," she concluded, "but still I am fond of the poor old palace."[1]

At the same time she took another decided step. She had determined that she would see no more of Sir John Conroy. She rewarded his past services with liberality: he was given a baronetcy and a pension of £3000 a year; he remained a member of the Duchess's household, but his per-

[1] *Girlhood*, I, 210-1.

sonal intercourse with the Queen came to an abrupt conclusion.[1]

II

It was clear that these interior changes—whatever else they might betoken—marked the triumph of one person—the Baroness Lehzen. The pastor's daughter observed the ruin of her enemies. Discreet and victorious, she remained in possession of the field. More closely than ever did she cleave to the side of her mistress, her pupil, and her friend; and in the recesses of the palace her mysterious figure was at once invisible and omnipresent. When the Queen's Ministers came in at one door, the Baroness went out by another; when they retired, she immediately returned.[2] Nobody knew —nobody ever will know—the precise extent and the precise nature of her influence. She herself declared that she never discussed public affairs with the Queen, that she was concerned with private matters only—with private letters and the details of private life.[3] Certainly her hand is everywhere discernible in Victoria's early correspondence. The Journal is written in the style of a child; the Letters are not so simple; they are the

1 Greville, IV, 15.   2 *Ibid.*, IV, 21-2.
3 Stockmar, 322-3; Maxwell, 159-60.

work of a child, rearranged—with the minimum of
alteration, no doubt, and yet perceptibly—by a
governess. And the governess was no fool: narrow, jealous, provincial, she might be; but she was
an acute and vigorous woman, who had gained by
a peculiar insight, a peculiar ascendancy. That
ascendancy she meant to keep. No doubt it was
true that technically she took no part in public
business; but the distinction between what is public and what is private is always a subtle one; and
in the case of a reigning sovereign—as the next
few years were to show—it is often imaginary.
Considering all things—the characters of the persons, and the character of the times—it was something more than a mere matter of private interest
that the bedroom of Baroness Lehzen at Buckingham Palace should have been next door to the bedroom of the Queen.

But the influence wielded by the Baroness, supreme as it seemed within its own sphere, was not
unlimited; there were other forces at work. For
one thing, the faithful Stockmar had taken up his
residence in the palace. During the twenty years
which had elapsed since the death of the Princess
Charlotte, his experiences had been varied and remarkable. The unknown counsellor of a disappointed princeling had gradually risen to a posi-

tion of European importance. His devotion to his
master had been not only whole-hearted but cautious and wise. It was Stockmar's advice that had
kept Prince Leopold in England during the critical years which followed his wife's death, and had
thus secured to him the essential requisite of a
point d'appui in the country of his adoption.[1] It
was Stockmar's discretion which had smoothed
over the embarrassments surrounding the Prince's
acceptance and rejection of the Greek crown. It
was Stockmar who had induced the Prince to become the constitutional Sovereign of Belgium.[2]
Above all, it was Stockmar's tact, honesty, and
diplomatic skill which, through a long series of
arduous and complicated negotiations, had led to
the guarantee of Belgian neutrality by the Great
Powers.[3] His labours had been rewarded by a
German barony and by the complete confidence of
King Leopold. Nor was it only in Brussels that
he was treated with respect and listened to with
attention. The statesmen who governed England
—Lord Grey, Sir Robert Peel, Lord Palmerston,
Lord Melbourne—had learnt to put a high value
upon his probity and his intelligence. " He is
one of the cleverest fellows I ever saw," said Lord

1 Stockmar, 109–10.   2 *Ibid.*, 165–6.
3 *Ibid.*, chaps. viii, ix, x, and xi.

Melbourne—"the most discreet man, the most well-judging, and most cool man."[1] And Lord Palmerston cited Baron Stockmar as the only absolutely disinterested man he had come across in life.[2] At last he was able to retire to Coburg, and to enjoy for a few years the society of the wife and children whom his labours in the service of his master had hitherto only allowed him to visit at long intervals for a month or two at a time. But in 1836 he had been again entrusted with an important negotiation, which he had brought to a successful conclusion in the marriage of Prince Ferdinand of Saxe-Coburg, a nephew of King Leopold's, with Queen Maria II of Portugal.[3] The House of Coburg was beginning to spread over Europe; and the establishment of the Baron at Buckingham Palace in 1837 was to be the prelude of another and a more momentous advance.[4]

King Leopold and his counsellor provide in their careers an example of the curious diversity of human ambitions. The desires of man are wonderfully various; but no less various are the means by which those desires may reach satisfaction: and so the work of the world gets done. The correct mind of Leopold craved for the whole apparatus

---

[1] *Girlhood*, II, 303.
[2] Stockmar, 324

[3] *Ibid.*, chap. xv, pt. 2.
[4] *Ibid.*, chap. xvii.

of royalty. Mere power would have held no attractions for him; he must be an actual king—the crowned head of a people. It was not enough to do; it was essential also to be recognised; anything else would not be fitting. The greatness that he dreamt of was surrounded by every appropriate circumstance. To be a Majesty, to be a cousin of Sovereigns, to marry a Bourbon for diplomatic ends, to correspond with the Queen of England, to be very stiff and very punctual, to found a dynasty, to bore ambassadresses into fits, to live, on the highest pinnacle, an exemplary life devoted to the public service—such were his objects, and such, in fact, were his achievements. The "Marquis Peu-à-peu," as George IV called him,[1] had what he wanted. But this would never have been the case if it had not happened that the ambition of Stockmar took a form exactly complementary to his own. The sovereignty that the Baron sought for was by no means obvious. The satisfaction of his essential being lay in obscurity, in invisibility —in passing, unobserved, through a hidden entrance, into the very central chamber of power, and in sitting there, quietly, pulling the subtle strings that set the wheels of the whole world in motion. A very few people, in very high places,

---

[1] Stein, VI, 932.

and exceptionally well-informed, knew that Baron
Stockmar was a most important person: that was
enough. The fortunes of the master and the servant, intimately interacting, rose together. The
Baron's secret skill had given Leopold his unexceptionable kingdom; and Leopold, in his turn, as
time went on, was able to furnish the Baron with
more and more keys to more and more back doors.

Stockmar took up his abode in the Palace partly
as the emissary of King Leopold, but more particularly as the friend and adviser of a queen who
was almost a child, and who, no doubt, would be
much in need of advice and friendship. For it
would be a mistake to suppose that either of these
two men was actuated by a vulgar selfishness. The
King, indeed, was very well aware on which side
his bread was buttered; during an adventurous and
chequered life he had acquired a shrewd knowledge of the world's workings; and he was ready
enough to use that knowledge to strengthen his
position and to spread his influence. But then,
the firmer his position and the wider his influence,
the better for Europe; of that he was quite certain. And besides, he was a constitutional monarch; and it would be highly indecorous in a constitutional monarch to have any aims that were
low or personal. As for Stockmar, the disinter-

estedness which Palmerston had noted was undoubtedly a basic element in his character. The
ordinary schemer is always an optimist; and Stockmar, racked by dyspepsia and haunted by gloomy
forebodings, was a constitutionally melancholy
man. A schemer, no doubt, he was; but he
schemed distrustfully, splenetically, to do good.
To do good! What nobler end could a man
scheme for? Yet it is perilous to scheme at all.

With Lehzen to supervise every detail of her
conduct, with Stockmar in the next room, so full
of wisdom and experience of affairs, with her
Uncle Leopold's letters, too, pouring out so constantly their stream of encouragements, general
reflections, and highly valuable tips, Victoria, even
had she been without other guidance, would have
stood in no lack of private counsellors. But other
guidance she had; for all these influences paled
before a new star, of the first magnitude, which,
rising suddenly upon her horizon, immediately
dominated her life.

III

William Lamb, Viscount Melbourne, was fifty-
eight years of age, and had been for the last three
years Prime Minister of England. In every outward respect he was one of the most fortunate

of mankind. He had been born into the midst of riches, brilliance, and power. His mother, fascinating and intelligent, had been a great Whig hostess, and he had been bred up as a member of that radiant society which, during the last quarter of the eighteenth century, concentrated within itself the ultimate perfections of a hundred years of triumphant aristocracy. Nature had given him beauty and brains; the unexpected death of an elder brother brought him wealth, a peerage, and the possibility of high advancement. Within that charmed circle, whatever one's personal disabilities, it was difficult to fail; and to him, with all his advantages, success was well-nigh unavoidable. With little effort, he attained political eminence. On the triumph of the Whigs he became one of the leading members of the Government; and when Lord Grey retired from the premiership he quietly stepped into the vacant place. Nor was it only in the visible signs of fortune that Fate had been kind to him. Bound to succeed, and to succeed easily, he was gifted with so fine a nature that his success became him. His mind, at once supple and copious, his temperament, at once calm and sensitive, enabled him not merely to work, but to live with perfect facility and with the grace of strength. In society he was a notable talker, a

captivating companion, a charming man. If one
looked deeper, one saw at once that he was not
ordinary, that the piquancies of his conversation
and his manner—his free-and-easy vaguenesses,
his abrupt questions, his lollings and loungings, his
innumerable oaths—were something more than an
amusing ornament, were the outward manifestation of an individuality that was fundamental.

The precise nature of this individuality was very
difficult to gauge: it was dubious, complex, perhaps self-contradictory. Certainly there was an
ironical discordance between the inner history of
the man and his apparent fortunes. He owed all
he had to his birth, and his birth was shameful; it
was known well enough that his mother had passionately loved Lord Egremont, and that Lord
Melbourne was not his father.[1] His marriage,
which had seemed to be the crown of his youthful
ardours, was a long, miserable, desperate failure:
the incredible Lady Caroline,

> . . . "with pleasures too refined to please,
> With too much spirit to be e'er at ease,
> With too much quickness to be ever taught,
> With too much thinking to have common thought,"

was very nearly the destruction of his life. When
at last he emerged from the anguish and confusion

[1] Greville, VI, 247; Torrens, 14; Hayward, I, 336.

of her folly, her extravagance, her rage, her despair, and her devotion, he was left alone with endless memories of intermingled farce and tragedy, and an only son, who was an imbecile. But there was something else that he owed to Lady Caroline. While she whirled with Byron in a hectic frenzy of love and fashion, he had stayed at home in an indulgence bordering on cynicism, and occupied his solitude with reading. It was thus that he had acquired those habits of study, that love of learning, and that wide and accurate knowledge of ancient and modern literature, which formed so unexpected a part of his mental equipment. His passion for reading never deserted him; even when he was Prime Minister he found time to master every new important book.[1] With an incongruousness that was characteristic, his favourite study was theology. An accomplished classical scholar, he was deeply read in the Fathers of the Church; heavy volumes of commentary and exegesis he examined with scrupulous diligence; and at any odd moment he might be found turning over the pages of the Bible.[2] To the ladies whom he most liked he would lend some learned

---

[1] Greville, VI, 248.

[2] Greville, III, 331; VI, 254; Haydon, III, 12: "March 1, 1835. Called on Lord Melbourne, and found him reading the Acts, with a quarto Greek Testament that belonged to Samuel Johnson."

work on the Revelation, crammed with marginal
notes in his own hand, or Dr. Lardner's " Observations upon the Jewish Errors with respect to the
Conversion of Mary Magdalene." The more pious
among them had high hopes that these studies
would lead him into the right way; but of this
there were no symptoms in his after-dinner conversations.[1]

The paradox of his political career was no less
curious. By temperament an aristocrat, by conviction a conservative, he came to power as the leader
of the popular party, the party of change. He
had profoundly disliked the Reform Bill, which
he had only accepted at last as a necessary evil;
and the Reform Bill lay at the root of the very
existence, of the very meaning, of his government.
He was far too sceptical to believe in progress of
any kind. Things were best as they were—or
rather, they were least bad. " You'd better try
to do no good," was one of his dictums, " and then
you'll get into no scrapes." Education at best was
futile; education of the poor was positively dangerous. The factory children? " Oh, if you'd only
have the goodness to leave them alone!" Free
Trade was a delusion; the ballot was nonsense;
and there was no such thing as a democracy. Nev-

[1] Greville, III, 142; Torrens, 545.

ertheless, he was not a reactionary; he was simply an opportunist. The whole duty of government, he said, was "to prevent crime and to preserve contracts." All one could really hope to do was to carry on. He himself carried on in a remarkable manner—with perpetual compromises, with fluctuations and contradictions, with every kind of weakness, and yet with shrewdness, with gentleness, even with conscientiousness, and a light and airy mastery of men and of events. He conducted the transactions of business with extraordinary nonchalance. Important persons, ushered up for some grave interview, found him in a towselled bed, littered with books and papers, or vaguely shaving in a dressing-room; but, when they went downstairs again, they would realise that somehow or other they had been pumped. When he had to receive a deputation, he could hardly ever do so with becoming gravity. The worthy delegates of the tallow-chandlers, or the Society for the Abolition of Capital Punishment, were distressed and mortified when, in the midst of their speeches, the Prime Minister became absorbed in blowing a feather, or suddenly cracked an unseemly joke. How could they have guessed that he had spent the night before diligently getting up the details of their case? He hated patronage and the making of appointments—a feeling rare in Ministers. "As for the Bishops," he burst out. " I positively believe they die to vex me." But when at last the appointment was made, it was made with keen discrimination. His colleagues observed another symptom—was it of his irresponsibility or his wisdom? He went to sleep in the Cabinet.[1]

Probably, if he had been born a little earlier, he would have been a simpler and a happier man. As it was, he was a child of the eighteenth century whose lot was cast in a new, difficult, unsympathetic age. He was an autumn rose. With all his gracious amenity, his humour, his happy-go-lucky ways, a deep disquietude possessed him. A sentimental cynic, a sceptical believer, he was restless and melancholy at heart. Above all, he could never harden himself; those sensitive petals shivered in every wind. Whatever else he might be, one thing was certain: Lord Melbourne was always human, supremely human—too human, perhaps.[2]

And now, with old age upon him, his life took a sudden, new, extraordinary turn. He became, in the twinkling of an eye, the intimate adviser and the daily companion of a young girl who had

[1] *Girlhood,* II, 148; Torrens, 278, 431, 517; Greville, IV, 331; VIII, 162.
[2] Greville, VI, 253–4; Torrens, 354.

stepped all at once from a nursery to a throne.
His relations with women had been, like everything else about him, ambiguous. Nobody had ever
been able quite to gauge the shifting, emotional
complexities of his married life; Lady Caroline
vanished; but his peculiar susceptibilities remained.
Female society of some kind or other was necessary to him, and he did not stint himself; a great
part of every day was invariably spent in it. The
feminine element in him made it easy, made it
natural and inevitable for him to be the friend of
a great many women; but the masculine element
in him was strong as well. In such circumstances
it is also easy, it is even natural, perhaps it is even
inevitable, to be something more than a friend.
There were rumours and combustions. Lord Melbourne was twice a co-respondent in a divorce
action; but on each occasion he won his suit. The
lovely Lady Brandon, the unhappy and brilliant
Mrs. Norton . . . the law exonerated them both.
Beyond that hung an impenetrable veil. But at
any rate it was clear that, with such a record, the
Prime Minister's position in Buckingham Palace
must be a highly delicate one. However, he was
used to delicacies, and he met the situation with
consummate success. His behaviour was from the
first moment impeccable. His manner towards

the young Queen mingled, with perfect facility, the watchfulness and the respect of a statesman and a courtier with the tender solicitude of a parent. He was at once reverential and affectionate, at once the servant and the guide. At the same time the habits of his life underwent a surprising change. His comfortable, unpunctual days became subject to the unaltering routine of a palace; no longer did he sprawl on sofas; not a single " damn " escaped his lips. The man of the world who had been the friend of Byron and the regent, the talker whose paradoxes had held Holland House enthralled, the cynic whose ribaldries had' enlivened so many deep potations, the lover whose soft words had captivated such beauty and such passion and such wit, might now be seen, evening after evening, talking with infinite politeness to a schoolgirl, bolt upright, amid the silence and the rigidity of Court etiquette.[1]

IV

On her side, Victoria was instantaneously fascinated by Lord Melbourne. The good report of Stockmar had no doubt prepared the way; Lehzen was wisely propitiated; and the first highly favourable impression was never afterwards belied. She

[1] Greville, IV, 135, 154; *Girlhood*, 1, 249.

found him perfect; and perfect in her sight he remained. Her absolute and unconcealed adoration
was very natural; what innocent young creature
could have resisted, in any circumstances, the
charm and the devotion of such a man? But, in
her situation, there was a special influence which
gave a peculiar glow to all she felt. After years
of emptiness and dullness and suppression, she had
come suddenly, in the heyday of youth, into freedom and power. She was mistress of herself, of
great domains and palaces; she was Queen of
England. Responsibilities and difficulties she
might have, no doubt, and in heavy measure; but
one feeling dominated and absorbed all others—
the feeling of joy. Everything pleased her. She
was in high spirits from morning till night. Mr.
Creevey, grown old now, and very near his end,
catching a glimpse of her at Brighton, was much
amused, in his sharp fashion, by the ingenuous
gaiety of " little Vic."—" A more homely little
being you never beheld, *when she is at her ease,*
and she is evidently dying to be always more so.
She laughs in real earnest, opening her mouth as
wide as it can go, showing not very pretty gums.
. . . She eats quite as heartily as she laughs, I
think I may say she gobbles. . . . She blushes
and laughs every instant in so natural a way as

to disarm anybody." [1]   But it was not merely
when she was laughing or gobbling that she enjoyed herself; the performance of her official duties gave her intense satisfaction. " I really have
immensely to do," she wrote in her Journal a few
days after her accession; " I receive so many communications from my Ministers, but I like it very
much." [2]   And again, a week later, " I repeat what
I said before that I have *so many* communications
from the Ministers, and from me to them, and I
get so many papers to sign every day, that I have
always a *very great* deal to do. I *delight* in this
work." [3]   Through the girl's immaturity the vigorous predestined tastes of the woman were pushing
themselves into existence with eager velocity, with
delicious force.

One detail of her happy situation deserves particular mention. Apart from the splendour of her
social position and the momentousness of her political one, she was a person of great wealth. As
soon as Parliament met, an annuity of £385,000
was settled upon her. When the expenses of her
household had been discharged, she was left with
£68,000 a year of her own. She enjoyed besides
the revenues of the Duchy of Lancaster, which
amounted annually to over £27,000. The first use

1 Creevey, II, 326.   2 *Girlhood*, I, 203.   3 *Ibid.*, I, 206.

to which she put her money was characteristic: she paid off her father's debts. In money matters, no less than in other matters, she was determined to be correct. She had the instincts of a man of business; and she never could have borne to be in a position that was financially unsound.[1]

With youth and happiness gilding every hour, the days passed merrily enough. And each day hinged upon Lord Melbourne. Her diary shows us, with undiminished clarity, the life of the young sovereign during the early months of her reign— a life satisfactorily regular, full of delightful business, a life of simple pleasures, mostly physical— riding, eating, dancing—a quick, easy, highly un-sophisticated life, sufficient unto itself. The light of the morning is upon it; and, in the rosy radiance, the figure of " Lord M." emerges, glorified and supreme. If she is the heroine of the story, he is the hero; but indeed they are more than hero and heroine, for there are no other characters at all. Lehzen, the Baron, Uncle Leopold, are un-substantial shadows—the incidental supers of the piece. Her paradise was peopled by two persons, and surely that was enough. One sees them to-gether still, a curious couple, strangely united in those artless pages, under the magical illumination

[1] Lee, 79–81.

of that dawn of eighty years ago: the polished high fine gentleman with the whitening hair and whiskers and the thick dark eyebrows and the mobile lips and the big expressive eyes; and beside him the tiny Queen—fair, slim, elegant, active, in her plain girl's dress and little tippet, looking up at him earnestly, adoringly, with eyes blue and projecting, and half-open mouth. So they appear upon every page of the Journal; upon every page Lord M. is present, Lord M. is speaking, Lord M. is being amusing, instructive, delightful, and affectionate at once, while Victoria drinks in the honied words, laughs till she shows her gums, tries hard to remember, and runs off, as soon as she is left alone, to put it all down. Their long conversations touched upon a multitude of topics. Lord M. would criticise books, throw out a remark or two on the British Constitution, make some passing reflections on human life, and tell story after story of the great people of the eighteenth century. Then there would be business—a despatch perhaps from Lord Durham in Canada, which Lord M. would read. But first he must explain a little. "He said that I must know that Canada originally belonged to the French, and was only ceded to the English in 1760, when it was taken in an expedition under Wolfe: 'a very daring enterprise,' he said. Canada was then entirely French, and the British only came afterwards. . . . Lord M. explained this very clearly (and much better than I have done) and said a good deal more about it. He then read me Durham's despatch, which is a very long one and took him more than ½ an hour to read. Lord M. read it beautifully with that fine soft voice of his, and with so much expression, so that it is needless to say I was much interested by it." [1] And then the talk would take a more personal turn. Lord M. would describe his boyhood, and she would learn that " he wore his hair long, as all boys then did, till he was 17; (*how* handsome he must have looked!)." [2] Or she would find out about his queer tastes and habits—how he never carried a watch, which seemed quite extraordinary. " ' I always ask the servant what o'clock it is, and then he tells me what he likes,' said Lord M." [3] Or, as the rooks wheeled about round the trees, " in a manner which indicated rain," he would say that he could sit looking at them for an hour, and " was quite surprised at my disliking them. . . . Lord M. said, ' The rooks are my delight.' " [4]

The day's routine, whether in London or at

[1] *Girlhood,* II, 3.
[2] *Ibid,* II, 29.
[3] *Ibid.,* II, 100.
[4] *Ibid.,* II, 57, 256.

Windsor, was almost invariable. The morning
was devoted to business and Lord M. In the
afternoon the whole Court went out riding. The
Queen, in her velvet riding-habit and a top-hat
with a veil draped about the brim, headed the cav-
alcade; and Lord M. rode beside her. The lively
troupe went fast and far, to the extreme exhilaration of Her Majesty. Back in the Palace again,
there was still time for a little more fun before
dinner—a game of battledore and shuttlecock perhaps, or a romp along the galleries with some children.[1] Dinner came, and the ceremonial decidedly
tightened. The gentleman of highest rank sat on
the right hand of the Queen; on her left—it soon
became an established rule—sat Lord Melbourne.
After the ladies had left the dining-room, the gentlemen were not permitted to remain behind for
very long; indeed, the short time allowed them for
their wine-drinking formed the subject—so it was
rumoured—of one of the very few disputes between the Queen and her Prime Minister;[2] but her

---

[1] Lee, 71.

[2] The Duke of Bedford told Greville he was " sure there was a
battle between her and Melbourne. . . . He is sure there was
one about the men's sitting after dinner, for he heard her say to him
rather angrily, ' it is a horrid custom '—but when the ladies left
the room (he dined there) directions were given that the men
should remain *five minutes* longer." Greville *Memoirs*, February 26,
1840 (unpublished).

determination carried the day, and from that moment after-dinner drunkenness began to go out of fashion. When the company was reassembled in the drawing-room the etiquette was stiff. For a few moments the Queen spoke in turn to each one of her guests; and during these short uneasy colloquies the aridity of royalty was apt to become painfully evident. One night Mr. Greville, the Clerk of the Privy Council, was present; his turn soon came; the middle-aged, hard-faced *viveur* was addressed by his young hostess. " Have you been riding to-day, Mr. Greville? " asked the Queen. " No, Madam, I have not," replied Mr. Greville. " It was a fine day," continued the Queen. " Yes, Madam, a very fine day," said Mr. Greville. " It was rather cold, though," said the Queen. " It *was* rather cold, Madam," said Mr. Greville. " Your sister, Lady Frances Egerton, rides, I think, doesn't she? " said the Queen. " She does ride sometimes, Madam," said Mr. Greville. There was a pause, after which Mr. Greville ventured to take the lead, though he did not venture to change the subject. " Has your Majesty been riding to-day? " asked Mr. Greville. " Oh yes, a very long ride," answered the Queen with animation. " Has your Majesty got a nice horse? " said Mr. Greville. " Oh, a very nice horse," said the Queen.

It was over. Her Majesty gave a smile and an inclination of the head, Mr. Greville a profound bow, and the next conversation began with the next gentleman.[1] When all the guests had been disposed of, the Duchess of Kent sat down to her whist, while everybody else was ranged about the round table. Lord Melbourne sat beside the Queen, and talked pertinaciously—very often *à propos* to the contents of one of the large albums of engravings with which the round table was covered—until it was half-past eleven and time to go to bed.[2]

Occasionally, there were little diversions: the evening might be spent at the opera or at the play. Next morning the royal critic was careful to note down her impressions. " It was Shakespeare's tragedy of *Hamlet*, and we came in at the beginning of it. Mr. Charles Kean (son of old Kean) acted the part of Hamlet, and I must say beautifully. His conception of this very difficult, and I may almost say incomprehensible, character is admirable; his delivery of all the fine long speeches quite beautiful; he is excessively graceful and all his actions and attitudes are good, though not at all good-looking in face. . . . I came away just

1 Greville, March 11, 1838 (unpublished).
2 Greville, IV, 152–3.

as *Hamlet* was over." [1]   Later on, she went to
see Macready in *King Lear*. The story was new
to her; she knew nothing about it, and at first she
took very little interest in what was passing on
the stage; she preferred to chatter and laugh with
the Lord Chamberlain. But, as the play went on,
her mood changed; her attention was fixed, and
then she laughed no more. Yet she was puzzled;
it seemed a strange, a horrible business. What did
Lord M. think? Lord M. thought it was a very
fine play, but to be sure, " a rough, coarse play,
written for those times, with exaggerated characters." " I'm glad you've seen it," he added.[2] But,
undoubtedly, the evenings which she enjoyed most
were those on which there was dancing. She was
always ready enough to seize any excuse—the arrival of cousins—a birthday—a gathering of young
people—to give the command for that. Then,
when the band played, and the figures of the dan-
cers swayed to the music, and she felt her own
figure swaying too, with youthful spirits so close
on every side—then her happiness reached its
height, her eyes sparkled, she must go on and on
into the small hours of the morning. For a moment Lord M. himself was forgotten.

[1] *Girlhood*, I, 265–6.
[2] Martineau, II, 119–20; *Girlhood*, II, 121–2.

V

The months flew past. The summer was over: "the pleasantest summer I EVER passed in *my life,* and I shall never forget this first summer of my reign."[1] With surprising rapidity, another summer was upon her. The coronation came and went—a curious dream. The antique, intricate, endless ceremonial worked itself out as best it could, like some machine of gigantic complexity which was a little out of order. The small central figure went through her gyrations. She sat; she walked; she prayed; she carried about an orb that was almost too heavy to hold; the Archbishop of Canterbury came and crushed a ring upon the wrong finger, so that she was ready to cry out with the pain; old Lord Rolle tripped up in his mantle and fell down the steps as he was doing homage; she was taken into a side chapel, where the altar was covered with a table-cloth, sandwiches, and bottles of wine; she perceived Lehzen in an upper box and exchanged a smile with her as she sat, robed and crowned, on the Confessor's throne. "I shall ever remember this day as the *proudest* of my life," she noted. But the pride was soon merged once more in youth and simplicity. When she returned to Buckingham Pal-

[1] *Girlhood,* I, 229.

ace at last she was not tired; she ran up to her
private rooms, doffed her splendours, and gave
her dog Dash its evening bath.[1]

Life flowed on again with its accustomed smoothness—though, of course, the smoothness was occasionally disturbed. For one thing, there was the
distressing behaviour of Uncle Leopold. The King
of the Belgians had not been able to resist attempting to make use of his family position to further
his diplomatic ends. But, indeed, why should there
be any question of resisting? Was not such a
course of conduct, far from being a temptation,
simply *selon les règles?* What were royal marriages for, if they did not enable sovereigns, in
spite of the hindrances of constitutions, to control
foreign politics? For the highest purposes, of
course; that was understood. The Queen of England was his niece—more than that—almost his
daughter; his confidential agent was living, in a
position of intimate favour, at her court. Surely,
in such circumstances, it would be preposterous,
it would be positively incorrect, to lose the opportunity of bending to his wishes by means of personal influence, behind the backs of the English
Ministers, the foreign policy of England.

He set about the task with becoming precau-

[1] *Girlhood,* I, 356–64; Leslie, II, 239.

tions. He continued in his letters his admirable advice. Within a few days of her accession, he recommended the young Queen to lay emphasis, on every possible occasion, upon her English birth; to praise the English nation; " the Established Church I also recommend strongly; you cannot, without *pledging* yourself to anything *particular, say too much on the subject."* And then " before you decide on anything important I should be glad if you would consult me; this would also have the advantage of giving you time "; nothing was more injurious than to be hurried into wrong decisions unawares. His niece replied at once with all the accustomed warmth of her affection; but she wrote hurriedly—and, perhaps, a trifle vaguely too. *" Your* advice is always of the *greatest importance* to me," she said.[1]

Had he, possibly, gone too far? He could not be certain; perhaps Victoria *had* been hurried. In any case, he would be careful; he would draw back—*pour mieux sauter,* he added to himself with a smile. In his next letters he made no reference to his suggestion of consultations with himself; he merely pointed out the wisdom, in general, of refusing to decide upon important questions off-hand. So far, his advice was taken; and it

[1] *Letters,* I, 79.

was noticed that the Queen, when applications were made to her, rarely gave an immediate answer. Even with Lord Melbourne, it was the same; when he asked for her opinion upon any subject, she would reply that she would think it over, and tell him her conclusions next day.[1]

King Leopold's counsels continued. The Princess de Lieven, he said, was a dangerous woman; there was reason to think that she would make attempts to pry into what did not concern her; let Victoria beware. "A rule which I cannot sufficiently recommend is *never to permit* people to speak on subjects concerning yourself or your affairs, without you having yourself desired them to do so." Should such a thing occur, "change the conversation, and make the individual feel that he has made a mistake." This piece of advice was also taken; for it fell out as the King had predicted. Madame de Lieven sought an audience, and appeared to be verging towards confidential topics; whereupon the Queen, becoming slightly embarrassed, talked of nothing but commonplaces. The individual felt that she had made a mistake.[2]

The King's next warning was remarkable. Letters, he pointed out, are almost invariably read in

1 *Letters*, I, 80; Greville, IV, 22.
2 Greville, I, 85–6; Greville, IV, 16.

the post. This was inconvenient, no doubt; but the fact, once properly grasped, was not without its advantages. " I will give you an example: we are still plagued by Prussia concerning those fort-resses; now to tell the Prussian Government many things, which we *should not like* to tell them offi-cially, the Minister is going to write a despatch to our man at Berlin, sending it *by post;* the Prus-sians *are sure* to read it, and to learn in this way what we wish them to hear." Analogous circum-stances might very probably occur in England. " I tell you the *trick*," wrote His Majesty, " that you should be able to guard against it." Such were the subtleties of constitutional sovereignty.[1]

It seemed that the time had come for another step. The King's next letter was full of foreign politics—the situation in Spain and Portugal, the character of Louis Philippe; and he received a favourable answer. Victoria, it is true, began by saying that she had shown the *political part* of his letter to Lord Melbourne; but she proceeded to a discussion of foreign affairs. It appeared that she was not unwilling to exchange observations on such matters with her uncle.[2] So far so good. But King Leopold was still cautious; though a crisis was impending in his diplomacy, he still hung

[1] *Letters,* I, 93.   [2] *Ibid.,* I, 93–5.

back; at last, however, he could keep silence no
longer. It was of the utmost importance to him
that, in his manœuvrings with France and Holland, he should have, or at any rate appear to
have, English support. But the English Government appeared to adopt a neutral attitude; it was
too bad; not to be for him was to be against him—
could they not see that? Yet, perhaps, they were
only wavering, and a little pressure upon them
from Victoria might still save all. He determined
to put the case before her, delicately yet forcibly—
just as he saw it himself. "All I want from your
kind Majesty," he wrote, "is, that you will *occasionally* express to your Ministers, and particularly to good Lord Melbourne, that, as far as it is
compatible with the interests *of your own* dominions, you do *not* wish that your Government should
take the lead in such measures as might in a short
time bring on the *destruction* of this country, as
well as that of your uncle and his family." [1] The
result of this appeal was unexpected; there was
dead silence for more than a week. When Victoria at last wrote, she was prodigal of her affection—"it would, indeed, my dearest Uncle, be
very wrong of you, if you thought my feelings of
warm and devoted attachment to you, and of great

[1] *Letters,* I, 116.

affection for you, could be changed—*nothing* can
ever change them "—but her references to foreign
politics, though they were lengthy and elaborate,
were non-committal in the extreme; they were almost cast in an official and diplomatic form. Her
Ministers, she said, entirely shared her views upon
the subject; she understood and sympathised with
the difficulties of her beloved uncle's position; and
he might rest assured " that both Lord Melbourne
and Lord Palmerston are most anxious at all times
for the prosperity and welfare of Belgium." That
was all. The King in his reply declared himself
delighted, and re-echoed the affectionate protestations of his niece. " My dearest and most beloved
Victoria," he said, " you have written me a *very
dear* and long letter, which has given me *great
pleasure and satisfaction.*" He would not admit
that he had had a rebuff.[1]

A few months later the crisis came. King Leopold determined to make a bold push, and to carry
Victoria with him, this time, by a display of royal
vigour and avuncular authority. In an abrupt,
an almost peremptory letter, he laid his case, once
more, before his niece. " You know from experience," he wrote, " that I *never ask anything of
you.* . . . But, as I said before, if we are not

[1] *Letters,* I. 117–20.

careful we may see serious consequences which may affect more or less everybody, and *this* ought to be the object of our most anxious attention. I remain, my dear Victoria, your affectionate uncle, Leopold R." [1] The Queen immediately despatched this letter to Lord Melbourne, who replied with a carefully thought-out form of words, signifying nothing whatever, which, he suggested, she should send to her uncle. She did so, copying out the elaborate formula, with a liberal scattering of " dear Uncles " interspersed; and she concluded her letter with a message of " affectionate love to Aunt Louise and the children." Then at last King Leopold was obliged to recognise the facts. His next letter contained no reference at all to politics. " I am glad," he wrote, " to find that you like Brighton better than last year. I think Brighton very agreeable at this time of the year, till the east winds set in. The pavilion, besides, is comfortable; that cannot be denied. Before my marriage, it was there that I met the Regent. Charlotte afterwards came with old Queen Charlotte. How distant all this already, but still how present to one's memory." Like poor Madame de Lieven, His Majesty felt that he had made a mistake.[2]

[1] *Letters*, I, 134. [2] *Ibid.*, I, 134–6, 140.

Nevertheless, he could not quite give up all hope. Another opportunity offered, and he made another effort—but there was not very much conviction in it, and it was immediately crushed. " My dear Uncle," the Queen wrote, " I have to thank you for your last letter which I received on Sunday. Though you seem not to dislike my political sparks, I think it is better not to increase them, as they might finally take fire, particularly as I see with regret that upon this one subject we cannot agree. I shall, therefore, limit myself to my expressions of very sincere wishes for the welfare and prosperity of Belgium." [1] After that, it was clear that there was no more to be said. Henceforward there is audible in the King's letters a curiously elegiac note. " My dearest Victoria, your *delightful* little letter has just arrived and went like *an arrow to my heart.* Yes, my beloved Victoria! I *do love you tenderly* . . . I love you *for yourself,* and I love in you the dear child whose welfare I tenderly watched." He had gone through much; yet, if life had its disappointments, it had its satisfactions too. " I have all the honours that can be given, and I am, politically speaking, very solidly established." But there were other things besides politics; there were romantic yearnings in

1 *Letters,* I, 154.

his heart. "The only longing I still have is for the Orient, where I perhaps shall once end my life, rising in the west and setting in the east." As for his devotion to his niece, that could never end. "I never press my services on you, nor my councils, though I may say with some truth that from the extraordinary fate which the higher powers had ordained for me, my experience, both political and of private life, is great. I am *always ready* to be useful to you *when and where* it may be, and I repeat it, *all I want in return is some little sincere affection from you.*" [1]

VI

The correspondence with King Leopold was significant of much that still lay partly hidden in the character of Victoria. Her attitude towards her uncle had never wavered for a moment. To all his advances she had presented an absolutely unyielding front. The foreign policy of England was not his province; it was hers and her Ministers'; his insinuations, his entreaties, his struggles—all were quite useless; and he must understand that this was so. The rigidity of her position was the more striking owing to the respectfulness and the affection with which it was accompanied. From

---

[1] *Letters,* I, 185.

start to finish the unmoved Queen remained the
devoted niece. Leopold himself must have envied
such perfect correctitude; but what may be admirable in an elderly statesman is alarming in a
maiden of nineteen. And privileged observers
were not without their fears. The strange mixture of ingenuous light-heartedness and fixed determination, of frankness and reticence, of child-
ishness and pride, seemed to augur a future that
was perplexed and full of dangers. As time
passed the less pleasant qualities in this curious
composition revealed themselves more often and
more seriously. There were signs of an imperious,
a peremptory temper, an egotism that was strong
and hard. It was noticed that the palace etiquette,
far from relaxing, grew ever more and more inflexible. By some, this was attributed to Lehzen's
influence; but, if that was so, Lehzen had a willing
pupil; for the slightest infringements of the freez-
ing rules of regularity and deference were invariably and immediately visited by the sharp and
haughty glances of the Queen.[1] Yet Her Majesty's eyes, crushing as they could be, were less
crushing than her mouth. The self-will depicted
in those small projecting teeth and that small re-
ceding chin was of a more dismaying kind than

---

[1] Greville, IV, 16–17; Crawford, 163–4.

that which a powerful jaw betokens; it was a self-will imperturbable, impenetrable, unintelligent; a self-will dangerously akin to obstinacy. And the obstinacy of monarchs is not as that of other men.

Within two years of her accession, the storm-clouds which, from the first, had been dimly visible on the horizon, gathered and burst. Victoria's relations with her mother had not improved. The Duchess of Kent, still surrounded by all the galling appearances of filial consideration, remained in Buckingham Palace a discarded figure, power-less and inconsolable. Sir John Conroy, banished from the presence of the Queen, still presided over the Duchess's household, and the hostilities of Kensington continued unabated in the new surroundings. Lady Flora Hastings still cracked her malicious jokes; the animosity of the Baroness was still unappeased. One day, Lady Flora found the joke was turned against her. Early in 1839, travelling in the suite of the Duchess, she had returned from Scotland in the same carriage with Sir John. A change in her figure became the subject of an unseemly jest; tongues wagged; and the jest grew serious. It was whispered that Lady Flora was with child.[1] The state of her health seemed to confirm the suspicion; she con-

[1] Greville, IV, 178, and August 15, 1839 (unpublished).

sulted Sir James Clark, the royal physician, and, after the consultation, Sir James let his tongue wag, too. On this, the scandal flared up sky-high. Everyone was talking; the Baroness was not surprised; the Duchess rallied tumultuously to the support of her lady; the Queen was informed. At last the extraordinary expedient of a medical examination was resorted to, during which Sir James, according to Lady Flora, behaved with brutal rudeness, while a second doctor was extremely polite. Finally, both physicians signed a certificate entirely exculpating the lady. But this was by no means the end of the business. The Hastings family, socially a very powerful one, threw itself into the fray with all the fury of outraged pride and injured innocence; Lord Hastings insisted upon an audience of the Queen, wrote to the papers, and demanded the dismissal of Sir James Clark. The Queen expressed her regret to Lady Flora, but Sir James Clark was not dismissed. The tide of opinion turned violently against the Queen and her advisers; high society was disgusted by all this washing of dirty linen in Buckingham Palace; the public at large was indignant at the ill-treatment of Lady Flora. By the end of March, the popularity, so radiant and so abundant, with which the young

Sovereign had begun her reign, had entirely disappeared.[1]

There can be no doubt that a great lack of discretion had been shown by the Court. Ill-natured tittle-tattle, which should have been instantly nipped in the bud, had been allowed to assume disgraceful proportions; and the Throne itself had become involved in the personal malignities of the palace. A particularly awkward question had been raised by the position of Sir James Clark. The Duke of Wellington, upon whom it was customary to fall back, in cases of great difficulty in high places, had been consulted upon this question, and he had given it as his opinion that, as it would be impossible to remove Sir James without a public enquiry, Sir James must certainly stay where he was.[2] Probably the Duke was right; but the fact that the peccant doctor continued in the Queen's service made the Hastings family irreconcilable and produced an unpleasant impression of unrepentant error upon the public mind. As for Victoria, she was very young and quite inexperienced; and she can hardly be blamed for having failed to control an extremely difficult situation. That

[1] " Nobody cares for the Queen, her popularity has sunk to zero, and loyalty is a dead letter." Greville, March 25, 1839; *Morning Post*, September 14, 1839.

[2] Greville, August 15, 1839 (unpublished).

was clearly Lord Melbourne's task; he was a man
of the world, and, with vigilance and circumspec-
tion, he might have quietly put out the ugly flames
while they were still smouldering. He did not do
so; he was lazy and easy-going; the Baroness was
persistent, and he let things slide. But doubtless
his position was not an easy one; passions ran high
in the palace; and Victoria was not only very
young, she was very headstrong, too. Did he possess the magic bridle which would curb that fiery
steed? He could not be certain. And then, suddenly, another violent crisis revealed more unmis-
takably than ever the nature of the mind with
which he had to deal.

VII

The Queen had for long been haunted by a
terror that the day might come when she would
be obliged to part with her Minister. Ever since
the passage of the Reform Bill, the power of the
Whig Government had steadily declined. The
General Election of 1837 had left them with a
very small majority in the House of Commons;
since then, they had been in constant difficulties—
abroad, at home, in Ireland; the Radical group
had grown hostile; it became highly doubtful how
much longer they could survive. The Queen

watched the development of events in great anxiety. She was a Whig by birth, by upbringing, by every association, public and private; and, even if those ties had never existed, the mere fact that Lord M. was the head of the Whigs would have amply sufficed to determine her politics. The fall of the Whigs would mean a sad upset for Lord M. But it would have a still more terrible consequence: Lord M. would have to leave her; and the daily, the hourly, presence of Lord M. had become an integral part of her life. Six months after her accession she had noted in her diary " I shall be very sorry to lose him *even* for *one* night ";[1] and this feeling of personal dependence on her Minister steadily increased. In these circumstances it was natural that she should have become a Whig partisan. Of the wider significance of political questions she knew nothing; all she saw was that her friends were in office and about her, and that it would be dreadful if they ceased to be so. " I cannot say," she wrote when a critical division was impending, "(though I feel *confident* of *our success*) HOW *low,* HOW *sad* I feel, when I think of the POSSIBILITY of this excellent and truly kind man not *remaining* my Minister! Yet I trust fervently that *He* who has so wonderfully pro-

[1] *Girlhood,* I, 254.

tected me through such manifold difficulties will not *now* desert me! I should have liked to have expressed to Lord M. my anxiety, but the tears were nearer than words throughout the time I saw him, and I felt I should have choked, had I attempted to say anything." [1]   Lord Melbourne realised clearly enough how undesirable was such a state of mind in a constitutional sovereign who might be called upon at any moment to receive as her Ministers the leaders of the opposite party; he did what he could to cool her ardour; but in vain.

With considerable lack of foresight, too, he had himself helped to bring about this unfortunate condition of affairs.   From the moment of her accession, he had surrounded the Queen with ladies of his own party; the Mistress of the Robes and all the Ladies of the Bedchamber were Whigs.   In the ordinary course, the Queen never saw a Tory: eventually she took pains never to see one in any circumstances.   She disliked the whole tribe; and she did not conceal the fact.   She particularly disliked Sir Robert Peel, who would almost certainly be the next Prime Minister.   His manners were detestable, and he wanted to turn out Lord M. His supporters, without exception, were equally

[1] *Girlhood*, I, 324.

PRINCESS VICTORIA IN 1836.

From the Portrait by F. Winterhalter.

LORD MELBOURNE.

From the Portrait by Sir Edwin Landseer, R.A.

bad; and as for Sir James Graham, she could not bear the sight of him; he was exactly like Sir John Conroy.[1]

The affair of Lady Flora intensified these party rumours still further. The Hastings were Tories, and Lord Melbourne and the Court were attacked by the Tory press in unmeasured language. The Queen's sectarian zeal proportionately increased. But the dreaded hour was now fast approaching. Early in May the Ministers were visibly tottering; on a vital point of policy they could only secure a majority of five in the House of Commons; they determined to resign. When Victoria heard the news she burst into tears. Was it possible, then, that all was over? Was she, indeed, about to see Lord M. for the last time? Lord M. came; and it is a curious fact that, even in this crowning moment of misery and agitation, the precise girl noted, to the minute, the exact time of the arrival and the departure of her beloved Minister. The conversation was touching and prolonged; but it could only end in one way—the Queen must send for the Duke of Wellington. When, next morning, the Duke came, he advised her Majesty to send for Sir Robert Peel. She was in " a state of dreadful grief," but she swallowed down her tears, and

[1] Greville, August 4, 1841 (unpublished); *Girlhood*, II, 154, 162.

braced herself, with royal resolution, for the odious, odious interview.

Peel was by nature reserved, proud, and shy. His manners were not perfect, and he knew it; he was easily embarrassed, and, at such moments, he grew even more stiff and formal than before, while his feet mechanically performed upon the carpet a dancing-master's measure. Anxious as he now was to win the Queen's good graces, his very anxiety to do so made the attainment of his object the more difficult. He entirely failed to make any headway whatever with the haughty hostile girl before him. She coldly noted that he appeared to be unhappy and " put out," and, while he stood in painful fixity, with an occasional uneasy pointing of the toe, her heart sank within her at the sight of that manner, " Oh! how different, how dreadfully different, to the frank, open, natural, and most kind warm manner of Lord Melbourne." Nevertheless, the audience passed without disaster. Only at one point had there been some slight hint of a disagreement. Peel had decided that a change would be necessary in the composition of the royal Household: the Queen must no longer be entirely surrounded by the wives and sisters of his opponents; some, at any rate, of the Ladies of the Bedchamber should be friendly to his Government. When this matter was touched upon, the Queen had intimated that she wished her Household to remain unchanged; to which Sir Robert had replied that the question could be settled later, and shortly afterwards withdrew to arrange the details of his Cabinet. While he was present, Victoria had remained, as she herself said, "very much collected, civil and high, and betrayed no agitation"; but as soon as she was alone she completely broke down. Then she pulled herself together to write to Lord Melbourne an account of all that had happened, and of her own wretchedness. "She feels," she said, "Lord Melbourne will understand it, amongst enemies to those she most relied on and most esteemed; but what is worst of all is the being deprived of seeing Lord Melbourne as she used to do."

Lord Melbourne replied with a very wise letter. He attempted to calm the Queen and to induce her to accept the new position gracefully; and he had nothing but good words for the Tory leaders. As for the question of the Ladies of the Household, the Queen, he said, should strongly urge what she desired, as it was a matter which concerned her personally, "but," he added, "if Sir Robert is unable to concede it, it will not do to refuse and to put off the negotiation upon it."

On this point there can be little doubt that Lord Melbourne was right. The question was a complicated and subtle one, and it had never arisen before; but subsequent constitutional practice has determined that a Queen Regnant must accede to the wishes of her Prime Minister as to the *personnel* of the female part of her Household. Lord Melbourne's wisdom, however, was wasted. The Queen would not be soothed, and still less would she take advice. It was outrageous of the Tories to want to deprive her of her Ladies, and that night she made up her mind that, whatever Sir Robert might say, she would refuse to consent to the removal of a single one of them. Accordingly, when, next morning, Peel appeared again, she was ready for action. He began by detailing the Cabinet appointments, and then he added " Now, ma'am, about the Ladies "—when the Queen sharply interrupted him. " I cannot give up *any* of my Ladies," she said. " What, ma'am! " said Sir Robert, " does your Majesty mean to retain them *all?* " " *All,*" said the Queen. Sir Robert's face worked strangely; he could not conceal his agitation. " The Mistress of the Robes and the Ladies of the Bedchamber? " he brought out at last. " *All,*" replied once more her Majesty. It was in vain that Peel pleaded and argued; in vain that he spoke, growing every moment more pompous and uneasy, of the constitution, and Queens Regnant, and the public interest; in vain that he danced his pathetic minuet. She was adamant; but he, too, through all his embarrassment, showed no sign of yielding; and when at last he left her nothing had been decided—the whole formation of the Government was hanging in the wind. A frenzy of excitement now seized upon Victoria. Sir Robert, she believed in her fury, had tried to outwit her, to take her friends from her, to impose his will upon her own; but that was not all: she had suddenly perceived, while the poor man was moving so uneasily before her, the one thing that she was desperately longing for—a loop-hole of escape. She seized a pen and dashed off a note to Lord Melbourne.

"Sir Robert has behaved very ill," she wrote, "he insisted on my giving up my Ladies, to which I replied that I *never* would consent, and I never saw a man so frightened. . . . I was calm but very decided, and I think you would have been pleased to see my composure and great firmness; the Queen of England will not submit to such trickery. Keep yourself in readiness, for you may soon be wanted." Hardly had she finished when the Duke of Wellington was announced. "Well,

Ma'am," he said as he entered, " I am very sorry
to find there is a difficulty." " Oh! " she instantly
replied, " *he* began it, not me." She felt that only
one thing now was needed: she must be firm. And
firm she was. The venerable conqueror of Napoleon was outfaced by the relentless equanimity of
a girl in her teens. He could not move the Queen
one inch. At last, she even ventured to rally him.
" Is Sir Robert so weak," she asked, " that even
the Ladies must be of his opinion? " On which the
Duke made a brief and humble expostulation,
bowed low, and departed.

Had she won? Time would show; and in the
meantime she scribbled down another letter.
" Lord Melbourne must not think the Queen rash
in her conduct. . . . The Queen felt this was an
attempt to see whether she could be led and managed like a child." The Tories were not only
wicked but ridiculous. Peel, having, as she understood, expressed a wish to remove only those members of the Household who were in Parliament,
now objected to her Ladies. " I should like to
know," she exclaimed in triumphant scorn, " if
they mean to give the *Ladies* seats in Parliament? "

The end of the crisis was now fast approaching.
Sir Robert returned, and told her that if she in-

sisted upon retaining all her Ladies he could not
form a Government. She replied that she would
send him her final decision in writing. Next morning the late Whig Cabinet met. Lord Melbourne
read to them the Queen's letters, and the group of
elderly politicians were overcome by an extraordinary wave of enthusiasm. They knew very well
that, to say the least, it was highly doubtful
whether the Queen had acted in strict accordance
with the constitution; that in doing what she had
done she had brushed aside Lord Melbourne's advice; that, in reality, there was no public reason
whatever why they should go back upon their decision to resign. But such considerations vanished
before the passionate urgency of Victoria. The
intensity of her determination swept them head-
long down the stream of her desire. They unanimously felt that "it was impossible to abandon
such a Queen and such a woman." Forgetting
that they were no longer her Majesty's Ministers,
they took the unprecedented course of advising the
Queen by letter to put an end to her negotiation
with Sir Robert Peel. She did so; all was over;
she had triumphed. That evening there was a ball
at the Palace. Everyone was present. "Peel and
the Duke of Wellington came by looking very
much put out." She was perfectly happy; Lord

M. was Prime Minister once more, and he was by her side.[1]

VIII

Happiness had returned with Lord M., but it was happiness in the midst of agitation. The domestic imbroglio continued unabated, until at last the Duke, rejected as a Minister, was called in once again in his old capacity as moral physician to the family. Something was accomplished when, at last, he induced Sir John Conroy to resign his place about the Duchess of Kent and leave the Palace for ever; something more when he persuaded the Queen to write an affectionate letter to her mother. The way seemed open for a reconciliation, but the Duchess was stormy still. She didn't believe that Victoria had written that letter; it was not in her handwriting; and she sent for the Duke to tell him so. The Duke, assuring her that the letter was genuine, begged her to forget the

---

[1] *Letters*, I, 154–72; *Girlhood*, II, 163–75; Greville, IV, 206–217, and unpublished passages; Broughton, V, 195; Clarendon, I, 165. The exclamation "They wished to treat me like a girl, but I will show them that I am Queen of England!" often quoted as the Queen's, is apocryphal. It is merely part of Greville's summary of the two letters to Melbourne, printed in *Letters*, 162 and 163. It may be noted that the phrase "the Queen of England will not submit to such trickery" is omitted in *Girlhood*, 169; and in general there are numerous verbal discrepancies between the versions of the journal and the letters in the two books.

past. But that was not so easy. "What am I to do if Lord Melbourne comes up to me?" "Do, ma'am? Why, receive him with civility." Well, she would make an effort. . . . "But what am I to do if Victoria asks me to shake hands with Lehzen?" "Do, ma'am? Why, take her in your arms and kiss her." "What!" The Duchess bristled in every feather, and then she burst into a hearty laugh. "No, ma'am, no," said the Duke, laughing too. "I don't mean you are to take *Lehzen* in your arms and kiss *her*, but the Queen."[1]

The Duke might perhaps have succeeded, had not all attempts at conciliation been rendered hopeless by a tragical event. Lady Flora, it was discovered, had been suffering from a terrible internal malady, which now grew rapidly worse. There could be little doubt that she was dying. The Queen's unpopularity reached an extraordinary height. More than once she was publicly insulted. "Mrs. Melbourne," was shouted at her when she appeared at her balcony; and, at Ascot, she was hissed by the Duchess of Montrose and Lady Sarah Ingestre as she passed. Lady Flora died. The whole scandal burst out again with redoubled vehemence; while, in the Palace, the two parties

[1] Greville, June 7, June 10, June 15, August 15, 1839 (unpublished).

were henceforth divided by an impassable, a
Stygian, gulf.[1]

Nevertheless, Lord M. was back, and every
trouble faded under the enchantment of his presence and his conversation. He, on his side, had
gone through much; and his distresses were intensified by a consciousness of his own shortcomings.
He realised clearly enough that, if he had intervened at the right moment, the Hastings scandal
might have been averted; and, in the bedchamber
crisis, he knew that he had allowed his judgment
to be overruled and his conduct to be swayed by
private feelings and the impetuosity of Victoria.[2]
But he was not one to suffer too acutely from the
pangs of conscience. In spite of the dullness and
the formality of the Court, his relationship with
the Queen had come to be the dominating interest
in his life; to have been deprived of it would have
been heartrending; that dread eventuality had
been—somehow—avoided; he was installed once
more, in a kind of triumph; let him enjoy the
fleeting hours to the full! And so, cherished by
the favour of a sovereign and warmed by the
adoration of a girl, the autumn rose, in those
autumn months of 1839, came to a wondrous

1 Greville, June 24 and July 7, 1839 (unpublished); Crawford, 222.
2 Greville, VI, 251–2.

blooming. The petals expanded, beautifully, for the last time. For the last time in this unlooked-for, this incongruous, this almost incredible intercourse, the old epicure tasted the exquisiteness of romance. To watch, to teach, to restrain, to encourage the royal young creature beside him—that was much; to feel with such a constant intimacy the impact of her quick affection, her radiant vitality—that was more; most of all, perhaps, was it good to linger vaguely in humorous contemplation, in idle apostrophe, to talk disconnectedly, to make a little joke about an apple or a furbelow, to dream. The springs of his sensibility, hidden deep within him, were overflowing. Often, as he bent over her hand and kissed it, he found himself in tears.[1]

Upon Victoria, with all her impermeability, it was inevitable that such a companionship should have produced, eventually, an effect. She was no longer the simple schoolgirl of two years since. The change was visible even in her public demeanour. Her expression, once " ingenuous and serene," now appeared to a shrewd observer to be " bold and discontented." [2] She had learnt something of the pleasures of power and the pains

[1] Greville, VI, 251; *Girlhood*, I, 236, 238; II, 267.
[2] Martineau, II, 120.

of it; but that was not all. Lord Melbourne with his gentle instruction had sought to lead her into the paths of wisdom and moderation, but the whole unconscious movement of his character had swayed her in a very different direction. The hard clear pebble, subjected for so long and so constantly to that encircling and insidious fluidity, had suffered a curious corrosion; it seemed to be actually growing a little soft and a little clouded. Humanity and fallibility are infectious things; was it possible that Lehzen's prim pupil had caught them? That she was beginning to listen to siren voices? That the secret impulses of self-expression, of self-indulgence even, were mastering her life? For a moment the child of a new age looked back, and wavered towards the eighteenth century. It was the most critical moment of her career. Had those influences lasted, the development of her character, the history of her life, would have been completely changed.

And why should they not last? She, for one, was very anxious that they should. Let them last for ever! She was surrounded by Whigs, she was free to do whatever she wanted, she had Lord M.; she could not believe that she could ever be happier. Any change would be for the worse; and the worst change of all . . . no, she would not hear of it; it would be quite intolerable, it would upset everything, if she were to marry. And yet everyone seemed to want her to—the general public, the Ministers, her Saxe-Coburg relations—it was always the same story. Of course, she knew very well that there were excellent reasons for it. For one thing, if she remained childless, and were to die, her uncle Cumberland, who was now the King of Hanover, would succeed to the Throne of England. That, no doubt, would be a most unpleasant event; and she entirely sympathised with everybody who wished to avoid it. But there was no hurry; naturally, she would marry in the end—but not just yet—not for three or four years. What was tiresome was that her uncle Leopold had apparently determined, not only that she ought to marry, but that her cousin Albert ought to be her husband. That was very like her uncle Leopold, who wanted to have a finger in every pie; and it was true that long ago, in far-off days, before her accession even, she had written to him in a way which might well have encouraged him in such a notion. She had told him then that Albert possessed " every quality that could be desired to render her perfectly happy," and had begged her " dearest uncle to take care of the health of one, now *so dear* to me, and to take him under *your special* protection," adding, " I hope and trust all will go on prosperously and well on this subject of so much importance to me." [1] But that had been years ago, when she was a mere child; perhaps, indeed, to judge from the language, the letter had been dictated by Lehzen; at any rate, her feelings, and all the circumstances, had now entirely changed. Albert hardly interested her at all.

In later life the Queen declared that she had never for a moment dreamt of marrying anyone but her cousin; [2] her letters and diaries tell a very different story. On August 26, 1837, she wrote in her journal: " To-day is my *dearest* cousin Albert's 18th birthday, and I pray Heaven to pour its choicest blessings on his beloved head!" In the subsequent years, however, the date passes unnoticed. It had been arranged that Stockmar should accompany the Prince to Italy, and the faithful Baron left her side for that purpose. He wrote to her more than once with sympathetic descriptions of his young companion; but her mind was by this time made up. She liked and admired Albert very much, but she did not want to marry him. " At present," she told Lord Melbourne in April, 1839, " *my* feeling is quite against ever

1 *Letters*, I, 49.   2 Grey, 219.

marrying." [1] When her cousin's Italian tour came to an end, she began to grow nervous; she knew that, according to a long-standing engagement, his next journey would be to England. He would probably arrive in the autumn, and by July her uneasiness was intense. She determined to write to her uncle, in order to make her position clear. It must be understood she said, that " there is *no engagement* between us." If she should like Albert, she could " make *no final promise this year,* for, at the *very earliest,* any such event could not take place till *two or three years hence."* She had, she said, " a *great* repugnance " to change her present position; and, if she should not like him, she was *" very* anxious that it should be understood that she would *not* be guilty of any breach of promise, for she *never gave any."* [2] To Lord Melbourne she was more explicit. She told him that she " had no great wish to see Albert, as the whole subject was an odious one "; she hated to have to decide about it; and she repeated once again that seeing Albert would be " a disagreeable thing." [3] But there was no escaping the horrid business; the visit must be made, and she must see him. The summer slipped by and was over;

[1] *Girlhood,* II, 153.   [2] *Letters,* I, 177–8.

[3] *Girlhood,* II, 215–6.

it was the autumn already; on the evening of
October 10 Albert, accompanied by his brother
Ernest, arrived at Windsor.

Albert arrived; and the whole structure of her
existence crumbled into nothingness like a house
of cards. He was beautiful—she gasped—she
knew no more. Then, in a flash, a thousand mysteries were revealed to her; the past, the present,
rushed upon her with a new significance; the delu-
sions of years were abolished, and an extraordinary,
an irresistible certitude leapt into being in the
light of those blue eyes, the smile of that lovely
mouth. The succeeding hours passed in a rapture.
She was able to observe a few more details—the
" exquisite nose," the " delicate moustachios and
slight but very slight whiskers," the " beautiful
figure, broad in the shoulders and a fine waist."
She rode with him, danced with him, talked with
him, and it was all perfection. She had no shadow
of a doubt. He had come on a Thursday evening,
and on the following Sunday morning she told
Lord Melbourne that she had " a good deal
changed her opinion as to marrying." Next morning, she told him that she had made up her mind
to marry Albert. The morning after that, she
sent for her cousin. She received him alone, and
" after a few minutes I said to him that I thought

he must be aware *why* I wished them to come here—and that it would make me *too happy* if he would consent to what I wished (to marry me)." Then "we embraced each other, and he was *so* kind, *so* affectionate." She said that she was quite unworthy of him, while he murmured that he would be very happy "Das Leben mit dir zu zubringen." They parted, and she felt "the happiest of human beings," when Lord M. came in. At first she beat about the bush, and talked of the weather, and indifferent subjects. Somehow or other she felt a little nervous with her old friend. At last, summoning up her courage, she said, "I have got well through this with Albert." "Oh! you have," said Lord M.[1]

---

[1] *Girlhood,* II, 262–9. Greville's statement (Nov. 27, 1839) that "the Queen settled everything about her marriage herself, and without consulting Melbourne at all on the subject, not even communicating to him her intention," has no foundation in fact. The Queen's journal proves that she consulted Melbourne at every point.

CHAPTER IV

MARRIAGE

I

IT was decidedly a family match. Prince Francis
Charles Augustus Albert Emmanuel of Saxe-
Coburg-Gotha—for such was his full title—had
been born just three months after his cousin Victoria, and the same midwife had assisted at the
two births. The children's grandmother, the Dowager Duchess of Coburg, had from the first looked
forward to their marriage; as they grew up, the
Duke, the Duchess of Kent, and King Leopold
came equally to desire it. The Prince, ever since
the time when, as a child of three, his nurse had
told him that some day " the little English May
flower " would be his wife, had never thought of
marrying anyone else. When eventually Baron
Stockmar himself signified his assent, the affair
seemed as good as settled.[1]

The Duke had one other child—Prince Ernest,
Albert's senior by one year, and heir to the principality. The Duchess was a sprightly and beau-

[1] Martin, I, 1–2; Grey, 213–4.

tiful woman, with fair hair and blue eyes; Albert
was very like her and was her declared favourite.
But in his fifth year he was parted from her for
ever. The ducal court was not noted for the
strictness of its morals; the Duke was a man of
gallantry, and it was rumoured that the Duchess
followed her husband's example. There were
scandals: one of the Court Chamberlains, a charming and cultivated man of Jewish extraction, was
talked of; at last there was a separation, followed
by a divorce. The Duchess retired to Paris, and
died unhappily in 1831. Her memory was always
very dear to Albert.[1]

He grew up a pretty, clever, and high-spirited
boy. Usually well-behaved, he was, however, sometimes violent. He had a will of his own, and asserted it; his elder brother was less passionate, less
purposeful, and, in their wrangles, it was Albert
who came out top. The two boys, living for the
most part in one or other of the Duke's country
houses, among pretty hills and woods and streams,
had been at a very early age—Albert was less than
four—separated from their nurses and put under
a tutor, in whose charge they remained until they
went to the University. They were brought up
in a simple and unostentatious manner, for the

[1] Grey, 7–9; Crawford, 245–6; Panam, 256–7.

Duke was poor and the duchy very small and very insignificant. Before long it became evident that Albert was a model lad. Intelligent and painstaking, he had been touched by the moral earnestness of his generation; at the age of eleven he surprised his father by telling him that he hoped to make himself " a good and useful man." And yet he was not over-serious; though, perhaps, he had little humour, he was full of fun—of practical jokes and mimicry. He was no milksop; he rode, and shot, and fenced; above all did he delight in being out of doors, and never was he happier than in his long rambles with his brother through the wild country round his beloved Rosenau—stalking the deer, admiring the scenery, and returning laden with specimens for his natural history collection. He was, besides, passionately fond of music. In one particular it was observed that he did not take after his father: owing either to his peculiar upbringing or to a more fundamental idiosyncrasy he had a marked distaste for the opposite sex. At the age of five, at a children's dance, he screamed with disgust and anger when a little girl was led up to him for a partner; and though, later on, he grew more successful in disguising such feelings, the feelings remained.[1]

[1] Grey, chaps. i to vi; Ernest, I, 18–23.

The brothers were very popular in Coburg, and, when the time came for them to be confirmed, the preliminary examination which, according to ancient custom, was held in public in the " Giants' Hall " of the Castle, was attended by an enthusiastic crowd of functionaries, clergy, delegates from the villages of the duchy, and miscellaneous onlookers. There were also present, besides the Duke and the Dowager Duchess, their Serene Highnesses the Princes Alexander and Ernest of Würtemberg, Prince Leiningen, Princess Hohenlohe-Langenburg, and Princess Hohenlohe-Schillingsfürst. Dr. Jacobi, the Court chaplain, presided at an altar, simply but appropriately decorated, which had been placed at the end of the hall; and the proceedings began by the choir singing the first verse of the hymn, " Come, Holy Ghost." After some introductory remarks, Dr. Jacobi began the examination. " The dignified and decorous bearing of the Princes," we are told in a contemporary account, " their strict attention to the questions, the frankness, decision, and correctness of their answers, produced a deep impression on the numerous assembly. Nothing was more striking in their answers than the evidence they gave of deep feeling and of inward strength of conviction. The questions put by the examiner

were not such as to be met by a simple " yes " or
" no." They were carefully considered in order
to give the audience a clear insight into the views
and feelings of the young princes. One of the
most touching moments was when the examiner
asked the hereditary prince whether he intended
steadfastly to hold to the Evangelical Church, and
the Prince answered not only " Yes! " but added
in a clear and decided tone: " I and my brother
are firmly resolved ever to remain faithful to the
acknowledged truth." The examination having
lasted an hour, Dr. Jacobi made some concluding
observations, followed by a short prayer; the second and third verses of the opening hymn were
sung; and the ceremony was over. The Princes,
stepping down from the altar, were embraced by
the Duke and the Dowager Duchess; after which
the loyal inhabitants of Coburg dispersed, well
satisfied with their entertainment.[1]

Albert's mental development now proceeded
apace. In his seventeenth year he began a careful
study of German literature and German philosophy. He set about, he told his tutor, " to follow
the thoughts of the great Klopstock into their
depths—though in this, for the most part," he
modestly added, " I do not succeed." He wrote

[1] Grey, App. B.

an essay on the " Mode of Thought of the Germans, and a Sketch of the History of German Civilisation," " making use," he said, " in its general outlines, of the divisions which the treatment of the subject itself demands," and concluding with " a retrospect of the shortcomings of our time, with an appeal to every one to correct those shortcomings in his own case, and thus set a good example to others." [1] Placed for some months under the care of King Leopold at Brussels, he came under the influence of Adolphe Quetelet, a mathematical professor, who was particularly interested in the application of the laws of probability to political and moral phenomena; this line of inquiry attracted the Prince, and the friendship thus begun continued till the end of his life.[2] From Brussels he went to the University of Bonn, where he was speedily distinguished both by his intellectual and his social activities; his energies were absorbed in metaphysics, law, political economy, music, fencing, and amateur theatricals. Thirty years later his fellow-students recalled with delight the fits of laughter into which they had been sent by Prince Albert's mimicry. The *verve* with which his Serene Highness reproduced the tones and gestures of one of the professors who used to point

[1] Grey, 124–7.   [2] Gossart; Ernest, I, 72–3.

to a picture of a row of houses in Venice with the remark, " That is the Ponte Realte," and of another who fell down in a race and was obliged to look for his spectacles, was especially appreciated.[1]

After a year at Bonn, the time had come for a foreign tour, and Baron Stockmar arrived from England to accompany the Prince on an expedition to Italy. The Baron had been already, two years previously, consulted by King Leopold as to his views upon the proposed marriage of Albert and Victoria. His reply had been remarkable. With a characteristic foresight, a characteristic absence of optimism, a characteristic sense of the moral elements in the situation, Stockmar had pointed out what were, in his opinion, the conditions essential to make the marriage a success. Albert, he wrote, was a fine young fellow, well grown for his age, with agreeable and valuable qualities; and it was probable that in a few years he would turn out a strong handsome man, of a kindly, simple, yet dignified demeanour. " Thus, externally, he possesses all that pleases the sex, and at all times and in all countries must please." Supposing, therefore, that Victoria herself was in favour of the marriage, the further question arose

[1] Grey, 169–73.

as to whether Albert's mental qualities were such as to fit him for the position of husband of the Queen of England. On this point, continued the Baron, one heard much to his credit; the Prince was said to be discreet and intelligent; but all such judgments were necessarily partial, and the Baron preferred to reserve his opinion until he could come to a trustworthy conclusion from personal observation. And then he added: " But all this is not enough. The young man ought to have not merely great ability, but a *right* ambition, and great force of will as well. To pursue for a life-time a political career so arduous demands more than energy and inclination—it demands also that earnest frame of mind which is ready of its own accord to sacrifice mere pleasure to real useful-ness. If he is not satisfied hereafter with the con-sciousness of having achieved one of the most influ-ential positions in Europe, how often will he feel tempted to repent his adventure! If he does not from the very outset accept it as a vocation of grave responsibility, on the efficient performance of which his honour and happiness depend, there is small likelihood of his succeeding." [1]

Such were the views of Stockmar on the qualifi-cations necessary for the due fulfilment of that

1 Stockmar, 310.

destiny which Albert's family had marked out for him; and he hoped, during the tour in Italy, to come to some conclusion as to how far the Prince possessed them. Albert on his side was much impressed by the Baron, whom he had previously seen but rarely; he also became acquainted, for the first time in his life, with a young Englishman, Lieut. Francis Seymour, who had been engaged to accompany him, whom he found *sehr liebenswürdig,* and with whom he struck up a warm friendship. He delighted in the galleries and scenery of Florence, though with Rome he was less impressed. " But for some beautiful palaces," he said, " it might just as well be any town in Germany." In an interview with Pope Gregory XVI, he took the opportunity of displaying his erudition. When the Pope observed that the Greeks had taken their art from the Etruscans, Albert replied that, on the contrary, in his opinion, they had borrowed from the Egyptians: his Holiness politely acquiesced. Wherever he went he was eager to increase his knowledge, and, at a ball in Florence, he was observed paying no attention whatever to the ladies, and deep in conversation with the learned Signor Capponi. " Voilà un prince dont nous pouvons être fiers," said the Grand Duke of Tuscany, who was standing

by: "la belle danseuse l'attend, le savant l'oc-
cupe." [1]

On his return to Germany, Stockmar's observations, imparted to King Leopold, were still critical. Albert, he said, was intelligent, kind, and
amiable; he was full of the best intentions and the
noblest resolutions, and his judgment was in many
things beyond his years. But great exertion was
repugnant to him; he seemed to be too willing to
spare himself, and his good resolutions too often
came to nothing. It was particularly unfortunate
that he took not the slightest interest in politics,
and never read a newspaper. In his manners, too,
there was still room for improvement. "He will
always," said the Baron, "have more success with
men than with women, in whose society he shows
too little *empressement,* and is too indifferent and
retiring." One other feature of the case was noted
by the keen eye of the old physician: the Prince's
constitution was not a strong one.[2] Yet, on the
whole, he was favourable to the projected marriage. But by now the chief obstacle seemed to
lie in another quarter, Victoria was apparently
determined to commit herself to nothing. And so
it happened that when Albert went to England
he had made up his mind to withdraw entirely

[1] Grey, 133, 415, 416, 419.   [2] Stockmar, 331-2.

from the affair. Nothing would induce him, he confessed to a friend, to be kept vaguely waiting; he would break it all off at once. His reception at Windsor threw an entirely new light upon the situation. The wheel of fortune turned with a sudden rapidity; and he found, in the arms of Victoria, the irrevocable assurance of his overwhelming fate.[1]

II

He was not in love with her. Affection, gratitude, the natural reactions to the unqualified devotion of a lively young cousin who was also a queen —such feelings possessed him, but the ardours of reciprocal passion were not his. Though he found that he liked Victoria very much, what immediately interested him in his curious position was less her than himself. Dazzled and delighted, riding, dancing, singing, laughing, amid the splendours of Windsor, he was aware of a new sensation—the stirrings of ambition in his breast. His place would indeed be a high, an enviable one! And then, on the instant, came another thought. The teaching of religion, the admonitions of Stockmar, his own inmost convictions, all spoke with the same utterance. He would not be there to

[1] Grey, 425.

please himself, but for a very different purpose—
to do good. He must be "noble, manly, and
princely in all things," he would have "to live
and to sacrifice himself for the benefit of his new
country"; to "use his powers and endeavours
for a great object—that of promoting the welfare
of multitudes of his fellowmen." One serious
thought led on to another. The wealth and the
bustle of the English Court might be delightful
for the moment, but, after all, it was Coburg that
had his heart. "While I shall be untiring," he
wrote to his grandmother, "in my efforts and
labours for the country to which I shall in future
belong, and where I am called to so high a position, I shall never cease *ein treuer Deutscher, Co-
burger, Gothaner zu sein.*" And now he must
part from Coburg for ever! Sobered and sad,
he sought relief in his brother Ernest's company;
the two young men would shut themselves up together, and, sitting down at the pianoforte, would
escape from the present and the future in the
sweet familiar gaiety of a Haydn duet.[1]

They returned to Germany; and while Albert,
for a few farewell months, enjoyed, for the last
time, the happiness of home, Victoria, for the last
time, resumed her old life in London and Wind-

---

[1] Grey, 421–5; *Letters,* I, 188,

sor. She corresponded daily with her future husband in a mingled flow of German and English; but the accustomed routine reasserted itself; the business and the pleasures of the day would brook no interruption; Lord M. was once more constantly beside her; and the Tories were as intolerable as ever. Indeed, they were more so. For now, in these final moments, the old feud burst out with redoubled fury.[1] The impetuous sovereign found, to her chagrin, that there might be disadvantages in being the declared enemy of one of the great parties in the State. On two occasions, the Tories directly thwarted her in a matter on which she had set her heart. She wished her husband's rank to be fixed by statute, and their opposition prevented it. She wished her husband to receive a settlement from the nation of £50,000 a year; and, again owing to the Tories, he was only allowed £30,000. It was too bad. When the question was discussed in Parliament, it had been pointed out that the bulk of the population was suffering from great

[1] "I had much talk with Lady Cowper about the Court. She lamented the obstinate character of the Queen, from which she thought that hereafter great evils might be apprehended. She said that her prejudices and antipathies were deep and strong, and her disposition very inflexible. Her hatred of Peel and her resentment against the Duke for having sided with him rather than with her in the old quarrel are unabated." Greville, November 3, 1839 (unpublished).

poverty, and that £30,000 was the whole revenue of Coburg; but her uncle Leopold had been given £50,000, and it would be monstrous to give Albert less. Sir Robert Peel—it might have been expected—had had the effrontery to speak and vote for the smaller sum. She was very angry; and determined to revenge herself by omitting to invite a single Tory to her wedding. She would make an exception in favour of old Lord Liverpool, but even the Duke of Wellington she refused to ask. When it was represented to her that it would amount to a national scandal if the Duke were absent from her wedding, she was angrier than ever. "What! That old rebel! I won't have him," she was reported to have said. Eventually she was induced to send him an invitation; but she made no attempt to conceal the bitterness of her feelings, and the Duke himself was only too well aware of all that had passed.[1]

Nor was it only against the Tories that her irritation rose. As the time for her wedding approached, her temper grew steadily sharper and more arbitrary. Queen Adelaide annoyed her. King Leopold, too, was "ungracious" in his correspondence; "Dear Uncle," she told Albert, "is given to believe that he must rule the roost every-

[1] Greville, January 29, February 15, 1840 (unpublished).

where. However," she added with asperity, "that is not a necessity."[1] Even Albert himself was not impeccable. Engulfed in Coburgs, he failed to appreciate the complexity of English affairs. There were difficulties about his household. He had a notion that he ought not to be surrounded by violent Whigs; very likely, but he would not understand that the only alternatives to violent Whigs were violent Tories; and it would be preposterous if his Lords and Gentlemen were to be found voting against the Queen's. He wanted to appoint his own Private Secretary. But how could he choose the right person? Lord M. was obviously best qualified to make the appointment; and Lord M. had decided that the Prince should take over his own Private Secretary—George Anson, a staunch Whig. Albert protested, but it was useless; Victoria simply announced that Anson was appointed, and instructed Lehzen to send the Prince an explanation of the details of the case. Then, again, he had written anxiously upon the necessity of maintaining unspotted the moral purity of the Court. Lord M.'s pupil considered that dear Albert was strait-laced, and, in a brisk Anglo-German missive, set forth her own views. "I like Lady A. very much," she told him, "only

[1] *Letters*, I, 201.

QUEEN VICTORIA IN 1838.

From the Painting by E. Corbould.

PRINCE ALBERT IN 1840.

From the Portrait by John Partridge.

she is a little *strict and particular,* and too severe
towards others, which is not right; for I think one
ought always to be indulgent towards other people, as I always think, if we had not been well
taken care of, we might also have gone astray.
That is always my feeling. Yet it is always right
to show that one does not like to see what is obviously wrong; but it is very dangerous to be *too*
severe, and I am certain that as a rule such people
always greatly regret that in their youth they
have not been so careful as they ought to have
been. I have explained this so badly and written
it so badly, that I fear you will hardly be able to
make it out." [1]

On one other matter she was insistent. Since
the affair of Lady Flora Hastings, a sad fate had
overtaken Sir James Clark. His flourishing practice had quite collapsed; nobody would go to him
any more. But the Queen remained faithful. She
would show the world how little she cared for
their disapproval, and she desired Albert to make
" poor Clark " his physician in ordinary. He did
as he was told; but, as it turned out, the appointment was not a happy one. [2]

The wedding-day was fixed, and it was time

[1] *Letters,* I, 200–8; *Girlhood,* II, 287.
[2] *Dictionary of National Biography,* Art. Sir James Clark;
Letters, I, 202.

for Albert to tear himself away from his family
and the scenes of his childhood. With an aching
heart, he had revisited his beloved haunts—the
woods and the valleys where he had spent so many
happy hours shooting rabbits and collecting botan-
ical specimens; in deep depression, he had sat
through the farewell banquets in the Palace and
listened to the *Freischutz* performed by the State
band. It was time to go. The streets were packed
as he drove through them; for a short space his
eyes were gladdened by a sea of friendly German
faces, and his ears by a gathering volume of good
guttural sounds. He stopped to bid a last adieu
to his grandmother. It was a heartrending moment. "Albert! Albert!" she shrieked, and fell
fainting into the arms of her attendants as his
carriage drove away. He was whirled rapidly to
his destiny. At Calais a steamboat awaited him,
and, together with his father and his brother, he
stepped, dejected, on board. A little later, he
was more dejected still. The crossing was a very
rough one; the Duke went hurriedly below; while
the two Princes, we are told, lay on either side of
the cabin staircase "in an almost helpless state."
At Dover a large crowd was collected on the pier,
and "it was by no common effort that Prince
Albert, who had continued to suffer up to the last

moment, got up to bow to the people." His sense
of duty triumphed. It was a curious omen: his
whole life in England was foreshadowed as he
landed on English ground.[1]

Meanwhile Victoria, in growing agitation, was
a prey to temper and to nerves. She grew feverish, and at last Sir James Clark pronounced that
she was going to have the measles. But, once
again, Sir James's diagnosis was incorrect. It was
not the measles that were attacking her, but a
very different malady; she was suddenly pros-
trated by alarm, regret, and doubt. For two years
she had been her own mistress—the two happiest
years, by far, of her life. And now it was all
to end! She was to come under an alien domination—she would have to promise that she would
honour and obey . . . someone, who might, after
all, thwart her, oppose her—and how dreadful that
would be! Why had she embarked on this hazardous experiment? Why had she not been contented with Lord M.? No doubt, she loved Albert;
but she loved power too. At any rate, one thing
was certain: she might be Albert's wife, but she
would always be Queen of England.[2] He reappeared, in an exquisite uniform, and her hesita-

---

[1] Grey, 292–303.
[2] Greville, February 15, 1840 (unpublished).

tions melted in his presence like mist before the sun. On February 10, 1840, the marriage took place. The wedded pair drove down to Windsor; but they were not, of course, entirely alone. They were accompanied by their suites, and, in particular, by two persons—the Baron Stockmar and the Baroness Lehzen.

III

Albert had foreseen that his married life would not be all plain sailing; but he had by no means realised the gravity and the complication of the difficulties which he would have to face. Politically, he was a cipher. Lord Melbourne was not only Prime Minister, he was in effect the Private Secretary of the Queen, and thus controlled the whole of the political existence of the sovereign. A queen's husband was an entity unknown to the British Constitution. In State affairs there seemed to be no place for him; nor was Victoria herself at all unwilling that this should be so. "The English," she had told the Prince when, during their engagement, a proposal had been made to give him a peerage, "are very jealous of any foreigner interfering in the government of this country, and have already in some of the papers expressed a

hope that you would not interfere. Now, though
I know you never would, still, if you were a Peer,
they would all say, the Prince meant to play a
political part."[1] "I know you never would!" In
reality, she was not quite so certain; but she wished
Albert to understand her views. He would, she
hoped, make a perfect husband; but, as for gov-
erning the country, he would see that she and
Lord M. between them could manage that very
well, without his help.

But it was not only in politics that the Prince
discovered that the part cut out for him was a
negligible one. Even as a husband, he found, his
functions were to be of an extremely limited kind.
Over the whole of Victoria's private life the Baroness reigned supreme; and she had not the slightest intention of allowing that supremacy to be
diminished by one iota. Since the accession, her
power had greatly increased. Besides the undefined and enormous influence which she exercised
through her management of the Queen's private
correspondence, she was now the superintendent
of the royal establishment and controlled the important office of Privy Purse.[2] Albert very soon
perceived that he was not master in his own house.[3]
Every detail of his own and his wife's existence

[1] *Letters,* I, 199.   [2] Martin, I, 71, 153.   [3] Grey, 319-20.

was supervised by a third person: nothing could be done until the consent of Lehzen had first been obtained. And Victoria, who adored Lehzen with unabated intensity, saw nothing in all this that was wrong.

Nor was the Prince happier in his social surroundings. A shy young foreigner, awkward in ladies' company, unexpansive and self-opinionated, it was improbable that, in any circumstances, he would have been a society success. His appearance, too, was against him. Though in the eyes of Victoria he was the mirror of manly beauty, her subjects, whose eyes were of a less Teutonic cast, did not agree with her. To them—and particularly to the high-born ladies and gentlemen who naturally saw him most—what was immediately and distressingly striking in Albert's face and figure and whole demeanour was his un-English look. His features were regular, no doubt, but there was something smooth and smug about them; he was tall, but he was clumsily put together, and he walked with a slight slouch. Really, they thought, this youth was more like some kind of foreign tenor than anything else. These were serious disadvantages; but the line of conduct which the Prince adopted from the first moment of his arrival was far from calculated to dispel them. Owing partly to a natural awkwardness, partly to a fear of undue familiarity, and partly to a desire to be absolutely correct, his manners were infused with an extraordinary stiffness and formality. Whenever he appeared in company, he seemed to be surrounded by a thick hedge of prickly etiquette. He never went out into ordinary society; he never walked in the streets of London; he was invariably accompanied by an equerry when he rode or drove. He wanted to be irreproachable and, if that involved friendlessness, it could not be helped. Besides, he had no very high opinion of the English. So far as he could see, they cared for nothing but fox-hunting and Sunday observances; they oscillated between an undue frivolity and an undue gloom; if you spoke to them of friendly joyousness they stared; and they did not understand either the Laws of Thought or the wit of a German University. Since it was clear that with such people he could have very little in common, there was no reason whatever for relaxing in their favour the rules of etiquette. In strict privacy, he could be natural and charming; Seymour and Anson were devoted to him, and he returned their affection; but they were subordinates—the receivers of his confidences and the agents of his will. From the support and

the solace of true companionship he was utterly
cut off.[1]

A friend, indeed, he had—or rather, a mentor.
The Baron, established once more in the royal
residence, was determined to work with as whole-
hearted a detachment for the Prince's benefit as,
more than twenty years before, he had worked for
his uncle's. The situations then and now, similar
in many respects, were yet full of differences.
Perhaps in either case the difficulties to be encoun-
tered were equally great; but the present problem was the more complex and the more interesting. The young doctor who, unknown and insignificant, had nothing at the back of him but his
own wits and the friendship of an unimportant
Prince, had been replaced by the accomplished
confidant of kings and ministers, ripe in years, in
reputation, and in the wisdom of a vast experience. It was possible for him to treat Albert with
something of the affectionate authority of a father;
but, on the other hand, Albert was no Leopold.
As the Baron was very well aware, he had none
of his uncle's rigidity of ambition, none of his overweening impulse to be personally great. He was
virtuous and well-intentioned; he was clever and

---

[1] Greville, April 3, 1840 (unpublished); Grey, 353–4; Ernest,
I, 93–4.

well-informed; but he took no interest in politics, and there were no signs that he possessed any commanding force of character. Left to himself, he would almost certainly have subsided into a high-minded nonentity, an aimless dilettante busy over culture, a palace appendage without influence or power. But he was not left to himself: Stockmar saw to that. For ever at his pupil's elbow, the hidden Baron pushed him forward, with tireless pressure, along the path which had been trod by Leopold so many years ago. But, this time, the goal at the end of it was something more than the mediocre royalty that Leopold had reached. The prize which Stockmar, with all the energy of disinterested devotion, had determined should be Albert's was a tremendous prize indeed.

The beginning of the undertaking proved to be the most arduous part of it. Albert was easily dispirited: what was the use of struggling to perform in a rôle which bored him and which, it was quite clear, nobody but the dear good Baron had any desire that he should take up? It was simpler, and it saved a great deal of trouble, to let things slide. But Stockmar would not have it.[1] Incessantly, he harped upon two strings—Albert's sense of duty and his personal pride. Had the

1 Stockmar, 351.

Prince forgotten the noble aims to which his life
was to be devoted? And was he going to allow
himself, his wife, his family, his whole existence,
to be governed by Baroness Lehzen? The latter
consideration was a potent one. Albert had never
been accustomed to giving way; and now, more
than ever before, it would be humiliating to do
so. Not only was he constantly exasperated by
the position of the Baroness in the royal household; there was another and a still more serious
cause of complaint. He was, he knew very well,
his wife's intellectual superior, and yet he found,
to his intense annoyance, that there were parts of
her mind over which he exercised no influence.
When, urged on by the Baron, he attempted to
discuss politics with Victoria, she eluded the subject, drifted into generalities, and then began to
talk of something else. She was treating him as
she had once treated their uncle Leopold. When
at last he protested, she replied that her conduct
was merely the result of indolence; that when she
was with *him* she could not bear to bother her
head with anything so dull as politics. The excuse was worse than the fault: was he the wife
and she the husband? It almost seemed so. But
the Baron declared that the root of the mischief
was Lehzen: that it was she who encouraged the

Queen to have secrets; who did worse—under-
mined the natural ingenuousness of Victoria, and
induced her to give, unconsciously no doubt, false
reasons to explain away her conduct.[1]

Minor disagreements made matters worse. The
royal couple differed in their tastes. Albert,
brought up in a régime of Spartan simplicity
and early hours, found the great Court functions
intolerably wearisome, and was invariably observed to be nodding on the sofa at half-past ten;
while the Queen's favourite form of enjoyment
was to dance through the night, and then, going
out into the portico of the Palace, watch the sun
rise behind St. Paul's and the towers of Westminster.[2] She loved London and he detested it.
It was only in Windsor that he felt he could really
breathe; but Windsor too had its terrors: though
during the day there he could paint and walk and
play on the piano, after dinner black tedium descended like a pall. He would have liked to summon distinguished scientific and literary men to his
presence, and after ascertaining their views upon
various points of art and learning, to set forth his
own; but unfortunately Victoria " had no fancy to
encourage such people "; knowing that she was
unequal to taking a part in their conversation,

[1] *Letters*, I, 224.   [2] Bloomfield, I, 19.

she insisted that the evening routine should remain unaltered; the regulation interchange of platitudes with official persons was followed as usual by the round table and the books of engravings, while the Prince, with one of his attendants, played game after game of double chess.[1]

It was only natural that in so peculiar a situation, in which the elements of power, passion, and pride were so strangely apportioned, there should have been occasionally something more than mere irritation—a struggle of angry wills. Victoria, no more than Albert, was in the habit of playing second fiddle. Her arbitrary temper flashed out. Her vitality, her obstinacy, her overweening sense of her own position, might well have beaten down before them his superiorities and his rights. But she fought at a disadvantage; she was, in very truth, no longer her own mistress; a profound preoccupation dominated her, seizing upon her inmost purposes for its own extraordinary ends. She was madly in love. The details of those curious battles are unknown to us; but Prince Ernest, who remained in England with his brother for some months, noted them with a friendly and startled eye.[2] One story, indeed, survives, ill-authenticated and perhaps mythical, yet summing

1 Grey, 340; *Letters*, I, 256.   2 Ernest, I, 93.

up, as such stories often do, the central facts of the case. When, in wrath, the Prince one day had locked himself into his room, Victoria, no less furious, knocked on the door to be admitted. " Who is there? " he asked. " The Queen of England " was the answer. He did not move, and again there was a hail of knocks. The question and the answer were repeated many times; but at last there was a pause, and then a gentler knocking. " Who is there? " came once more the relentless question. But this time the reply was different. " Your wife, Albert." And the door was immediately opened.[1]

Very gradually the Prince's position changed. He began to find the study of politics less uninteresting than he had supposed; he read Blackstone, and took lessons in English Law; he was occasionally present when the Queen interviewed her Ministers; and at Lord Melbourne's suggestion he was shown all the despatches relating to Foreign Affairs. Sometimes he would commit his views to paper, and read them aloud to the Prime Minister, who, infinitely kind and courteous, listened with attention, but seldom made any reply.[2] An important step was taken when, before the birth of the Princess Royal, the Prince, without any

---

[1] Jerrold, *Married Life*, 56.   [2] Grey 320–1, 361–2.

opposition in Parliament, was appointed Regent in case of the death of the Queen.[1] Stockmar, owing to whose intervention with the Tories this happy result had been brought about, now felt himself at liberty to take a holiday with his family in Coburg; but his solicitude, poured out in innumerable letters, still watched over his pupil from afar. " Dear Prince," he wrote, " I am satisfied with the news you have sent me. Mistakes, misunderstandings, obstructions, which come in vexatious opposition to one's views, are always to be taken for just what they are—namely, natural phenomena of life, which represent one of its sides, and that the shady one. In overcoming them with dignity, your mind has to exercise, to train, to enlighten itself; and your character to gain force, endurance, and the necessary hardness." The Prince had done well so far; but he must continue in the right path; above all, he was " never to relax."—" Never to relax in putting your magnanimity to the proof; never to relax in logical separation of what is great and essential from what is trivial and of no moment; never to relax in keeping yourself up to a high standard—in the determination, daily renewed, to be consistent, patient, courageous." It was a hard programme,

[1] Stockmar, 352–7.

perhaps, for a young man of twenty-one; and yet
there was something in it which touched the very
depths of Albert's soul. He sighed, but he listened—listened as to the voice of a spiritual direc-
tor inspired with divine truth. " The stars which
are needful to you now," the voice continued,
" and perhaps for some time to come, are *Love,
Honesty, Truth.* All those whose minds are
warped, or who are destitute of true feeling, will
be apt to mistake you," and to persuade themselves and the world that you are not the man
you are—or, at least, may become. . . . Do you,
therefore, be on the alert betimes, with your eyes
open in every direction. . . . I wish for my Prince
a great, noble, warm, and true heart, such as shall
serve as the richest and surest basis for the noblest
views of human nature, and the firmest resolve to
give them development." [1]

Before long, the decisive moment came. There
was a General Election, and it became certain that
the Tories, at last, must come into power. The
Queen disliked them as much as ever; but, with a
large majority in the House of Commons, they
would now be in a position to insist upon their
wishes being attended to. Lord Melbourne himself was the first to realise the importance of car-

[1] Martin, I, 90-2.

rying out the inevitable transition with as little
friction as possible; and with his consent, the
Prince, following up the *rapprochement* which had
begun over the Regency Act, opened, through
Anson, a negotiation with Sir Robert Peel. In
a series of secret interviews, a complete understanding was reached upon the difficult and complex question of the Bedchamber. It was agreed
that the constitutional point should not be raised,
but that on the formation of the Tory Government, the principal Whig ladies should retire, and
their places be filled by others appointed by Sir
Robert.[1] Thus, in effect, though not in form, the
Crown abandoned the claims of 1839, and they
have never been subsequently put forward. The
transaction was a turning point in the Prince's
career. He had conducted an important negotiation with skill and tact; he had been brought into
close and friendly relations with the new Prime
Minister; it was obvious that a great political
future lay before him. Victoria was much impressed and deeply grateful. " My dearest
Angel," she told King Leopold, " is indeed a
great comfort to me. He takes the greatest interest in what goes on, feeling with and for me, and
yet abstaining as he ought from biasing me either

[1] *Letters.* I, 271–4, 284–6.

way, though we talk much on the subject, and his judgment is, as you say, good and mild." [1] She was in need of all the comfort and assistance he could give her. Lord M. was going; and she ·could hardly bring herself to speak to Peel. Yes; she would discuss everything with Albert now!

Stockmar, who had returned to England, watched the departure of Lord Melbourne with satisfaction. If all went well, the Prince should now wield a supreme political influence over Victoria. But would all go well? An unexpected development put the Baron into a serious fright. When the dreadful moment finally came, and the Queen, in anguish, bade adieu to her beloved Minister, it was settled between them that, though it would be inadvisable to meet very often, they could continue to correspond. Never were the inconsistencies of Lord Melbourne's character shown more clearly than in what followed. So long as he was in office, his attitude towards Peel had been irreproachable; he had done all he could to facilitate the change of government; he had even, through more than one channel, transmitted privately to his successful rival advice as to the best means of winning the Queen's good graces. [2] Yet, no sooner was he in opposition than his heart

---

[1] *Letters,* I, 280.   [2] *Letters,* I, 305; Greville, V, 39–40.

failed him. He could not bear the thought of sur-
rendering altogether the privilege and the pleasure
of giving counsel to Victoria—of being cut off
completely from the power and the intimacy which
had been his for so long and in such abundant
measure. Though he had declared that he would
be perfectly discreet in his letters, he could not
resist taking advantage of the opening they afforded. He discussed in detail various public
questions, and, in particular, gave the Queen a
great deal of advice in the matter of appointments.
This advice was followed. Lord Melbourne recommended that Lord Heytesbury, who, he said,
was an able man, should be made Ambassador at
Vienna; and a week later the Queen wrote to the
Foreign Secretary urging that Lord Heytesbury,
whom she believed to be a very able man, should
be employed " on some important mission." Stockmar was very much alarmed. He wrote a memorandum, pointing out the unconstitutional nature
of Lord Melbourne's proceedings and the unpleasant position in which the Queen might find herself
if they were discovered by Peel; and he instructed
Anson to take this memorandum to the ex-Min-
ister. Lord Melbourne, lounging on a sofa, read
it through with compressed lips. " This is quite
an apple-pie opinion," he said. When Anson ven-

tured to expostulate further, suggesting that it
was unseemly in the leader of the Opposition to
maintain an intimate relationship with the Sovereign, the old man lost his temper. " God eternally damn it! " he exclaimed, leaping up from
his sofa, and dashing about the room. " Flesh and
blood cannot stand this! " He continued to write
to the Queen, as before; and two more violent
bombardments from the Baron were needed before
he was brought to reason. Then, gradually, his
letters grew less and less frequent, with fewer
and fewer references to public concerns; at last,
they were entirely innocuous. The Baron smiled;
Lord M. had accepted the inevitable.[1]

The Whig Ministry resigned in September,
1841; but more than a year was to elapse before
another and an equally momentous change was
effected—the removal of Lehzen. For, in the
end, the mysterious governess was conquered.
The steps are unknown by which Victoria was at
last led to accept her withdrawal with composure
—perhaps with relief; but it is clear that Albert's
domestic position must have been greatly strengthened by the appearance of children. The birth of
the Princess Royal had been followed in November, 1841, by that of the Prince of Wales; and

[1] *Letters,* I, 325-6, 329, 330-1, 339-42, 352-4, 360-3, 368.

before very long another baby was expected. The Baroness, with all her affection, could have but a remote share in such family delights. She lost ground perceptibly. It was noticed as a phenomenon that, once or twice, when the Court travelled, she was left behind at Windsor.[1] The Prince was very cautious; at the change of Ministry, Lord Melbourne had advised him to choose that moment for decisive action; but he judged it wiser to wait.[2] Time and the pressure of inevitable circumstances were for him; every day his predominance grew more assured—and every night. At length he perceived that he need hesitate no longer—that every wish, every velleity of his had only to be expressed to be at once Victoria's. He spoke, and Lehzen vanished for ever. No more would she reign in that royal heart and those royal halls. No more, watching from a window at Windsor, would she follow her pupil and her sovereign walking on the terrace among the obsequious multitude, with the eye of triumphant love.[3] Returning to her native Hanover she established herself at Bückeburg in a small but comfortable house, the walls of which were entirely covered by portraits of Her Majesty.[4] The Baron, in spite of his dyspepsia, smiled again: Albert was supreme.

[1] *Letters.*, I, 291, 295.
[2] *Ibid.*, I, 303.
[3] Lyttelton, 282–3.
[4] Bloomfield, I, 215.

IV

The early discords had passed away completely —resolved into the absolute harmony of married life. Victoria, overcome by a new, an unimagined revelation, had surrendered her whole soul to her husband. The beauty and the charm which so suddenly had made her his at first were, she now saw, no more than but the outward manifestation of the true Albert. There was an inward beauty, an inward glory which, blind that she was, she had then but dimly apprehended, but of which now she was aware in every fibre of her being—he was good—he was great! How could she ever have dreamt of setting up her will against his wisdom, her ignorance against his knowledge, her fancies against his perfect taste? Had she really once loved London and late hours and dissipation? She who now was only happy in the country, she who jumped out of bed every morning—oh, so early! —with Albert, to take a walk, before breakfast, with Albert alone! How wonderful it was to be taught by him! To be told by him which trees were which; and to learn all about the bees! And then to sit doing cross-stitch while he read aloud to her Hallam's Constitutional History of England! Or to listen to him playing on his new organ (" The organ is the first of instruments," he said); or to sing to him a song by Mendelssohn, with a great deal of care over the time and the breathing, and only a very occasional false note! And, after dinner, too—oh, how good of him! He had given up his double chess! And so there could be round games at the round table, or everyone could spend the evening in the most amusing way imaginable—spinning counters and rings.[1] When the babies came it was still more wonderful. Pussy was such a clever little girl ("I am not Pussy! I am the Princess Royal!" she had angrily exclaimed on one occasion); and Bertie—well, she could only pray *most* fervently that the little Prince of Wales would grow up to "resemble his angelic dearest Father in *every, every* respect, both in body and mind."[2] Her dear Mamma, too, had been drawn once more into the family circle, for Albert had brought about a reconciliation, and the departure of Lehzen had helped to obliterate the past.[3] In Victoria's eyes, life had become an idyll, and, if the essential elements of an idyll are happiness, love and simplicity, an idyll it was; though, indeed, it was of a kind that might have disconcerted Theocritus. "Albert brought in

---

[1] Grey 338–9; Bloomfield, I, 28, 123; Lyttelton, 300, 303, 305–6, 312, 334–5; Martin, I, 488; *Letters,* I, 369.

[2] *Letters,* I, 366.

[3] *Ibid.,* III, 439.

dearest little Pussy," wrote Her Majesty in her
journal, "in such a smart white merino dress
trimmed with blue, which Mamma had given her,
and a pretty cap, and placed her on my bed, seat-
ing himself next to her, and she was very dear
and good. And, as my precious, invaluable Albert
sat there, and our little Love between us, I felt
quite moved with happiness and gratitude to
God." [1]

The past—the past of only three years since—
when she looked back upon it, seemed a thing so
remote and alien that she could explain it to herself in no other way than as some kind of delusion
—an unfortunate mistake. Turning over an old
volume of her diary, she came upon this sentence
—"As for 'the confidence of the Crown,' God
knows! No *Minister, no friend* EVER possessed it
so entirely as this truly excellent Lord Melbourne
possesses mine!" A pang shot through her—she
seized a pen, and wrote upon the margin—"Reading this again, I cannot forbear remarking what
an artificial sort of happiness *mine* was *then,* and
what a blessing it is I have now in my beloved
Husband *real* and solid happiness, which no Politics, no worldly reverses *can* change; it could not
have lasted long as it was then, for after all, kind

1 Martin, I, 125.

and excellent as Lord M. is, and kind as he was
to me, it was but in Society that I had amusement,
and I was only living on that superficial resource,
which I *then fancied* was happiness! Thank God!
for *me* and others, this is changed, and I *know
what* REAL *happiness* is—V. R." [1] How did she
know? What is the distinction between happiness
that is real and happiness that is felt? So a philosopher—Lord M. himself perhaps—might have
inquired. But she was no philosopher, and Lord
M. was a phantom, and Albert was beside her,
and that was enough.

Happy, certainly, she was; and she wanted
everyone to know it. Her letters to King Leopold
are sprinkled thick with raptures. "Oh! my dearest uncle, I am sure if you knew *how* happy, how
blessed I feel, and how *proud* I feel in possessing
such a perfect being as my husband . . ." such
ecstasies seemed to gush from her pen unceasingly
and almost of their own accord.[2] When, one day,
without thinking, Lady Lyttelton described someone to her as being "as happy as a queen," and
then grew a little confused, "Don't correct yourself, Lady Lyttelton," said Her Majesty. "A
queen *is* a very happy woman." [3]

---

[1] *Girlhood,* II, 135.   [2] *Letters,* I, 366, 464–5, 475, etc.
[3] Lyttelton, 306.

But this new happiness was no lotus dream. On the contrary, it was bracing, rather than relaxing. Never before had she felt so acutely the necessity for doing her duty. She worked more methodically than ever at the business of State; she watched over her children with untiring vigilance. She carried on a large correspondence; she was occupied with her farm—her dairy—a whole multitude of household avocations—from morning till night. Her active, eager little body hurrying with quick steps after the long strides of Albert down the corridors and avenues of Windsor,[1] seemed the very expression of her spirit. Amid all the softness, the deliciousness of unmixed joy, all the liquescence, the overflowings of inexhaustible sentiment, her native rigidity remained. "A vein of iron," said Lady Lyttelton, who, as royal governess, had good means of observation, "runs through her most extraordinary character."[2]

Sometimes the delightful routine of domestic existence had to be interrupted. It was necessary to exchange Windsor for Buckingham Palace, to open Parliament, or to interview official personages, or, occasionally, to entertain foreign visitors at the Castle. Then the quiet Court put on a sudden magnificence, and sovereigns from over the

---

[1] Crawford, 243.   [2] Lyttelton, 348.

seas—Louis Philippe, or the King of Prussia, or
the King of Saxony—found at Windsor an entertainment that was indeed a royal one. Few spectacles in Europe, it was agreed, produced an effect
so imposing as the great Waterloo banqueting hall,
crowded with guests in sparkling diamonds and
blazing uniforms, the long walls hung with the
stately portraits of heroes, and the tables loaded
with the gorgeous gold plate of the kings of England.[1] But, in that wealth of splendour, the most
imposing spectacle of all was the Queen. The
little *hausfrau,* who had spent the day before
walking out with her children, inspecting her livestock, practising shakes at the piano, and filling up
her journal with adoring descriptions of her husband, suddenly shone forth, without art, without
effort, by a spontaneous and natural transition, the
very culmination of Majesty. The Tsar of Russia himself was deeply impressed. Victoria on her
side viewed with secret awe the tremendous Nich-
olas. " A great event and a great compliment *his*
visit certainly is," she told her uncle, " and the
people *here* are extremely flattered at it. He is
certainly a *very striking* man; still very handsome.
His profile is *beautiful,* and his manners *most*
dignified and graceful; extremely civil—quite

[1] *Letters,* II, 13; Bunsen, II, 6; Bloomfield, I, 53–4.

alarmingly so, as he is so full of attentions and
politeness. But the expression of the *eyes* is *formidable,* and unlike anything I ever saw before." [1]
She and Albert and " the good King of Saxony,"
who happened to be there at the same time, and
whom, she said, " we like much—he is *so* unassum-
ing "—drew together like tame villatic fowl in the
presence of that awful eagle. When he was gone,
they compared notes about his face, his unhappi-
ness, and his despotic power over millions. Well!
She for her part could not help pitying him, and
she thanked God she was Queen of England.[2]

When the time came for returning some of these
visits, the royal pair set forth in their yacht, much
to Victoria's satisfaction. " I do love a ship! "
she exclaimed, ran up and down ladders with the
greatest agility, and cracked jokes with the sailors.[3]
The Prince was more aloof. They visited Louis
Philippe at the Château d'Eu; they visited King
Leopold in Brussels. It happened that a still
more remarkable Englishwoman was in the Belgian capital, but she was not remarked; and Queen
Victoria passed unknowing before the steady gaze
of one of the mistresses in M. Héger's *pensionnat.*
" A little stout, vivacious lady, very plainly dressed

1 *Letters,* II, 12–16.   2 Martin, I, 224.
3 Lyttelton. 292; Bloomfield, I, 76–7.

—not much dignity or pretension about her," was Charlotte Brontë's comment as the royal carriage and six flashed by her, making her wait on the pavement for a moment, and interrupting the train of her reflections.[1] Victoria was in high spirits, and even succeeded in instilling a little cheerfulness into her uncle's sombre Court. King Leopold, indeed, was perfectly contented. His dearest hopes had been fulfilled; all his ambitions were satisfied; and for the rest of his life he had only to enjoy, in undisturbed decorum, his throne, his respectability, the table of precedence, and the punctual discharge of his irksome duties. But unfortunately the felicity of those who surrounded him was less complete. His Court, it was murmured, was as gloomy as a conventicle, and the most dismal of all the sufferers was his wife. " Pas de plaisanteries, madame! " he had exclaimed to the unfortunate successor of the Princess Charlotte, when, in the early days of their marriage, she had attempted a feeble joke. Did she not understand that the consort of a constitutional sovereign must not be frivolous? She understood, at last, only too well; and when the startled walls of the state apartments re-echoed to the chattering and the laughter of Victoria, the poor lady

[1] Gaskell, I, 313.

found that she had almost forgotten how to smile.

Another year, Germany was visited, and Albert displayed the beauties of his home. When Victoria crossed the frontier, she was much excited— and she was astonished as well. "To hear the people speak German," she noted in her diary, "and to see the German soldiers, etc., seemed to me so singular." Having recovered from this slight shock, she found the country charming. She was fêted everywhere, crowds of the surrounding royalties swooped down to welcome her, and the prettiest groups of peasant children, dressed in their best clothes, presented her with bunches of flowers. The principality of Coburg, with its romantic scenery and its well-behaved inhabitants, particularly delighted her; and when she woke up one morning to find herself in "dear Rosenau, my Albert's birthplace," it was "like a beautiful dream." On her return home, she expatiated, in a letter to King Leopold, upon the pleasures of the trip, dwelling especially upon the intensity of her affection for Albert's native land. "I have a feeling," she said, "for our dear little Germany, which I cannot describe. I felt it at Rosenau so much. It is a something which touches me, and which goes to my heart, and makes me inclined to cry. I never felt at any other place that sort of pensive pleasure and peace which I felt there. I fear I almost like it too much." [1]

V

The husband was not so happy as the wife. In spite of the great improvement in his situation, in spite of a growing family and the adoration of Victoria, Albert was still a stranger in a strange land, and the serenity of spiritual satisfaction was denied him. It was something, no doubt, to have dominated his immediate environment; but it was not enough; and, besides, in the very completeness of his success, there was a bitterness. Victoria idolised him; but it was understanding that he craved for, not idolatry; and how much did Victoria, filled to the brim though she was with him, understand him? How much does the bucket understand the well? He was lonely. He went to his organ and improvised with learned modulations until the sounds, swelling and subsiding through elaborate cadences, brought some solace to his heart. Then, with the elasticity of youth, he hurried off to play with the babies, or to design a new pigsty, or to read aloud the " Church History of Scotland " to Victoria, or to pirouette before her

1 Martin, I, 275, 306.

on one toe, like a ballet-dancer, with a fixed smile,
to show her how she ought to behave when she
appeared in public places.[1] Thus did he amuse
himself; but there was one distraction in which
he did not indulge. He never flirted—no, not
with the prettiest ladies of the Court. When, dur·
ing their engagement, the Queen had remarked
with pride to Lord Melbourne that the Prince paid
no attention to any other woman, the cynic had
answered, " No, that sort of thing is apt to come
later "; upon which she had scolded him severely,
and then hurried off to Stockmar to repeat what
Lord M. had said. But the Baron had reassured
her; though in other cases, he had replied, that
might happen, he did not think it would in Albert's. And the Baron was right. Throughout
their married life no rival female charms ever had
cause to give Victoria one moment's pang of jealousy.[1]

What more and more absorbed him—bringing
with it a curious comfort of its own—was his work.
With the advent of Peel, he began to intervene
actively in the affairs of the State. In more ways
than one—in the cast of their intelligence, in their
moral earnestness, even in the uneasy formalism of

1 Lyttelton, 303, 354, 402.
2 Clarendon, I, 181–2; *Girlhood*, II, 299, 306.

their manners—the two men resembled each other;
there was a sympathy between them; and thus
Peel was ready enough to listen to the advice of
Stockmar, and to urge the Prince forward into
public life. A royal commission was about to be
formed to enquire whether advantage might not
be taken of the rebuilding of the Houses of Parliament to encourage the Fine Arts in the United
Kingdom; and Peel, with great perspicacity, asked
the Prince to preside over it. The work was of
a kind which precisely suited Albert: his love of
art, his love of method, his love of coming into
contact—close yet dignified—with distinguished
men—it satisfied them all; and he threw himsel;
into it *con amore*. Some of the members of the
commission were somewhat alarmed when, in his
opening speech, he pointed out the necessity of
dividing the subjects to be considered into " cate-
gories "—the word, they thought, smacked dangerously of German metaphysics; but their confidence returned when they observed His Royal
Highness's extraordinary technical acquaintance
with the processes of fresco painting. When the
question arose as to whether the decorations upon
the walls of the new buildings should, or should
not, have a moral purpose, the Prince spoke
strongly for the affirmative. Although many, he

observed, would give but a passing glance to the
works, the painter was not therefore to forget
that others might view them with more thoughtful
eyes. This argument convinced the commission,
and it was decided that the subjects to be depicted
should be of an improving nature. The frescoes
were carried out in accordance with the commission's instructions, but unfortunately before very
long they had become, even to the most thoughtful eyes, totally invisible. It seems that His
Royal Highness's technical acquaintance with the
processes of fresco painting was incomplete.[1]

The next task upon which the Prince embarked
was a more arduous one: he determined to reform
the organisation of the royal household. This
reform had been long overdue. For years past
the confusion, discomfort, and extravagance in
the royal residences, and in Buckingham Palace
particularly, had been scandalous; no reform had
been practicable under the rule of the Baroness;
but her functions had now devolved upon the
Prince, and in 1844, he boldly attacked the problem. Three years earlier, Stockmar, after careful enquiry, had revealed in an elaborate memorandum an extraordinary state of affairs. The
control of the household, it appeared, was divided

---

[1] Martin, I, 119–25, 167; Stockmar, 660.

in the strangest manner between a number of authorities, each independent of the other, each possessed of vague and fluctuating powers, without responsibility, and without co-ordination. Of these authorities, the most prominent were the Lord Steward and the Lord Chamberlain—noblemen of high rank and political importance, who changed office with every administration, who did not reside with the Court, and had no effective representatives attached to it. The distribution of their respective functions was uncertain and peculiar. In Buckingham Palace, it was believed that the Lord Chamberlain had charge of the whole of the rooms, with the exception of the kitchen, sculleries, and pantries, which were claimed by the Lord Steward. At the same time, the outside of the Palace was under the control of neither of these functionaries—but of the Office of Woods and Forests; and thus, while the insides of the windows were cleaned by the Department of the Lord Chamberlain—or possibly, in certain cases, of the Lord Steward—the Office of Woods and Forests cleaned their outsides. Of the servants, the housekeepers, the pages, and the housemaids were under the authority of the Lord Chamberlain; the clerk of the kitchen, the cooks, and the porters were under that of the Lord Steward; but the footmen,

the livery-porters, and the under-butlers took their
orders from yet another official—the Master of
the Horse. Naturally, in these circumstances the
service was extremely defective and the lack of
discipline among the servants disgraceful. They
absented themselves for as long as they pleased
and whenever the fancy took them; " and if," as
the Baron put it, " smoking, drinking, and other
irregularities occur in the dormitories, where footmen, etc., sleep ten and twelve in each room, no
one can help it." As for Her Majesty's guests,
there was nobody to show them to their rooms,
and they were often left, having utterly lost their
way in the complicated passages, to wander helpless by the hour. The strange divisions of authority extended not only to persons but to things.
The Queen observed that there was never a fire
in the dining-room. She enquired why. The answer was " the Lord Steward lays the fire, and
the Lord Chamberlain lights it "; the underlings
of those two great noblemen having failed to come
to an accommodation, there was no help for it—
the Queen must eat in the cold.[1]

A surprising incident opened everyone's eyes
to the confusion and negligence that reigned in
the Palace. A fortnight after the birth of the

[1] Stockmar, 404–10; Martin, I, 156–60.

Princess Royal the nurse heard a suspicious noise in the room next to the Queen's bedroom. She called to one of the pages, who, looking under a large sofa, perceived there a crouching figure " with a most repulsive appearance." It was " the boy Jones." This enigmatical personage, whose escapades dominated the newspapers for several ensuing months, and whose motives and character remained to the end ambiguous, was an undersized lad of 17, the son of a tailor, who had apparently gained admittance to the Palace by climbing over the garden wall and walking in through an open window. Two years before he had paid a similar visit in the guise of a chimney-sweep. He now declared that he had spent three days in the Palace, hiding under various beds, that he had " helped himself to soup and other eatables," and that he had " sat upon the throne, seen the Queen, and heard the Princess Royal squall." Every detail of the strange affair was eagerly canvassed. *The Times* reported that the boy Jones had " from his infancy been fond of reading," but that " his countenance is exceedingly sullen." It added: " The sofa under which the boy Jones was discovered, we understand, is one of the most costly and magnificent material and workmanship, and ordered expressly for the accommodation of the royal and illustrious visitors who call to pay their respects to Her Majesty." The culprit was sent for three months to the " House of Correction." When he emerged, he immediately returned to Buckingham Palace. He was discovered, and sent back to the " House of Correction " for another three months, after which he was offered £4 a week by a music hall to appear upon the stage. He refused this offer, and shortly afterwards was found by the police loitering round Buckingham Palace. The authorities acted vigorously, and, without any trial or process of law, shipped the boy Jones off to sea. A year later his ship put into Portsmouth to refit, and he at once disembarked and walked to London. He was re-arrested before he reached the Palace, and sent back to his ship, the *Warspite*. On this occasion it was noticed that he had " much improved in personal appearance and grown quite corpulent "; and so the boy Jones passed out of history, though we catch one last glimpse of him in 1844 falling overboard in the night between Tunis and Algiers. He was fished up again; but it was conjectured—as one of the *Warspite's* officers explained in a letter to *The Times*—that his fall had not been accidental, but that he had deliberately jumped into the Mediterranean in order to " see the life-buoy

light burning." Of a boy with such a record, what
else could be supposed?[1]

But discomfort and alarm were not the only
results of the mismanagement of the household;
the waste, extravagance, and peculation that also
flowed from it were immeasurable. There were
preposterous perquisites and malpractices of every
kind. It was, for instance, an ancient and immu-
table rule that a candle that had once been lighted
should never be lighted again; what happened to
the old candles, nobody knew. Again, the Prince,
examining the accounts, was puzzled by a weekly
expenditure of thirty-five shillings on " Red Room
Wine." He enquired into the matter, and after
great difficulty discovered that in the time of
George III a room in Windsor Castle with red
hangings had once been used as a guard-room, and
that five shillings a day had been allowed to provide wine for the officers. The guard had long
since been moved elsewhere, but the payment for
wine in the Red Room continued, the money being
received by a half-pay officer who held the sinecure
position of under-butler.[2]

After much laborious investigation, and a stiff
struggle with the multitude of vested interests

[1] *The Times*, December, 1840; March, July, December, 1841;
February, October, 1842; July, 1844.
[2] *The Times*, " Life," 45.

which had been brought into being by long years of neglect, the Prince succeeded in effecting a complete reform. The various conflicting authorities were induced to resign their powers into the hands of a single official, the Master of the Household, who became responsible for the entire management of the royal palaces. Great economies were made, and the whole crowd of venerable abuses was swept away. Among others, the unlucky half-pay officer of the Red Room was, much to his surprise, given the choice of relinquishing his weekly emolument or of performing the duties of an under-butler. Even the irregularities among the footmen, etc., were greatly diminished. There were outcries and complaints; the Prince was accused of meddling, of injustice, and of saving candle-ends; but he held on his course, and before long the admirable administration of the royal household was recognised as a convincing proof of his perseverance and capacity.[1]

At the same time his activity was increasing enormously in a more important sphere. He had become the Queen's Private Secretary, her confidential adviser, her second self. He was now always present at her interviews with Ministers.[2] He took, like the Queen, a special interest in for-

[1] Stockmar, 409–10; Martin, I, 161.   [2] Greville, VII, 132.

eign policy; but there was no public question in which his influence was not felt. A double process was at work; while Victoria fell more and more absolutely under his intellectual predominance, he, simultaneously, grew more and more completely absorbed by the machinery of high politics—the incessant and multifarious business of a great State. Nobody any more could call him a dilettante; he was a worker, a public personage, a man of affairs. Stockmar noted the change with exultation. " The Prince," he wrote, " has improved very much lately. He has evidently a head for politics. He has become, too, far more independent. His mental activity is constantly on the increase, and he gives the greater part of his time to business, without complaining." " The relations between husband and wife," added the Baron, " are all one could desire." [1]

Long before Peel's ministry came to an end, there had been a complete change in Victoria's attitude towards him. His appreciation of the Prince had softened her heart; the sincerity and warmth of his nature, which, in private intercourse with those whom he wished to please, had the power of gradually dissipating the awkwardness of his manners, did the rest.[2] She came in time

[1] Stockmar, 466–7.   [2] Disraeli, 311; Greville, VI, 367–8.

to regard him with intense feelings of respect and attachment. She spoke of " our worthy Peel," for whom, she said, she had " an *extreme* admiration " and who had shown himself ." a man of unbounded *loyalty, courage,* patriotism, and *high-mindedness,* and his conduct towards me has been *chivalrous* almost, I might say." [1] She dreaded his removal from office almost as frantically as she had once dreaded that of Lord M. It would be, she declared, a *great calamity.* Six years before, what would she have said, if a prophet had told her that the day would come when she would be horrified by the triumph of the Whigs? Yet there was no escaping it; she had to face the return of her old friends. In the ministerial crises of 1845 and 1846, the Prince played a dominating part. Everybody recognised that he was the real centre of the negotiations—the actual controller of the forces and the functions of the Crown. The process by which this result was reached had been so gradual as to be almost imperceptible; but it may be said with certainty that, by the close of Peel's administration, Albert had become, in effect, the King of England.[2]

[1] *Letters,* II, 64.   [2] Greville, V, 329–30.

VI

With the final emergence of the Prince came the final extinction of Lord Melbourne. A year after his loss of office, he had been struck down by a paralytic seizure; he had apparently recovered, but his old elasticity had gone for ever. Moody, restless, and unhappy, he wandered like a ghost about the town, bursting into soliloquies in public places, or asking odd questions, suddenly, *à propos de bottes.* " I'll be hanged if I'll do it for you, my Lord," he was heard to say in the hall at Brooks's, standing by himself, and addressing the air after much thought. "Don't you consider," he abruptly asked a fellow-guest at Lady Holland's, leaning across the dinner-table in a pause of the conversation, " that it was a most damnable act of Henri Quatre to change his religion with a view to securing the Crown?" He sat at home, brooding for hours in miserable solitude. He turned over his books—his classics and his Testaments—but they brought him no comfort at all. He longed for the return of the past, for the impossible, for he knew not what, for the devilries of Caro, for the happy platitudes of Windsor. His friends had left him, and no wonder, he said in bitterness—the fire was out. He secretly hoped for a return to power, scanning the newspapers with solicitude,

and occasionally making a speech in the House of
Lords. His correspondence with the Queen continued, and he appeared from time to time at
Court; but he was a mere simulacrum of his former self; " the dream," wrote Victoria, " is *past*."
As for his political views, they could no longer be
tolerated. The Prince was an ardent Free Trader,
and so, of course, was the Queen; and when, din-
ing at Windsor at the time of the repeal of the
Corn Laws, Lord Melbourne suddenly exclaimed,
" Ma'am, it's a damned dishonest act! " everyone
was extremely embarrassed. Her Majesty laughed
and tried to change the conversation, but without
avail; Lord Melbourne returned to the charge
again and again with—" I say, Ma'am, it's damned
dishonest! "—until the Queen said " Lord Melbourne, I must beg you not to say anything more
on this subject now "; and then he held his
tongue. She was kind to him, writing him long
letters, and always remembering his birthday; but
it was kindness at a distance, and he knew it. He
had become " poor Lord Melbourne." A profound disquietude devoured him. He tried to fix
his mind on the condition of Agriculture and the
Oxford Movement. He wrote long memoranda
in utterly undecipherable handwriting. He was
convinced that he had lost all his money, and could

not possibly afford to be a Knight of the Garter. He had run through everything, and yet—if Peel went out, he might be sent for—why not? He was never sent for. The Whigs ignored him in their consultations, and the leadership of the party passed to Lord John Russell. When Lord John became Prime Minister, there was much politeness, but Lord Melbourne was not asked to join the Cabinet. He bore the blow with perfect amenity; but he understood, at last, that that was the end.[1]

For two years more he lingered, sinking slowly into unconsciousness and imbecility. Sometimes, propped up in his chair, he would be heard to murmur, with unexpected appositeness, the words of Samson:—

> " So much I feel my general spirit droop,
> My hopes all flat, nature within me seems
> In all her functions weary of herself,
> My race of glory run, and race of shame,
> And I shall shortly be with them that rest." [2]

A few days before his death, Victoria, learning that there was no hope of his recovery, turned her mind for a little towards that which had once been Lord M. " You will grieve to hear," she told King Leopold, " that our good, dear, old friend

[1] Torrens, 502, chap. xxxiii; *Letters,* I, 451; II, 140; Greville V, 359; VI, 125.

[2] Greville, VI, 255.

Melbourne is dying. . . . One cannot forget how good and kind and amiable he was, and it brings back so many recollections to my mind, though, God knows! I never wish that time back again." [1]

She was in little danger. The tide of circumstance was flowing now with irresistible fullness towards a very different consummation. The seriousness of Albert, the claims of her children, her own inmost inclinations, and the movement of the whole surrounding world, combined to urge her forward along the narrow way of public and domestic duty. Her family steadily increased. Within eighteen months of the birth of the Prince of Wales the Princess Alice appeared, and a year later the Prince Alfred, and then the Princess Helena, and, two years afterwards, the Princess Louise; and still there were signs that the pretty row of royal infants was not complete. The parents, more and more involved in family cares and family happiness, found the pomp of Windsor galling, and longed for some more intimate and remote retreat. On the advice of Peel they purchased the estate of Osborne, in the Isle of Wight. Their skill and economy in financial matters had enabled them to lay aside a substantial sum of

[1] *Letters*, II, 203.

money; and they could afford, out of their savings, not merely to buy the property but to build a new house for themselves and to furnish it at a cost of £200,000.[1] At Osborne, by the sea-shore, and among the woods, which Albert, with memories of Rosenau in his mind, had so carefully planted, the royal family spent every hour that could be snatched from Windsor and London—delightful hours of deep retirement and peaceful work.[2] The public looked on with approval. A few aristocrats might sniff or titter; but with the nation at large the Queen was now once more extremely popular. The middle-classes, in particular, were pleased. They liked a love-match; they liked a household which combined the advantages of royalty and virtue, and in which they seemed to see, reflected as in some resplendent looking-glass, the ideal image of the very lives they led themselves. Their own existences, less exalted, but oh! so soothingly similar, acquired an added excellence, an added succulence, from the early hours, the regularity, the plain tuckers, the round games, the roast beef and Yorkshire pudding of Osborne. It was indeed a model Court. Not only were its central personages the patterns of propriety, but no breath of scandal, no shadow of in-

[1] Greville, VI, 68-9.   [2] Martin, I, 247-9; Grey, 113.

decorum, might approach its utmost boundaries.[1]
For Victoria, with all the zeal of a convert, upheld
now the standard of moral purity with an inflexi-
bility surpassing, if that were possible, Albert's
own. She blushed to think how she had once believed—how she had once actually told *him*—that
one might be too strict and particular in such matters, and that one ought to be indulgent towards
other people's dreadful sins. But she was no
longer Lord M.'s pupil: she was Albert's wife.
She was more—the embodiment, the living apex
of a new era in the generations of mankind. The
last vestige of the eighteenth century had disappeared; cynicism and subtlety were shrivelled into
powder; and duty, industry, morality, and domes-
ticity triumphed over them. Even the very chairs
and tables had assumed, with a singular respon-
siveness, the forms of prim solidity. The Victorian Age was in full swing.

VII

Only one thing more was needed: material expression must be given to the new ideals and the
new forces so that they might stand revealed, in
visible glory, before the eyes of an astonished

[1] Stockmar, 363; Martin, I, 316.

world. It was for Albert to supply this want. He mused, and was inspired: the Great Exhibition came into his head.

Without consulting anyone, he thought out the details of his conception with the minutest care. There had been exhibitions before in the world, but this should surpass them all. It should contain specimens of what every country could produce in raw materials, in machinery and mechanical inventions, in manufactures, and in the applied and plastic arts. It should not be merely useful and ornamental; it should teach a high moral lesson. It should be an international monument to those supreme blessings of civilisation—peace, progress, and prosperity. For some time past the Prince had been devoting much of his attention to the problems of commerce and industry. He had a taste for machinery of every kind, and his sharp eye had more than once detected, with the precision of an expert, a missing cog-wheel in some vast and complicated engine.[1] A visit to Liverpool, where he opened the Albert Dock, impressed upon his mind the immensity of modern industrial forces, though in a letter to Victoria describing his experiences, he was careful to retain his customary lightness of touch. " As I write," he play-

[1] Martin, II, 87.

fully remarked, " you will be making your evening
toilette, and not be ready in time for dinner. I
must set about the same task, and not, let me hope,
with the same result. . . . The loyalty and enthusiasm of the inhabitants are great; but the heat
is greater still. I am satisfied that if the population of Liverpool had been weighed this morning,
and were to be weighed again now, they would
be found many degrees lighter. The docks are
wonderful, and the mass of shipping incredible." [1]
In art and science he had been deeply interested
since boyhood; his reform of the household had put
his talent for organisation beyond a doubt; and
thus from every point of view the Prince was well
qualified for his task. Having matured his plans,
he summoned a small committee and laid an outline of his scheme before it. The committee approved, and the great undertaking was set on foot
without delay.[2]

Two years, however, passed before it was completed. For two years the Prince laboured with
extraordinary and incessant energy. At first all
went smoothly. The leading manufacturers warmly
took up the idea; the colonies and the East India
Company were sympathetic; the great foreign nations were eager to send in their contributions;

[1] Martin, I, 334.   [2] *Ibid.*, II, 224–5.

the powerful support of Sir Robert Peel was obtained, and the use of a site in Hyde Park, selected by the Prince, was sanctioned by the Government. Out of 234 plans for the exhibition building, the Prince chose that of Joseph Paxton, famous as a designer of gigantic conservatories; and the work was on the point of being put in hand when a series of unexpected difficulties arose. Opposition to the whole scheme, which had long been smouldering in various quarters, suddenly burst forth. There was an outcry, headed by *The Times,* against the use of the park for the exhibition; for a moment it seemed as if the building would be relegated to a suburb; but, after a fierce debate in the House, the supporters of the site in the Park won the day. Then it appeared that the project lacked a sufficient financial backing; but this obstacle, too, was surmounted, and eventually £200,000 was subscribed as a guarantee fund. The enormous glass edifice rose higher and higher, covering acres and enclosing towering elm trees beneath its roof: and then the fury of its enemies reached a climax. The fashionable, the cautious, the Protectionists, the pious, all joined in the hue and cry. It was pointed out that the Exhibition would serve as a rallying point for all the ruffians in England, for all the malcontents in Europe;

and that on the day of its opening there would certainly be a riot and probably a revolution. It was asserted that the glass roof was porous, and that the droppings of fifty million sparrows would utterly destroy every object beneath it. Agitated nonconformists declared that the Exhibition was an arrogant and wicked enterprise which would infallibly bring down God's punishment upon the nation. Colonel Sibthorpe, in the debate on the Address, prayed that hail and lightning might descend from heaven on the accursed thing. The Prince, with unyielding perseverance and infinite patience, pressed on to his goal. His health was seriously affected; he suffered from constant sleeplessness; his strength was almost worn out. But he remembered the injunctions of Stockmar and never relaxed. The volume of his labours grew more prodigious every day; he toiled at committees, presided over public meetings, made speeches, and carried on communications with every corner of the civilised world—and his efforts were rewarded. On May 1, 1851, the Great Exhibition was opened by the Queen before an enormous concourse of persons, amid scenes of dazzling brilliancy and triumphant enthusiasm.[1]

---

[1] Martin, II, 225, 243–51, 289, 297–9, 358–9; *Dictionary of National Biography*, Art. "Joseph Paxton"; Bloomfield, II, 3–4.

Victoria herself was in a state of excitement which bordered on delirium. She performed her duties in a trance of joy, gratitude, and amazement, and, when it was all over, her feelings poured themselves out into her journal in a torrential flood. The day had been nothing but an endless succession of glories—or rather one vast glory— one vast radiation of Albert. Everything she had seen, everything she had felt or heard, had been so beautiful, so wonderful that even the royal underlinings broke down under the burden of emphasis, while her remembering pen rushed on, regardless, from splendour to splendour—the huge crowds, so well-behaved and loyal—flags of all the nations floating—the inside of the building, so immense, with myriads of people and the sun shining through the roof—a little side room, where we left our shawls—palm-trees and machinery—dear Albert—the place so big that we could hardly hear the organ—thankfulness to God—a curious assemblage of political and distinguished men—the March from Athalie—God bless my dearest Albert, God bless my dearest country!—a glass fountain—the Duke and Lord Anglesey walking arm in arm—a beautiful Amazon, in bronze, by Kiss—Mr. Paxton, who might be justly proud, and rose from being a common gardener's boy—

Sir George Grey in tears, and everybody astonished and delighted.[1]

A striking incident occurred when, after a short prayer by the Archbishop of Canterbury, the choir of 600 voices burst into the "Hallelujah Chorus." At that moment a Chinaman, dressed in full national costume, stepped out into the middle of the central nave, and, advancing slowly towards the royal group, did obeisance to Her Majesty. The Queen, much impressed, had no doubt that he was an eminent mandarin; and, when the final procession was formed, orders were given that, as no representative of the Celestial Empire was present, he should be included in the diplomatic cortège. He accordingly, with the utmost gravity, followed immediately behind the Ambassadors. He subsequently disappeared, and it was rumoured, among ill-natured people, that, far from being a mandarin, the fellow was a mere impostor. But nobody ever really discovered the nature of the comments that had been lurking behind the matchless impassivity of that yellow face.[2]

A few days later Victoria poured out her heart to her uncle. The first of May, she said, was "the *greatest* day in our history, the most *beautiful* and *imposing* and *touching* spectacle ever seen, and

[1] Martin, II, 364–8.   [2] Martin, II, 367 and note.

the triumph of my beloved Albert. . . . It was the *happiest, proudest* day in my life, and I can think of nothing else. Albert's dearest name is immortalised with this *great* conception, *his* own, and my *own* dear country *showed* she was *worthy* of it. The triumph is *immense.*" [1]

It was. The enthusiasm was universal; even the bitterest scoffers were converted, and joined in the chorus of praise. [2] Congratulations from public bodies poured in; the City of Paris gave a great *fête* to the Exhibition committee; and the Queen and the Prince made a triumphal progress through the North of England. The financial results were equally remarkable. The total profit made by the Exhibition amounted to a sum of £165,000, which was employed in the purchase of land for the erection of a permanent National Museum in South Kensington. During the six months of its existence in Hyde Park over six million persons visited it, and not a single accident occurred. But there is an end to all things; and the time had come for the Crystal Palace to be removed to the salubrious seclusion of Sydenham. Victoria, sad but resigned, paid her final visit. " It looked so beautiful," she said. " I could not believe it was the last time I was to see it. An organ, accompa-

nied by a fine and powerful wind instrument called
the sommerophone, was being played, and it nearly
upset me. The canvas is very dirty, the red curtains are faded and many things are very much
soiled, still the effect is fresh and new as ever and
most beautiful. The glass fountain was already
removed . . . and the sappers and miners were
rolling about the little boxes just as they did at
the beginning. It made us all very melancholy."
But more cheerful thoughts followed. When all
was over, she expressed her boundless satisfaction
in a dithyrambic letter to the Prime Minister. Her
beloved husband's name, she said, was for ever
immortalised, and that this was universally recognised by the country was a source to her of immense happiness and gratitude. " She feels grateful to Providence," Her Majesty concluded, " to
have permitted her to be united to so great, so
noble, so excellent a Prince, and this year will ever
remain the proudest and happiest of her life. The
day of the closing of the Exhibition (which the
Queen regretted much she could not witness), was
the twelfth anniversary of her betrothal to the
Prince, which is a curious coincidence." [1]

[1] Martin, II, 369–72, 386–92, 403–5.

CHAPTER V

LORD PALMERSTON

I

In 1851 the Prince's fortunes reached their high-water mark. The success of the Great Exhibition enormously increased his reputation and seemed to assure him henceforward a leading place in the national life. But before the year was out another triumph, in a very different sphere of action, was also his. This triumph, big with fateful consequences, was itself the outcome of a series of complicated circumstances which had been gathering to a climax for many years.

The unpopularity of Albert in high society had not diminished with time. Aristocratic persons continued to regard him with disfavour; and he on his side, withdrew further and further into a contemptuous reserve. For a moment, indeed, it appeared as if the dislike of the upper classes was about to be suddenly converted into cordiality; for they learnt with amazement that the Prince, during a country visit, had ridden to hounds and acquitted himself remarkably well. They had always taken it for granted that his horsemanship was of some second-rate foreign quality, and here he was jumping five-barred gates and tearing after the fox as if he had been born and bred in Leicestershire. They could hardly believe it; was it possible that they had made a mistake, and that Albert was a good fellow after all? Had he wished to be thought so he would certainly have seized this opportunity, purchased several hunters, and used them constantly. But he had no such desire; hunting bored him, and made Victoria nervous. He continued, as before, to ride, as he himself put it, for exercise or convenience, not for amusement; and it was agreed that though the Prince, no doubt, could keep in his saddle well enough, he was no sportsman.[1]

This was a serious matter. It was not merely that Albert was laughed at by fine ladies and sneered at by fine gentlemen; it was not merely that Victoria, who before her marriage had cut some figure in society, had, under her husband's influence, almost completely given it up. Since Charles the Second the sovereigns of England had, with a single exception, always been unfashionable; and the fact that the exception was George the Fourth seemed to give an added significance

[1] Martin, I, 194–6; *Letters*, I, 510–11.

to the rule. What was grave was not the lack of fashion, but the lack of other and more important qualities. The hostility of the upper classes was symptomatic of an antagonism more profound than one of manners or even of tastes. The Prince, in a word, was un-English. What that word precisely meant it was difficult to say; but the fact was patent to every eye. Lord Palmerston, also, was not fashionable; the great Whig aristocrats looked askance at him, and only tolerated him as an unpleasant necessity thrust upon them by fate. But Lord Palmerston was English through and through; there was something in him that expressed, with extraordinary vigour, the fundamental qualities of the English race. And he was the very antithesis of the Prince. By a curious chance it so happened that this typical Englishman was brought into closer contact than any other of his countrymen with the alien from over the sea. It thus fell out that differences which, in more fortunate circumstances, might have been smoothed away and obliterated, became accentuated to the highest pitch. All the mysterious forces in Albert's soul leapt out to do battle with his adversary, and, in the long and violent conflict that followed, it almost seemed as if he was struggling with England herself.

Palmerston's whole life had been spent in the government of the country. At twenty-two he had been a Minister; at twenty-five he had been offered the Chancellorship of the Exchequer, which, with that prudence which formed so unexpected a part of his character, he had declined to accept. His first spell of office had lasted uninterruptedly for twenty-one years. When Lord Grey came into power he received the Foreign Secretaryship, a post which he continued to occupy, with two intervals, for another twenty-one years. Throughout this period his reputation with the public had steadily grown, and when, in 1846, he became Foreign Secretary for the third time, his position in the country was almost, if not quite, on an equality with that of the Prime Minister, Lord John Russell. He was a tall, big man of sixty-two, with a jaunty air, a large face, dyed whiskers, and a long sardonic upper lip. His private life was far from respectable, but he had greatly strengthened his position in society by marrying, late in life, Lady Cowper, the sister of Lord Melbourne, and one of the most influential of the Whig hostesses. Powerful, experienced, and supremely self-confident, he naturally paid very little attention to Albert. Why should he? The Prince was interested in foreign affairs? Very

well, then; let the Prince pay attention to *him*—
to him, who had been a Cabinet Minister when
Albert was in the cradle, who was the chosen
leader of a great nation, and who had never failed
in anything he had undertaken in the whole course
of his life. Not that he wanted the Prince's attention—far from it: so far as he could see, Albert
was merely a young foreigner, who suffered from
having no vices, and whose only claim to distinction was that he had happened to marry the Queen
of England. This estimate, as he found out to
his cost, was a mistaken one. Albert was by no
means insignificant, and, behind Albert, there was
another figure by no means insignificant either—
there was Stockmar.

But Palmerston, busy with his plans, his ambitions, and the management of a great department,
brushed all such considerations on one side; it was
his favourite method of action. He lived by instinct—by a quick eye and a strong hand, a dex-
terous management of every crisis as it arose, a
half-unconscious sense of the vital elements in a
situation. He was very bold; and nothing gave
him more exhilaration than to steer the ship of
state in a high wind, on a rough sea, with every
stitch of canvas on her that she could carry. But
there is a point beyond which boldness becomes

rashness—a point perceptible only to intuition and not to reason; and beyond that point Palmerston never went. When he saw that the case demanded it, he could go slow—very slow indeed; in fact, his whole career, so full of vigorous adventure, was nevertheless a masterly example of the proverb, "tout vient à point à qui sait attendre." But when he decided to go quick, nobody went quicker. One day, returning from Osborne, he found that he had missed the train to London; he ordered a special, but the station-master told him that to put a special train upon the line at that time of day would be dangerous, and he could not allow it. Palmerston insisted, declaring that he had important business in London, which could not wait. The station-master, supported by all the officials, continued to demur; the company, he said, could not possibly take the responsibility. "On *my* responsibility, then!" said Palmerston, in his off-hand, peremptory way; whereupon the station-master ordered up the train, and the Foreign Secretary reached London in time for his work, without an accident.[1] The story is typical of the happy valiance with which he conducted both his own affairs and those of the nation. "England," he used to say, "is strong

[1] Bunsen, II, 152.

enough to brave consequences."[1] Apparently, under Palmerston's guidance, she was. While the officials protested and shook in their shoes, he would wave them away with his airy "*My* responsibility!" and carry the country swiftly along the line of his choice, to a triumphant destination,— without an accident. His immense popularity was the result partly of his diplomatic successes, partly of his extraordinary personal affability, but chiefly of the genuine intensity with which he responded to the feelings and supported the interests of his countrymen. The public knew that it had in Lord Palmerston not only a high-mettled master, but also a devoted servant—that he was, in every sense of the word, a public man. When he was Prime Minister, he noticed that iron hurdles had been put up on the grass in the Green Park; he immediately wrote to the Minister responsible, ordering, in the severest language, their instant removal, declaring that they were " an intolerable nuisance," and that the purpose of the grass was " to be walked upon freely and without restraint by the people, old and young, for whose enjoyment the parks are maintained."[2] It was in this spirit that, as Foreign Secretary, he watched over the interests of Englishmen abroad. Noth-

1 Dalling, I, 346.   2 Dalling, III, 413–5.

ing could be more agreeable for Englishmen; but foreign governments were less pleased. They found Lord Palmerston interfering, exasperating, and alarming. In Paris they spoke with bated breath of " ce terrible milord Palmerston "; and in Germany they made a little song about him—

"Hat der Teufel einen Sohn,
So ist er sicher Palmerston." [1]

But their complaints, their threats, and their agitations were all in vain. Palmerston, with his upper lip sardonically curving, braved consequences, and held on his course.

The first diplomatic crisis which arose after his return to office, though the Prince and the Queen were closely concerned with it, passed off without serious disagreement between the Court and the Minister. For some years past a curious problem had been perplexing the chanceries of Europe. Spain, ever since the time of Napoleon a prey to civil convulsions, had settled down for a short interval to a state of comparative quiet under the rule of Christina, the Queen Mother, and her daughter Isabella, the young Queen. In 1846, the question of Isabella's marriage, which had for long been the subject of diplomatic speculations,

[1] Ashley, II, 213.

suddenly became acute. Various candidates for her hand were proposed—among others, two cousins of her own, another Spanish prince, and Prince Leopold of Saxe-Coburg, a first cousin of Victoria's and Albert's; for different reasons, however, none of these young men seemed altogether satisfactory. Isabella was not yet sixteen; and it might have been supposed that her marriage could be put off for a few years more; but this was considered to be out of the question. " Vous ne savez pas," said a high authority, " ce que c'est que ces princesses espagnoles; elles ont le diable au corps, et on a toujours dit que si nous ne nous hâtions pas, l'héritier viendrait avant le mari." [1] It might also have been supposed that the young Queen's marriage was a matter to be settled by herself, her mother, and the Spanish Government; but this again was far from being the case. It had become, by one of those periodical reversions to the ways of the eighteenth century, which, it is rumoured, are still not unknown in diplomacy, a question of dominating importance in the foreign policies both of France and England. For several years, Louis Philippe and his Prime Minister Guizot had been privately maturing a very subtle plan. It was the object of the French King to repeat

[1] Greville, VI, 33.

the glorious *coup* of Louis XIV, and to abolish
the Pyrenees by placing one of his grandsons on
the throne of Spain. In order to bring this about,
he did not venture to suggest that his younger
son, the Duc de Montpensier, should marry Isabella; that would have been too obvious a move,
which would have raised immediate and insurmountable opposition. He therefore proposed
that Isabella should marry her cousin, the Duke
of Cadiz, while Montpensier married Isabella's
younger sister, the Infanta Fernanda; and pray,
what possible objection could there be to that?
The wily old King whispered into the chaste ears
of Guizot the key to the secret; he had good reason to believe that the Duke of Cadiz was incapable of having children, and therefore the offspring
of Fernanda would inherit the Spanish crown.
Guizot rubbed his hands, and began at once to
set the necessary springs in motion; but, of course,
the whole scheme was very soon divulged and
understood. The English Government took an
extremely serious view of the matter; the balance
of power was clearly at stake, and the French intrigue must be frustrated at all hazards. A diplomatic struggle of great intensity followed; and
it occasionally appeared that a second War of the
Spanish Succession was about to break out. This

was avoided, but the consequences of this strange imbroglio were far-reaching and completely different from what any of the parties concerned could have guessed.

In the course of the long and intricate negotiations there was one point upon which Louis Philippe laid a special stress—the candidature of Prince Leopold of Saxe-Coburg. The prospect of a marriage between a Coburg Prince and the Queen of Spain was, he declared, at least as threatening to the balance of power in Europe as that of a marriage between the Duc de Montpensier and the Infanta; and, indeed, there was much to be said for this contention. The ruin which had fallen upon the House of Coburg during the Napoleonic wars had apparently only served to multiply its vitality, for that princely family had by now extended itself over Europe in an extraordinary manner. King Leopold was firmly fixed in Belgium; his niece was Queen of England; one of his nephews was the husband of the Queen of England, and another the husband of the Queen of Portugal; yet another was Duke of Würtemberg. Where was this to end? There seemed to be a Coburg Trust ready to send out one of its members at any moment to fill up any vacant place among the ruling families of Europe. And

even beyond Europe there were signs of this infec-
tion spreading.   An American who had arrived in
Brussels had assured King Leopold that there was
a strong feeling in the United States in favour of
monarchy instead of the misrule of mobs, and had
suggested, to the delight of His Majesty, that
some branch of the Coburg family might be available for the position.[1]   That danger might, perhaps, be remote; but the Spanish danger was close
at hand; and if Prince Leopold were to marry
Queen Isabella the position of France would be
one of humiliation, if not of positive danger. Such
were the asseverations of Louis Philippe.   The
English Government had no wish to support
Prince Leopold, and though Albert and Victoria
had some hankerings for the match, the wisdom
of Stockmar had induced them to give up all
thoughts of it. The way thus seemed open for a
settlement: England would be reasonable about
Leopold, if France would be reasonable about
Montpensier. At the Château d'Eu, the agreement was made, in a series of conversations between the King and Guizot on the one side, and
the Queen, the Prince, and Lord Aberdeen on the
other. Aberdeen, as Foreign Minister, declared
that England would neither recognise nor support

[1] *Letters*, I, 511.

Prince Leopold as a candidate for the hand of the
Queen of Spain; while Louis Philippe solemnly
promised, both to Aberdeen and to Victoria, that
the Duc de Montpensier should not marry the
Infanta Fernanda until after the Queen was married and had issue. All went well, and the crisis
seemed to be over, when the whole question was
suddenly re-opened by Palmerston, who had succeeded Aberdeen at the Foreign Office. In a
despatch to the English Minister at Madrid, he
mentioned, in a list of possible candidates for
Queen Isabella's hand, Prince Leopold of Coburg;
and at the same time he took occasion to denounce
in violent language the tyranny and incompetence
of the Spanish Government. This despatch, in-
discreet in any case, was rendered infinitely more
so by being communicated to Guizot. Louis
Philippe saw his opportunity and pounced on it.
Though there was nothing in Palmerston's language to show that he either recognised or supported Prince Leopold, the King at once assumed
that the English had broken their engagement,
and that he was therefore free to do likewise. He
then sent the despatch to the Queen Mother, declared that the English were intriguing for the
Coburg marriage, bade her mark the animosity
of Palmerston against the Spanish Government,

and urged her to escape from her difficulties and
ensure the friendship of France by marrying Isabella to the Duke of Cadiz and Fernanda to Montpensier. The Queen Mother, alarmed and furious, was easily convinced. There was only one
difficulty: Isabella loathed the very sight of her
cousin. But this was soon surmounted; there was
a wild supper-party at the Palace, and in the
course of it the young girl was induced to consent
to anything that was asked of her. Shortly after,
and on the same day, both the marriages took
place.

The news burst like a bomb on the English
Government, who saw with rage and mortification
that they had been completely outmanœuvred by
the crafty King. Victoria, in particular, was outraged. Not only had she been the personal recip-
ient of Louis Philippe's pledge, but he had won
his way to her heart by presenting the Prince of
Wales with a box of soldiers and sending the Princess Royal a beautiful Parisian doll with eyes that
opened and shut. And now insult was added to
injury. The Queen of the French wrote her a
formal letter, calmly announcing, as a family
event in which she was sure Victoria would be interested, the marriage of her son, Montpensier—
" qui ajoutera à notre bonheur intérieur, le seul

vrai dans ce monde, et que vous, madame, savez
si bien apprécier." [1]   But the English Queen had
not long to wait for her revenge. Within eighteen
months the monarchy of Louis Philippe, discredited, unpopular, and fatally weakened by the withdrawal of English support, was swept into limbo,
while he and his family threw themselves as sup-
pliant fugitives at the feet of Victoria.[2]

II

In this affair both the Queen and the Prince had
been too much occupied with the delinquencies of
Louis Philippe to have any wrath to spare for
those of Palmerston; and, indeed, on the main
issue, Palmerston's attitude and their own had
been in complete agreement. But in this the case
was unique. In every other foreign complication
—and they were many and serious—during the
ensuing years, the differences between the royal
couple and the Foreign Secretary were constant
and profound. There was a sharp quarrel over
Portugal, where violently hostile parties were flying at each other's throats. The royal sympathy
was naturally enlisted on behalf of the Queen and
her Coburg husband, while Palmerston gave his

---

[1] *Letters*, II, 100–1.
[2] Dalling, III, chaps. vii and viii; Stockmar, chap. xxi.

support to the progressive elements in the country. It was not until 1848, however, that the strain became really serious. In that year of revolutions, when, in all directions and with alarming frequency, crowns kept rolling off royal heads, Albert and Victoria were appalled to find that the policy of England was persistently directed—in Germany, in Switzerland, in Austria, in Italy, in Sicily—so as to favour the insurgent forces. The situation, indeed, was just such an one as the soul of Palmerston loved. There was danger and excitement, the necessity of decision, the opportunity for action, on every hand. A disciple of Canning, with an English gentleman's contempt and dislike of foreign potentates deep in his heart, the spectacle of the popular uprisings, and of the oppressors bundled ignominiously out of the palaces they had disgraced, gave him unbounded pleasure, and he was determined that there should be no doubt whatever, all over the Continent, on which side in the great struggle England stood. It was not that he had the slightest tincture in him of philosophical radicalism; he had no philosophical tinctures of any kind; he was quite content to be inconsistent—to be a Conservative at home and a Liberal abroad. There were very good reasons for keeping the Irish in their places; but

what had that to do with it? The point was this
—when any decent man read an account of the
political prisons in Naples his gorge rose. He did
not want war; but he saw that without war a skil-
ful and determined use of England's power might
do much to further the cause of the Liberals in
Europe. It was a difficult and a hazardous game
to play, but he set about playing it with delighted
alacrity. And then, to his intense annoyance, just
as he needed all his nerve and all possible freedom
of action, he found himself being hampered and
distracted at every turn by . . . those people at
Osborne. He saw what it was; the opposition was
systematic and informed, and the Queen alone
would have been incapable of it; the Prince was
at the bottom of the whole thing. It was exceedingly vexatious; but Palmerston was in a hurry,
and could not wait; the Prince, if he would insist
upon interfering, must be brushed on one side.

Albert was very angry. He highly disapproved
both of Palmerston's policy and of his methods of
action. He was opposed to absolutism; but in his
opinion Palmerston's proceedings were simply calculated to substitute for absolutism, all over Europe, something no better and very possibly worse
—the anarchy of faction and mob violence. The
dangers of this revolutionary ferment were grave;

even in England Chartism was rampant—a sinister movement, which might at any moment upset the Constitution and abolish the Monarchy. Surely, with such dangers at home, this was a very bad time to choose for encouraging lawlessness abroad. He naturally took a particular interest in Germany. His instincts, his affections, his prepossessions, were ineradicably German; Stockmar was deeply involved in German politics; and he had a multitude of relatives among the ruling German families, who, from the midst of the hurly-burly of revolution, wrote him long and agitated letters once a week. Having considered the question of Germany's future from every point of view, he came to the conclusion, under Stockmar's guidance, that the great aim for every lover of Germany should be her unification under the sovereignty of Prussia. The intricacy of the situation was extreme, and the possibilities of good or evil which every hour might bring forth were incalculable; yet he saw with horror that Palmerston neither understood nor cared to understand the niceties of this momentous problem, but rushed on blindly, dealing blows to right and left, quite—so far as he could see—without system, and even without motive—except, indeed, a totally unreasonable distrust of the Prussian State.

But his disagreement with the details of Palmerston's policy was in reality merely a symptom of the fundamental differences between the characters of the two men. In Albert's eyes Palmerston was a coarse, reckless egotist, whose combined arrogance and ignorance must inevitably have their issue in folly and disaster. Nothing could be more antipathetic to him than a mind so strangely lacking in patience, in reflection, in principle, and in the habits of ratiocination. For to him it was intolerable to think in a hurry, to jump to slapdash decisions, to act on instincts that could not be explained. Everything must be done in due order, with careful premeditation; the premises of the position must first be firmly established; and he must reach the correct conclusion by a regular series of rational steps. In complicated questions—and what questions, rightly looked at, were not complicated?—to commit one's thoughts to paper was the wisest course, and it was the course which Albert, laborious though it might be, invariably adopted. It was as well, too, to draw up a reasoned statement after an event, as well as before it; and accordingly, whatever happened, it was always found that the Prince had made a memorandum. On one occasion he reduced to six pages of foolscap the substance of a confidential

conversation with Sir Robert Peel, and, having
read them aloud to him, asked him to append his
signature; Sir Robert, who never liked to commit
himself, became extremely uneasy; upon which the
Prince, understanding that it was necessary to
humour the singular susceptibilities of Englishmen, with great tact dropped that particular memorandum into the fire. But as for Palmerston, he
never even gave one so much as a chance to read
him a memorandum; he positively seemed to dislike discussion; and, before one knew where one
was, without any warning whatever, he would
plunge into some hare-brained, violent project,
which, as likely as not, would logically involve a
European war. Closely connected, too, with this
cautious, painstaking reasonableness of Albert's,
was his desire to examine questions thoroughly
from every point of view, to go down to the roots
of things, and to act in strict accordance with
some well-defined principle. Under Stockmar's
tutelage he was constantly engaged in enlarging
his outlook and in endeavouring to envisage vital
problems both theoretically and practically—both
with precision and with depth. To one whose
mind was thus habitually occupied, the empirical
activities of Palmerston, who had no notion what
a principle meant, resembled the incoherent vaga-

ries of a tiresome child. What did Palmerston know of economics, of science, of history? What did he care for morality and education? How much consideration had he devoted in the whole course of his life to the improvement of the condition of the working-classes and to the general amelioration of the human race? The answers to such questions were all too obvious; and yet it is easy to imagine, also, what might have been Palmerston's jaunty comment. "Ah! your Royal Highness is busy with fine schemes and beneficent calculations—exactly! Well, as for me, I must say I'm quite satisfied with my morning's work— I've had the iron hurdles taken out of the Green Park."

The exasperating man, however, preferred to make no comment, and to proceed in smiling silence on his inexcusable way. The process of "brushing on one side" very soon came into operation. Important Foreign Office despatches were either submitted to the Queen so late that there was no time to correct them, or they were not submitted to her at all; or, having been submitted, and some passage in them being objected to and an alteration suggested, they were after all sent off in their original form. The Queen complained; the Prince complained; both complained together.

It was quite useless. Palmerston was most apologetic—could not understand how it had occurred—must give the clerks a wigging—certainly Her Majesty's wishes should be attended to, and such a thing should never happen again. But, of course, it very soon happened again, and the royal remonstrances redoubled. Victoria, her partisan passions thoroughly aroused, imported into her protests a personal vehemence which those of Albert lacked. Did Lord Palmerston forget that she was Queen of England? How could she tolerate a state of affairs in which despatches written in her name were sent abroad without her approval or even her knowledge? What could be more derogatory to her position than to be obliged to receive indignant letters from the crowned heads to whom those despatches were addressed—letters which she did not know how to answer, since she so thoroughly agreed with them? She addressed herself to the Prime Minister. " No remonstrance has any effect with Lord Palmerston," she said.[1] " Lord Palmerston," she told him on another occasion, " has as usual pretended not to have had time to submit the draft to the Queen before he had sent it off." [2] She summoned Lord John to her presence, poured out her indignation, and after-

[1] *Letters,* II, 181.　　　　　　　[2] *Ibid.,* II, 194.

wards, on the advice of Albert, noted down what
had passed in a memorandum: "I said that I
thought that Lord Palmerston often endangered
the honour of England by taking a very preju-
diced and one-sided view of a question; that his
writings were always as bitter as gall and did
great harm, which Lord John entirely assented to,
and that I often felt quite ill from anxiety."[1]
Then she turned to her uncle. "The state of
Germany," she wrote in a comprehensive and de-
spairing review of the European situation, "is
dreadful, and one does feel quite ashamed about
that once really so peaceful and happy country.
That there are still good people there I am sure,
but they allow themselves to be worked upon in a
frightful and shameful way. In France a crisis
seems at hand. *What* a very bad figure we cut
in this mediation! Really it is quite immoral, with
Ireland quivering in our grasp and ready to throw
off her allegiance at any moment, for us to force
Austria to give up her lawful possessions.[2] What
shall we say if Canada, Malta, etc., begin to trouble us? It hurts me terribly."[3]   But what did
Lord Palmerston care?

Lord John's position grew more and more irksome. He did not approve of his colleague's treat-

[1] *Letters*, II, 195.   [2] Venice and Lombardy.
[3] *Letters*, 11, 199.

ment of the Queen. When he begged him to be
more careful, he was met with the reply that
28,000 despatches passed through the Foreign
Office in a single year, that, if every one of these
were to be subjected to the royal criticism, the delay would be most serious, that, as it was, the waste
of time and the worry involved in submitting
drafts to the meticulous examination of Prince
Albert was almost too much for an overworked
Minister, and that, as a matter of fact, the post-
ponement of important decisions owing to this
cause had already produced very unpleasant diplomatic consequences.[1] These excuses would have
impressed Lord John more favourably if he had
not himself had to suffer from a similar neglect.
As often as not Palmerston failed to communicate
even to him the most important despatches. The
Foreign Secretary was becoming an almost independent power, acting on his own initiative, and
swaying the policy of England on his own responsibility. On one occasion, in 1847, he had actually
been upon the point of threatening to break off
diplomatic relations with France without consulting either the Cabinet or the Prime Minister.[2] And
such incidents were constantly recurring. When
this became known to the Prince, he saw that his

[1] *Letters,* II, 221; Ashley, II, 195–6.   [2] Greville, VI, 63–4.

opportunity had come. If he could only drive in to the utmost the wedge between the two statesmen, if he could only secure the alliance of Lord John, then the suppression or the removal of Lord Palmerston would be almost certain to follow. He set about the business with all the pertinacity of his nature. Both he and the Queen put every kind of pressure upon the Prime Minister. They wrote, they harangued, they relapsed into awful silence. It occurred to them that Lord Clarendon, an important member of the Cabinet, would be a useful channel for their griefs. They commanded him to dine at the Palace, and, directly the meal was over, " the Queen," as he described it afterwards, " exploded, and went with the utmost vehemence and bitterness into the whole of Palmerston's conduct, all the effects produced all over the world, and all her own feelings and sentiments about it." When she had finished, the Prince took up the tale, with less excitement, but with equal force. Lord Clarendon found himself in an awkward situation; he disliked Palmerston's policy, but he was his colleague, and he disapproved of the attitude of his royal hosts. In his opinion, they were " wrong in wishing that courtiers rather than Ministers should conduct the affairs of the country," and he thought that they " laboured

under the curious mistake that the Foreign Office
was their peculiar department, and that they had
the right to control, if not to direct, the foreign
policy of England." He, therefore, with extreme
politeness, gave it to be understood that he would
not commit himself in any way.[1] But Lord John,
in reality, needed no pressure. Attacked by his
Sovereign, ignored by his Foreign Secretary, he
led a miserable life.[2] With the advent of the
dreadful Schleswig-Holstein question—the most
complex in the whole diplomatic history of Europe
—his position, crushed between the upper and the
nether mill-stones, grew positively unbearable. He
became anxious above all things to get Palmerston
out of the Foreign Office. But then—supposing
Palmerston refused to go?

In a memorandum made by the Prince, at about
this time, of an interview between himself, the
Queen, and the Prime Minister, we catch a curious
glimpse of the states of mind of those three high
personages—the anxiety and irritation of Lord
John, the vehement acrimony of Victoria, and the
reasonable animosity of Albert—drawn together,
as it were, under the shadow of an unseen Presence, the cause of that celestial anger—the gay,

[1] Greville, VI, 324-6; Clarendon, I, 341.
[2] Clarendon, I, 337, 342.

portentous Palmerston. At one point in the conversation Lord John observed that he believed the Foreign Secretary would consent to a change of offices; Lord Palmerston, he said, realised that he had lost the Queen's confidence—though only on public, and not on personal, grounds. But on that, the Prince noted, "the Queen interrupted Lord John by remarking that she distrusted him on *personal* grounds also, but I remarked that Lord Palmerston had so far at least seen rightly; that he had become disagreeable to the Queen, not on account of his person, but of his political doings—to which the Queen assented." Then the Prince suggested that there was a danger of the Cabinet breaking up, and of Lord Palmerston returning to office as Prime Minister. But on that point Lord John was reassuring: he "thought Lord Palmerston too old to do much in the future (having passed his sixty-fifth year)." Eventually it was decided that nothing could be done for the present, but that the *utmost secrecy* must be observed; and so the conclave ended.[1]

At last, in 1850, deliverance seemed to be at hand. There were signs that the public were growing weary of the alarums and excursions of Palmerston's diplomacy; and when his support of

[1] *Letters,* II, 235-7.

Don Pacifico, a British subject, in a quarrel with
the Greek Government, seemed to be upon the
point of involving the country in a war not only
with Greece but also with France, and possibly
with Russia into the bargain, a heavy cloud of
distrust and displeasure appeared to be gathering
and about to burst over his head. A motion directed against him in the House of Lords was
passed by a substantial majority. The question
was next to be discussed in the House of Commons, where another adverse vote was not improbable, and would seal the doom of the Minister.
Palmerston received the attack with complete nonchalance, and then, at the last possible moment, he
struck. In a speech of over four hours, in which
exposition, invective, argument, declamation, plain
talk and resounding eloquence were mingled together with consummate art and extraordinary
felicity, he annihilated his enemies. The hostile
motion was defeated, and Palmerston was once
more the hero of the hour. Simultaneously, Atro-
pos herself conspired to favour him. Sir Robert
Peel was thrown from his horse and killed. By
this tragic chance, Palmerston saw the one rival
great enough to cope with him removed from his
path. He judged—and judged rightly—that he
was the most popular man in England; and when

Lord John revived the project of his exchanging
the Foreign Office for some other position in the
Cabinet, he absolutely refused to stir.[1]

Great was the disappointment of Albert; great
was the indignation of Victoria. "The House of
Commons," she wrote, "is becoming very unman-
ageable and troublesome."[2] The Prince, perceiv-
ing that Palmerston was more firmly fixed in the
saddle than ever, decided that something drastic
must be done. Five months before, the prescient
Baron had drawn up, in case of emergency, a
memorandum, which had been carefully docketed,
and placed in a pigeon-hole ready to hand. The
emergency had now arisen, and the memorandum
must be used. The Queen copied out the words
of Stockmar, and sent them to the Prime Minister, requesting him to show her letter to Palmerston. "She thinks it right," she wrote, "in order
to prevent any mistake for the *future,* shortly to
explain *what it is she expects from her Foreign
Secretary.* She requires: (1) That he will distinctly state what he proposes in a given case, in
order that the Queen may know as distinctly to
what she has given her Royal sanction; (2) Having *once given* her sanction to a measure, that it
be not arbitrarily altered or modified by the Min-

[1] *Letters,* II. 261–4.   [2] *Ibid.,* II, 253.

ister; such an act she must consider as failing in sincerity towards the Crown, and justly to be visited by the exercise of her Constitutional right of dismissing that Minister." [1] Lord John Russell did as he was bid, and forwarded the Queen's letter to Lord Palmerston. This transaction, which was of grave constitutional significance, was entirely unknown to the outside world.

If Palmerston had been a sensitive man, he would probably have resigned on the receipt of the Queen's missive. But he was far from sensitive; he loved power, and his power was greater than ever; an unerring instinct told him that this was not the time to go. Nevertheless, he was seriously perturbed. He understood at last that he was struggling with a formidable adversary, whose skill and strength, unless they were mollified, might do irreparable injury to his career. He therefore wrote to Lord John, briefly acquiescing in the Queen's requirements—"I have taken a copy of this memorandum of the Queen and will not fail to attend to the directions which it contains "—and at the same time, he asked for an interview with the Prince. Albert at once summoned him to the Palace, and was astonished to observe, as he noted in a memorandum, that when

[1] *Letters*, II, 238 and 264.

Palmerston entered the room " he was very much agitated, shook, and had tears in his eyes, so as quite to move me, who never under any circumstances had known him otherwise than with a bland smile on his face." The old statesman was profuse in protestations and excuses; the young one was coldly polite. At last, after a long and inconclusive conversation, the Prince, drawing himself up, said that, in order to give Lord Palmerston " an example of what the Queen wanted," he would " ask him a question point-blank." Lord Palmerston waited in respectful silence, while the Prince proceeded as follows:—" You are aware that the Queen has objected to the Protocol about Schleswig, and of the grounds on which she has done so. Her opinion has been overruled, the Protocol stating the desire of the Great Powers to see the integrity of the Danish monarchy preserved has been signed, and upon this the King of Denmark has invaded Schleswig, where the war is raging. If Holstein is attacked also, which is likely, the Germans will not be restrained from flying to her assistance; Russia has menaced to interfere with arms, if the Schleswigers are successful. What will you do, if this emergency arises (provoking most likely an European war), and which will arise very probably when we shall be at Bal-

moral and Lord John in another part of Scotland?
The Queen expects from your foresight that you
have contemplated this possibility, and requires a
categorical answer as to what you would do in the
event supposed." Strangely enough, to this point-
blank question, the Foreign Secretary appeared to
be unable to reply. The whole matter, he said,
was extremely complicated, and the contingencies
mentioned by His Royal Highness were very un-
likely to arise. The Prince persisted; but it was
useless; for a full hour he struggled to extract a
categorical answer, until at length Palmerston
bowed himself out of the room. Albert threw up
his hands in shocked amazement: what could one
do with such a man?[1]

What indeed? For, in spite of all his apologies
and all his promises, within a few weeks the incorrigible reprobate was at his tricks again. The
Austrian General Haynau, notorious as a rigorous suppressor of rebellion in Hungary and Italy,
and in particular as a flogger of women, came to
England and took it into his head to pay a visit
to Messrs. Barclay and Perkins's brewery. The
features of " General Hyæna," as he was everywhere called—his grim thin face, his enormous
pepper-and-salt moustaches—had gained a horrid

[1] Martin, II, 307–10.

celebrity; and it so happened that among the clerks
at the brewery there was a refugee from Vienna,
who had given his fellow-workers a first-hand account of the General's characteristics. The Austrian Ambassador, scenting danger, begged his
friend not to appear in public, or, if he must do
so, to cut off his moustaches first. But the General would take no advice. He went to the brewery, was immediately recognised, surrounded by a
crowd of angry draymen, pushed about, shouted
at, punched in the ribs, and pulled by the moustaches until, bolting down an alley with the mob
at his heels brandishing brooms and roaring
"Hyæna!" he managed to take refuge in a public
house, whence he was removed under the protection of several policemen. The Austrian Government was angry and demanded explanations. Palmerston, who, of course, was privately delighted
by the incident, replied regretting what had occurred, but adding that in his opinion the General
had "evinced a want of propriety in coming to
England at the present moment"; and he delivered his note to the Ambassador without having
previously submitted it to the Queen or to the
Prime Minister. Naturally, when this was discovered, there was a serious storm. The Prince was
especially indignant; the conduct of the draymen

he regarded, with disgust and alarm, as "a slight foretaste of what an unregulated mass of illiterate people is capable "; and Palmerston was requested by Lord John to withdraw his note, and to substitute for it another from which all censure of the General had been omitted. On this the Foreign Secretary threatened resignation, but the Prime Minister was firm. For a moment the royal hopes rose high, only to be dashed to the ground again by the cruel compliance of the enemy. Palmerston, suddenly lamblike, agreed to everything; the note was withdrawn and altered, and peace was patched up once more.[1]

It lasted for a year, and then, in October, 1851, the arrival of Kossuth in England brought on another crisis. Palmerston's desire to receive the Hungarian patriot at his house in London was vetoed by Lord John; once more there was a sharp struggle; once more Palmerston, after threatening resignation, yielded. But still the insubordinate man could not keep quiet. A few weeks later a deputation of Radicals from Finsbury and Islington waited on him at the Foreign Office and presented him with an address, in which the Emperors of Austria and Russia were stigmatised as "odious and detestable assassins" and "merciless

[1] *Letters*, II, 267–70; Martin, II, 324–7; Ashley, II, 169–70.

tyrants and despots." The Foreign Secretary in his reply, while mildly deprecating these expressions, allowed his real sentiments to appear with a most undiplomatic *insouciance*. There was an immediate scandal, and the Court flowed over with rage and vituperation. " I think," said the Baron, " the man has been for some time insane." Victoria, in an agitated letter, urged Lord John to assert his authority. But Lord John perceived that on this matter the Foreign Secretary had the support of public opinion, and he judged it wiser to bide his time.[1]

He had not long to wait. The culmination of the long series of conflicts, threats, and exacerbations came before the year was out. On December 2, Louis Napoleon's *coup d'état* took place in Paris; and on the following day Palmerston, without consulting anybody, expressed in a conversation with the French Ambassador his approval of Napoleon's act. Two days later, he was instructed by the Prime Minister, in accordance with a letter from the Queen, that it was the policy of the English Government to maintain an attitude of strict neutrality towards the affairs of France. Nevertheless, in an official despatch to the British Am-

---

[1] *Letters,* II, 324–31; Martin, II, 406–11; Spencer Walpole, II, 33–7; Stockmar, 642; Greville, VI, 421–4.

bassador in Paris, he repeated the approval of the
coup d'état which he had already given verbally to
the French Ambassador in London.   This despatch was submitted neither to the Queen nor to
the Prime Minister.   Lord John's patience, as he
himself said, " was drained to the last drop."   He
dismissed Lord Palmerston.[1]

Victoria was in ecstasies; and Albert knew that
the triumph was his even more than Lord John's.
It was his wish that Lord Granville, a young man
whom he believed to be pliant to his influence,
should be Palmerston's successor; and Lord Granville was appointed.   Henceforward, it seemed
that the Prince would have his way in foreign
affairs.   After years of struggle and mortification,
success greeted him on every hand.   In his family,
he was an adored master; in the country, the Great
Exhibition had brought him respect and glory;
and now in the secret seats of power he had gained
a new supremacy.   He had wrestled with the terrible Lord Palmerston, the embodiment of all that
was most hostile to him in the spirit of England,
and his redoubtable opponent had been over-
thrown.[2]   Was England herself at his feet?   It
might be so; and yet . . . it is said that the sons

[1] *Letters,* II, 334–43; Martin, II, 411–18; Ashley, II, 200–12;
Walpole, II, 138–42; Clarendon, I, 338.
[2] Ernest, III, 14.

of England have a certain tiresome quality: they
never know when they are beaten. It was odd,
but Palmerston was positively still jaunty. Was
it possible? Could he believe, in his blind arrogance, that even his ignominious dismissal from
office was something that could be brushed aside?

III

The Prince's triumph was short-lived. A few
weeks later, owing to Palmerston's influence, the
Government was defeated in the House, and Lord
John resigned. Then, after a short interval, a
coalition between the Whigs and the followers of
Peel came into power, under the premiership of
Lord Aberdeen. Once more, Palmerston was in
the Cabinet. It was true that he did not return
to the Foreign Office; that was something to the
good; in the Home Department it might be hoped
that his activities would be less dangerous and
disagreeable. But the Foreign Secretary was no
longer the complacent Granville; and in Lord
Clarendon the Prince knew that he had a Minister
to deal with, who, discreet and courteous as he was,
had a mind of his own.

These changes, however, were merely the pre-
liminaries of a far more serious development.
Events, on every side, were moving towards a

catastrophe. Suddenly the nation found itself under the awful shadow of imminent war. For several months, amid the shifting mysteries of diplomacy and the perplexed agitations of politics, the issue grew more doubtful and more dark, while the national temper was strained to the breaking-point. At the very crisis of the long and ominous negotiations, it was announced that Lord Palmerston had resigned. Then the pent-up fury of the people burst forth. They had felt that in the terrible complexity of events they were being guided by weak and embarrassed counsels; but they had been reassured by the knowledge that at the centre of power there was one man with strength, with courage, with determination, in whom they could put their trust. They now learnt that that man was no longer among their leaders. Why? In their rage, anxiety, and nervous exhaustion, they looked round desperately for some hidden and horrible explanation of what had occurred. They suspected plots, they smelt treachery in the air. It was easy to guess the object upon which their frenzy would vent itself. Was there not a foreigner in the highest of high places, a foreigner whose hostility to their own adored champion was unrelenting and unconcealed? The moment that Palmerston's resignation was known,

there was a universal outcry and an extraordinary tempest of anger and hatred burst,
with unparalleled violence, upon the head of the
Prince.

It was everywhere asserted and believed that
the Queen's husband was a traitor to the country,
that he was a tool of the Russian Court, that in
obedience to Russian influences he had forced Palmerston out of the Government, and that he was
directing the foreign policy of England in the interests of England's enemies. For many weeks
these accusations filled the whole of the press; repeated at public meetings, elaborated in private
talk, they flew over the country, growing every
moment more extreme and more improbable.
While respectable newspapers thundered out their
grave invectives, halfpenny broadsides, hawked
through the streets of London, re-echoed in dog-
gerel vulgarity the same sentiments and the same
suspicions.[1] At last the wildest rumours began to
spread.

[1] "The Turkish war both far and near
   Has played the very deuce then,
And little Al, the royal pal,
   They say has turned a Russian;
Old Aberdeen, as may be seen,
   Looks woeful pale and yellow,
And Old John Bull had his belly full
   Of dirty Russian tallow.

In January, 1854, it was whispered that the Prince had been seized, that he had been found guilty of high treason, that he was to be committed to the Tower. The Queen herself, some declared, had been arrested, and large crowds actually collected round the Tower to watch the incarceration of the royal miscreants.[1]

These fantastic hallucinations, the result of the fevered atmosphere of approaching war, were devoid of any basis in actual fact. Palmerston's res-

Chorus.

"We'll send him home and make him groan,
Oh, Al! you've played the deuce then;
The German lad has acted sad
And turned tail with the Russians.

.   .   .   .

"Last Monday night, all in a fright,
Al out of bed did tumble.
The German lad was raving mad,
How he did groan and grumble!
He cried to Vic, ' I've cut my stick:
To St. Petersburg go right slap.'
When Vic, 'tis said, jumped out of bed,
And wopped him with her night-cap."

From *Lovely Albert!* a broadside preserved at the British Museum; Martin, II, 539–41; Greville, VII, 127–9.
[1] Martin, II, 540, 562.

"You Jolly Turks, now go to work,
And show the Bear your power.
It is rumoured over Britain's isle
That A——— is in the Tower;
The postmen some suspicion had,
And opened the two letters,
'Twas a pity sad the German lad
Should not have known much better!"

Lovely Albert!

ignation had been in all probability totally disconnected with foreign policy; it had certainly been
entirely spontaneous, and had surprised the Court
as much as the nation. Nor had Albert's influence
been used in any way to favour the interests of
Russia. As often happens in such cases, the Government had been swinging backwards and forwards between two incompatible policies—that of
non-interference and that of threats supported by
force—either of which, if consistently followed,
might well have had a successful and peaceful issue,
but which, mingled together, could only lead to war.
Albert, with characteristic scrupulosity, attempted
to thread his way through the complicated labyrinth
of European diplomacy, and eventually was lost
in the maze. But so was the whole of the Cabinet;
and, when war came, his anti-Russian feelings were
quite as vehement as those of the most bellicose of
Englishmen.

Nevertheless, though the specific charges levelled
against the Prince were without foundation, there
were underlying elements in the situation which explained, if they did not justify, the popular state of
mind. It was true that the Queen's husband was a
foreigner, who had been brought up in a foreign
Court, was impregnated with foreign ideas, and
was closely related to a multitude of foreign

princes. Clearly this, though perhaps an unavoidable, was an undesirable, state of affairs; nor were the objections to it merely theoretical; it had in fact produced unpleasant consequences of a serious kind. The Prince's German proclivities were perpetually lamented by English Ministers; Lord Palmerston, Lord Clarendon, Lord Aberdeen,[1] all told the same tale; and it was constantly necessary, in grave questions of national policy, to combat the prepossessions of a Court in which German views and German sentiments held a disproportionate place. As for Palmerston, his language on this topic was apt to be unbridled. At the height of his annoyance over his resignation, he roundly declared that he had been made a victim to foreign intrigue.[2] He afterwards toned down this accusation; but the mere fact that such a suggestion from such a quarter was possible at all showed to what unfortunate consequences Albert's foreign birth and foreign upbringing might lead.

But this was not all. A constitutional question of the most profound importance was raised by the position of the Prince in England. His pres-

---

[1] " Aberdeen spoke much of the Queen and Prince, of course with great praise. He said the Prince's views were generally sound and wise, with one exception, which was his violent and incorrigible German unionism. He goes all lengths with Prussia."—Greville, VI, 305.

[2] Ashley, II, 218.

ence gave a new prominence to an old problem—
the precise definition of the functions and the
powers of the Crown. Those functions and powers had become, in effect, his; and what sort of use
was he making of them? His views as to the
place of the Crown in the Constitution are easily
ascertainable; for they were Stockmar's; and it
happens that we possess a detailed account of
Stockmar's opinions upon the subject in a long
letter addressed by him to the Prince at the time
of this very crisis, just before the outbreak of the
Crimean War. Constitutional Monarchy, according to the Baron, had suffered an eclipse since the
passing of the Reform Bill. It was now " constantly in danger of becoming a pure Ministerial
Government." The old race of Tories, who " had
a direct interest in upholding the prerogatives of
the Crown," had died out; and the Whigs were
" nothing but partly conscious, partly unconscious
Republicans, who stand in the same relation to the
Throne as the wolf does to the lamb." There was
a rule that it was unconstitutional to introduce
" the name and person of the irresponsible Sovereign " into parliamentary debates on constitutional matters; this was " a constitutional fiction,
which, although undoubtedly of old standing, was
fraught with danger "; and the Baron warned

the Prince that " if the English Crown permit a
Whig Ministry to follow this rule in practice,
without exception, you must not wonder if in a
little time you find the majority of the people
impressed with the belief that the King, in the
view of the law, is nothing but a mandarin figure,
which has to nod its head in assent, or shake it in
denial, as his Minister pleases." To prevent this
from happening, it was of extreme importance,
said the Baron, " that no opportunity should be
let slip of vindicating the legitimate position of the
Crown." " And this is not hard to do," he added,
" and can never embarrass a Minister where such
straightforward loyal personages as the Queen
and the Prince are concerned." In his opinion,
the very lowest claim of the Royal Prerogative
should include " a right on the part of the King to
be the permanent President of his Ministerial
Council." The Sovereign ought to be " in the
position of a permanent Premier, who takes rank
above the temporary head of the Cabinet, and in
matters of discipline exercises supreme authority."
The Sovereign " may even take a part in the initi-
ation and the maturing of the Government measures; for it would be unreasonable to expect that
a king, himself as able, as accomplished, and as
patriotic as the best of his Ministers, should be

prevented from making use of these qualities at the deliberations of his Council." "The judicious exercise of this right," concluded the Baron, "which certainly requires a master mind, would not only be the best guarantee for Constitutional Monarchy, but would raise it to a height of power, stability, and symmetry, which has never been attained."[1]

Now it may be that this reading of the Constitution is a possible one, though indeed it is hard to see how it can be made compatible with the fundamental doctrine of ministerial responsibility. William III presided over his Council, and he was a constitutional monarch; and it seems that Stockmar had in his mind a conception of the Crown which would have given it a place in the Constitution analogous to that which it filled at the time of William III. But it is clear that such a theory, which would invest the Crown with more power than it possessed even under George III, runs counter to the whole development of English public life since the Revolution; and the fact that it was held by Stockmar, and instilled by him into Albert, was of very serious importance. For there was good reason to believe not only that these doctrines were held by Albert in theory, but that he

[1] Martin, II, 545–57.

was making a deliberate and sustained attempt to
give them practical validity. The history of the
struggle between the Crown and Palmerston provided startling evidence that this was the case.
That struggle reached its culmination when, in
Stockmar's memorandum of 1850, the Queen asserted her "constitutional right" to dismiss the
Foreign Secretary if he altered a despatch which
had received her sanction. The memorandum
was, in fact, a plain declaration that the Crown
intended to act independently of the Prime Minister. Lord John Russell, anxious at all costs to
strengthen himself against Palmerston, accepted
the memorandum, and thereby implicitly allowed
the claim of the Crown. More than that; after the
dismissal of Palmerston, among the grounds on
which Lord John justified that dismissal in the
House of Commons he gave a prominent place to
the memorandum of 1850. It became apparent
that the displeasure of the Sovereign might be a
reason for the removal of a powerful and popular
Minister. It seemed indeed as if, under the guidance of Stockmar and Albert, the "Constitutional
Monarchy" might in very truth be rising "to a
height of power, stability, and symmetry, which
had never been attained."

But this new development in the position of the

Crown, grave as it was in itself, was rendered
peculiarly disquieting by the unusual circumstances which surrounded it. For the functions of
the Crown were now, in effect, being exercised by
a person unknown to the Constitution, who
wielded over the Sovereign an undefined and unbounded influence. The fact that this person was
the Sovereign's husband, while it explained his
influence and even made it inevitable, by no means
diminished its strange and momentous import. An
ambiguous, prepotent figure had come to disturb
the ancient, subtle, and jealously guarded balance
of the English Constitution. Such had been the
unexpected outcome of the tentative and faint-
hearted opening of Albert's political life. He
himself made no attempt to minimise either the
multiplicity or the significance of the functions he
performed. He considered that it was his duty, he
told the Duke of Wellington in 1850, to " sink his
own individual existence in that of his wife . . .
—assume no separate responsibility before the
public, but make his position entirely a part of
hers—fill up every gap which, as a woman, she
would naturally leave in the exercise of her regal
functions—continually and anxiously watch every
part of the public business, in order to be able to
advise and assist her at any moment in any of the

multifarious and difficult questions or duties
brought before her, sometimes international, sometimes political, or social, or personal. As the natural head of her family, superintendent of her
household, manager of her private affairs, sole
confidential adviser in politics, and only assistant
in her communications with the officers of the Government, he is, besides, the husband of the Queen,
the tutor of the royal children, the private secretary of the Sovereign, and her permanent minister." [1] Stockmar's pupil had assuredly gone far
and learnt well. Stockmar's pupil!—precisely;
the public, painfully aware of Albert's predominance, had grown, too, uneasily conscious that
Victoria's master had a master of his own. Deep
in the darkness the Baron loomed. Another foreigner! Decidedly, there were elements in the situation which went far to justify the popular
alarm. A foreign Baron controlled a foreign
Prince, and the foreign Prince controlled the
Crown of England. And the Crown itself was
creeping forward ominously; and when, from under its shadow, the Baron and the Prince had
frowned, a great Minister, beloved of the people,
had fallen. Where was all this to end?

Within a few weeks Palmerston withdrew his

[1] Martin, II, 259–60.

resignation, and the public frenzy subsided as quickly as it had arisen. When Parliament met, the leaders of both the parties in both the Houses made speeches in favour of the Prince, asserting his unimpeachable loyalty to the country and vindicating his right to advise the Sovereign in all matters of State. Victoria was delighted. " The position of my beloved lord and master," she told the Baron, " has been defined for *once and all* and his merits have been acknowledged on all sides most duly. There was an immense concourse of people assembled when we went to the House of Lords, and the people were very friendly." [1] Immediately afterwards, the country finally plunged into the Crimean War. In the struggle that followed, Albert's patriotism was put beyond a doubt, and the animosities of the past were forgotten. But the war had another consequence, less gratifying to the royal couple: it crowned the ambition of Lord Palmerston. In 1855, the man who five years before had been pronounced by Lord John Russell to be " too old to do much in the future," became Prime Minister of England, and, with one short interval, remained in that position for ten years.

[1] Martin, II, 563–4.

CHAPTER VI

LAST YEARS OF PRINCE CONSORT

I

THE weak-willed youth who took no interest in politics and never read a newspaper had grown into a man of unbending determination whose tireless energies were incessantly concentrated upon the laborious business of government and the highest questions of State. He was busy now from morning till night. In the winter, before the dawn, he was to be seen, seated at his writing-table, working by the light of the green reading-lamp which he had brought over with him from Germany, and the construction of which he had much improved by an ingenious device. Victoria was early too, but she was not so early as Albert; and when, in the chill darkness, she took her seat at her own writing-table, placed side by side with his, she invariably found upon it a neat pile of papers arranged for her inspection and her signature.[1] The day, thus begun, continued in unremitting industry. At breakfast, the newspapers—

---

[1] Martin, II, 161.

the once hated newspapers—made their appearance, and the Prince, absorbed in their perusal,
would answer no questions, or, if an article struck
him, would read it aloud. After that there were
ministers and secretaries to interview; there was
a vast correspondence to be carried on; there were
numerous memoranda to be made. Victoria, treas-
uring every word, preserving every letter, was all
breathless attention and eager obedience. Sometimes Albert would actually ask her advice. He
consulted her about his English: " Lese recht auf-
merksam, und sage wenn irgend ein Fehler ist," [1]
he would say; or, as he handed her a draft for her
signature, he would observe, " Ich hab' Dir hier
ein Draft gemacht, lese es mal! Ich dächte es
wäre recht so." [2] Thus the diligent, scrupulous,
absorbing hours passed by. Fewer and fewer
grew the moments of recreation and of exercise.
The demands of society were narrowed down to
the smallest limits, and even then but grudgingly
attended to. It was no longer a mere pleasure,
it was a positive necessity, to go to bed as early
as possible in order to be up and at work on the
morrow betimes. [3]

[1] " Read this carefully, and tell me if there are any mistakes in it."
[2] " Here is a draft I have made for you. Read it. I should
think this would do."
[3] Martin, V, 273–5.

The important and exacting business of government, which became at last the dominating preoccupation in Albert's mind, still left unimpaired his old tastes and interests; he remained devoted to art, to science, to philosophy; and a multitude of subsidiary activities showed how his energies increased as the demands upon them grew. For whenever duty called, the Prince was all alertness. With indefatigable perseverance he opened museums, laid the foundation stones of hospitals, made speeches to the Royal Agricultural Society, and attended meetings of the British Association.[1] The National Gallery particularly interested him: he drew up careful regulations for the arrangement of the pictures according to schools; and he attempted —though in vain—to have the whole collection transported to South Kensington.[2] Feodora, now the Princess Hohenlohe, after a visit to England, expressed in a letter to Victoria her admiration of Albert both as a private and a public character. Nor did she rely only on her own opinion. " I must just copy out," she said, " what Mr. Klumpp wrote to me some little time ago, and which is quite true—'Prince Albert is one of the few Royal personages who can sacrifice to any principle (as soon as it has become evident to them to

be good and noble) all those notions (or sentiments) to which others, owing to their narrow-
mindedness, or to the prejudices of their rank, are
so thoroughly inclined strongly to cling.'—There
is something so truly religious in this," the Princess added, "as well as humane and just, most
soothing to my feelings which are so often hurt
and disturbed by what I hear and see." [1]

Victoria, from the depth of her heart, subscribed
to all the eulogies of Feodora and Mr. Klumpp.
She only found that they were insufficient. As
she watched her beloved Albert, after toiling with
state documents and public functions, devoting
every spare moment of his time to domestic duties, to artistic appreciation, and to intellectual
improvements; as she listened to him cracking his
jokes at the luncheon table, or playing Mendelssohn on the organ, or pointing out the merits of Sir
Edwin Landseer's pictures; as she followed him
round while he gave instructions about the breed-
ing of cattle, or decided that the Gainsboroughs
must be hung higher up so that the Winterhalters
might be properly seen—she felt perfectly certain
that no other wife had ever had such a husband.
His mind was apparently capable of everything,
and she was hardly surprised to learn that he had

[1] Martin, II, 479.

made an important discovery for the conversion
of sewage into agricultural manure. Filtration
from below upwards, he explained, through some
appropriate medium, which retained the solids and
set free the fluid sewage for irrigation, was the
principle of the scheme. "All previous plans," he
said, "would have cost millions; mine costs next
to nothing." Unfortunately, owing to a slight
miscalculation, the invention proved to be imprac-
ticable; but Albert's intelligence was unrebuffed,
and he passed on, to plunge with all his accustomed ardour into a prolonged study of the rudi-
ments of lithography.[1]

But naturally it was upon his children that his
private interests and those of Victoria were concentrated most vigorously. The royal nurseries
showed no sign of emptying. The birth of the
Prince Arthur in 1850 was followed, three years
later, by that of the Prince Leopold; and in 1857
the Princess Beatrice was born. A family of nine
must be, in any circumstances, a grave responsibility; and the Prince realised to the full how much
the high destinies of his offspring intensified the
need of parental care. It was inevitable that he
should believe profoundly in the importance of
education; he himself had been the product of

[1] Martin, II, 251-2; Bloomfield, II, 110.

education; Stockmar had made him what he was; it was for him, in his turn, to be a Stockmar—to be even more than a Stockmar—to the young creatures he had brought into the world. Victoria would assist him; a Stockmar, no doubt, she could hardly be; but she could be perpetually vigilant, she could mingle strictness with her affection, and she could always set a good example. These considerations, of course, applied pre-eminently to the education of the Prince of Wales. How tremendous was the significance of every particle of influence which went to the making of the future King of England! Albert set to work with a will. But, watching with Victoria the minutest details of the physical, intellectual, and moral training of his children, he soon perceived, to his distress, that there was something unsatisfactory in the development of his eldest son. The Princess Royal was an extremely intelligent child; but Bertie, though he was good-humoured and gentle, seemed to display a deep-seated repugnance to every form of mental exertion. This was most regrettable, but the remedy was obvious: the parental efforts must be redoubled; instruction must be multiplied; not for a single instant must the educational pressure be allowed to relax. Accordingly, more tutors were selected, the curriculum was revised, the

time-table of studies was rearranged, elaborate
memoranda dealing with every possible contin-
gency were drawn up. It was above all essential
that there should be no slackness: " work," said
the Prince, " must be work." And work indeed it
was. The boy grew up amid a ceaseless round of
paradigms, syntactical exercises, dates, genealogical tables, and lists of capes. Constant notes flew
backwards and forwards between the Prince, the
Queen, and the tutors, with inquiries, with reports
of progress, with detailed recommendations; and
these notes were all carefully preserved for future
reference. It was, besides, vital that the heir to
the throne should be protected from the slightest
possibility of contamination from the outside
world. The Prince of Wales was not as other
boys; he might, occasionally, be allowed to invite
some sons of the nobility, boys of good character,
to play with him in the garden of Buckingham
Palace; but his father presided, with alarming precision, over their sports. In short, every possible
precaution was taken, every conceivable effort was
made. Yet, strange to say, the object of all this
vigilance and solicitude continued to be unsatisfactory—appeared, in fact, to be positively growing worse. It was certainly very odd: the more
lessons that Bertie had to do, the less he did them;

and the more carefully he was guarded against excitements and frivolities, the more desirous of mere amusement he seemed to become. Albert was deeply grieved and Victoria was sometimes very angry; but grief and anger produced no more effect than supervision and time-tables. The Prince of Wales, in spite of everything, grew up into manhood without the faintest sign of " adherence to and perseverance in the plan both of studies and life "—as one of the Royal memoranda put it—which had been laid down with such extraordinary forethought by his father.[1]

II

Against the insidious worries of politics, the boredom of society functions, and the pompous publicity of state ceremonies, Osborne had afforded a welcome refuge; but it soon appeared that even Osborne was too little removed from the world. After all, the Solent was a feeble barrier. Oh, for some distant, some almost inaccessible sanctuary, where, in true domestic privacy, one could make happy holiday, just as if—or at least very, very, nearly—one were anybody else! Victoria, ever since, together with Albert, she had visited Scot-

---

[1] *D.N.B.*, Second Supplement, Art. " Edward VII "; *Quarterly Review*, ccxiii, 4–7, 16

land in the early years of her marriage, had felt
that her heart was in the Highlands. She had
returned to them a few years later, and her passion had grown. How romantic they were! And
how Albert enjoyed them too! His spirits rose
quite wonderfully as soon as he found himself
among the hills and the conifers. " It is a happiness to see him," she wrote. "Oh! What can
equal the beauties of nature!" she exclaimed in
her journal, during one of these visits. "What
enjoyment there is in them! Albert enjoys it so
much; he is in ecstasies here." "Albert said,"
she noted next day, "that the chief beauty of
mountain scenery consists in its frequent changes.
We came home at six o'clock." Then she went
on a longer expedition—up to the very top of a
high hill. " It was quite romantic. Here we were
with only this Highlander behind us holding the
ponies (for we got off twice and walked about).
. . . We came home at half-past eleven,—the
most delightful, most romantic ride and walk I
ever had. I had never been up such a mountain,
and then the day was so fine." The Highlanders,
too, were such astonishing people. They "never
make difficulties," she noted, "but are cheerful,
and happy, and merry, and ready to walk, and
run, and do anything." As for Albert he "highly

appreciated the good-breeding, simplicity, and intelligence, which make it so pleasant and even instructive to talk to them." "We were always in the habit," wrote Her Majesty, "of conversing with the Highlanders—with whom one comes so much in contact in the Highlands." She loved everything about them—their customs, their dress, their dances, even their musical instruments. "There were nine pipers at the castle," she wrote, after staying with Lord Breadalbane; "sometimes one and sometimes three played. They always played about breakfast-time, again during the morning, at luncheon, and also whenever we went in and out; again before dinner, and during most of dinner-time. We both have become quite fond of the bag-pipes." [1]

It was quite impossible not to wish to return to such pleasures again and again; and in 1848 the Queen took a lease of Balmoral House, a small residence near Braemar in the wilds of Aberdeenshire. Four years later she bought the place outright. Now she could be really happy every summer; now she could be simple and at her ease; now she could be romantic every evening, and dote upon Albert, without a single distraction, all day long. The diminutive scale of the house was in

[1] *Leaves*, 18, 33, 34, 36, 127–8, 132*n*.

itself a charm. Nothing was more amusing than
to find oneself living in two or three little sitting-
rooms, with the children crammed away upstairs,
and the minister in attendance with only a tiny
bedroom to do all his work in. And then to be
able to run in and out of doors as one liked, and
to sketch, and to walk, and to watch the red deer
coming so surprisingly close, and to pay visits to
the cottagers! And occasionally one could be
more adventurous still—one could go and stay for
a night or two at the Bothie at Alt-na-giuthasach
—a mere couple of huts with " a wooden addition "—and only eleven people in the whole party!
And there were mountains to be climbed and
cairns to be built in solemn pomp. " At last, when
the cairn, which is, I think, seven or eight feet
high, was nearly completed, Albert climbed up to
the top of it, and placed the last stone; after which
three cheers were given. It was a gay, pretty,
and touching sight; and I felt almost inclined to
cry. The view was so beautiful over the dear hills;
the day so fine; the whole so *gemüthlich*." [1] And
in the evening there were sword-dances and reels.

But Albert had determined to pull down the
little old house, and to build in its place a castle
of his own designing. With great ceremony, in

[1] *Leaves*, 73–4, 95–6; Greville, VI, 303–4.

accordance with a memorandum drawn up by the
Prince for the occasion, the foundation-stone of
the new edifice was laid,[1] and by 1855 it was habit-
able. Spacious, built of granite in the Scotch
baronial style, with a tower 100 feet high, and
minor turrets and castellated gables, the castle was
skilfully arranged to command the finest views of
the surrounding mountains and of the neighbouring river Dee. Upon the interior decorations Albert and Victoria lavished all their care. The wall
and the floors were of pitch-pine, and covered with
specially manufactured tartans. The Balmoral
tartan, in red and grey, designed by the Prince, and
the Victoria tartan, with a white stripe, designed by
the Queen, were to be seen in every room: there
were tartan curtains, and tartan chair-covers, and
even tartan linoleums. Occasionally the Royal
Stuart tartan appeared, for Her Majesty always
maintained that she was an ardent Jacobite.
Water-colour sketches by Victoria hung upon the
walls, together with innumerable stags' antlers,
and the head of a boar, which had been shot by
Albert in Germany. In an alcove in the hall,
stood a life-sized statue of Albert in Highland
dress.[2]

---

[1] *Leaves*, 99–100.
[2] *Private Life*, 209–11; *Quarterly Review*, cxciii, 335.

Victoria declared that it was perfection. " Every year," she wrote, " my heart becomes more fixed in this dear paradise, and so much more so now, that *all* has become my dear Albert's *own* creation, own work, own building, own lay-out; . . . and his great taste, and the impress of his dear hand, have been stamped everywhere." [1]

And here, in very truth, her happiest days were passed. In after years, when she looked back upon them, a kind of glory, a radiance as of an unearthly holiness, seemed to glow about these golden hours. Each hallowed moment stood out clear, beautiful, eternally significant. For, at the time, every experience there, sentimental, or grave, or trivial, had come upon her with a peculiar vividness, like a flashing of marvellous lights. Albert's stalkings—an evening walk when she lost her way—Vicky sitting down on a wasps' nest—a torchlight dance—with what intensity such things, and ten thousand like them, impressed themselves upon her eager consciousness! And how she flew to her journal to note them down! The news of the Duke's death! What a moment!—when, as she sat sketching after a picnic by a loch in the lonely hills, Lord Derby's letter had been brought to her, and she had learnt that " *England's,* or

[1] *Leaves,* 103, 111.

rather *Britain's* pride, her glory, her hero, **the**
greatest man she had ever produced, was no
more!" For such were here reflections upon the
"old rebel" of former days. But that past had
been utterly obliterated—no faintest memory of
it remained. For years she had looked up to the
Duke as a figure almost superhuman. Had he not
been a supporter of good Sir Robert? Had he
not asked Albert to succeed him as commander-
in-chief? And what a proud moment it had been
when he stood as sponsor to her son Arthur, who
was born on his eighty-first birthday! So now
she filled a whole page of her diary with pane-
gyrical regrets. "His position was the highest
a subject ever had—above party,—looked up to
by all,—revered by the whole nation,—the friend
of the Sovereign . . . The Crown never possessed,—and I fear never *will*—so *devoted,* loyal,
and faithful a subject, so staunch a supporter!
To *us* his loss is *irreparable* . . . To Albert he
showed the greatest kindness and the utmost confidence . . . Not an eye will be dry in the whole
country." [1] These were serious thoughts; but they
were soon succeeded by others hardly less moving
—by events as impossible to forget—by Mr. Mac-
Leod's sermon on Nicodemus,—by the gift of a

[1] *Leaves,* 92–4.

red flannel petticoat to Mrs. P. Farquharson, and another to old Kitty Kear.[1]

But, without doubt, most memorable, most delightful of all were the expeditions—the rare, exciting expeditions up distant mountains, across broad rivers, through strange country, and lasting several days. With only two gillies—Grant and Brown—for servants, and with assumed names . . . it was more like something in a story than real life. " We had decided to call ourselves *Lord and Lady Churchill and party*—Lady Churchill passing as *Miss Spencer* and General Grey as *Dr. Grey!* Brown once forgot this and called me ' Your Majesty ' as I was getting into the carriage, and Grant on the box once called Albert ' Your Royal Highness,' which set us off laughing, but no one observed it." Strong, vigorous, enthusiastic, bringing, so it seemed, good fortune with her—the Highlanders declared she had " a lucky foot "—she relished everything—the scrambles and the views and the contretemps and the rough inns with their coarse fare and Brown and Grant waiting at table. She could have gone on for ever and ever, absolutely happy with Albert beside her and Brown at her pony's head. But the time came for turning homewards; alas! the

[1] *Leaves*, 102, 113-4.

time came for going back to England. She could
hardly bear it; she sat disconsolate in her room
and watched the snow falling. The last day! Oh!
If only she could be snowed up![1]

III

The Crimean War brought new experiences, and
most of them were pleasant ones. It was pleasant
to be patriotic and pugnacious, to look out appropriate prayers to be read in the churches, to have
news of glorious victories, and to know oneself,
more proudly than ever, the representative of
England. With that spontaneity of feeling which
was so peculiarly her own, Victoria poured out
her emotion, her admiration, her pity, her love,
upon her " dear soldiers." When she gave them
their medals her exultation knew no bounds.
" Noble fellows! " she wrote to the King of the
Belgians. " I own I feel as if these were *my
own children;* my heart beats for *them* as for my
nearest and dearest. They were so touched, so
pleased; many, I hear, cried—and they won't hear
of giving up their medals to have their names engraved upon them for fear they should *not* receive the *identical one* put into *their hands by me,*
which is quite touching. Several came by in a

[1] *Leaves,* 72, 117, 137.

sadly mutilated state."[1] She and they were at
one. They felt that she had done them a splendid
honour, and she, with perfect genuineness, shared
their feeling. Albert's attitude towards such
things was different; there was an austerity in
him which quite prohibited the expansions of emotion. When General Williams returned from the
heroic defence of Kars and was presented at
Court, the quick, stiff, distant bow with which the
Prince received him struck like ice upon the be-
holders.[2] He was a stranger still.

But he had other things to occupy him, more
important, surely, than the personal impressions
of military officers and people who went to Court.
He was at work—ceaselessly at work—on the tremendous task of carrying through the war to a
successful conclusion. State papers, despatches,
memoranda, poured from him in an overwhelming
stream. Between 1853 and 1857 fifty folio volumes were filled with the comments of his pen
upon the Eastern question.[3] Nothing would induce him to stop. Weary ministers staggered
under the load of his advice; but his advice continued, piling itself up over their writing-tables,
and flowing out upon them from red box after red

[1] *Letters*, III, 127.   [2] Private information.
[3] Martin, III, v.

box. Nor was it advice to be ignored. The talent
for administration which had reorganised the royal
palaces and planned the Great Exhibition asserted
itself no less in the confused complexities of war.
Again and again the Prince's suggestions, rejected
or unheeded at first, were adopted under the stress
of circumstances and found to be full of value.
The enrolment of a foreign legion, the establishment of a depôt for troops at Malta, the institution of periodical reports and tabulated returns
as to the condition of the army at Sebastopol—
such were the contrivances and the achievements
of his indefatigable brain. He went further: in a
lengthy minute he laid down the lines for a radical reform in the entire administration of the
army. This was premature, but his proposal that
" a camp of evolution " should be created, in which
troops should be concentrated and drilled, proved
to be the germ of Aldershot.[1]

Meanwhile Victoria had made a new friend:
she had suddenly been captivated by Napoleon
III. Her dislike of him had been strong at first.
She considered that he was a disreputable adven-
turer who had usurped the throne of poor old
Louis Philippe; and besides he was hand-in-glove
with Lord Palmerston. For a long time, although

[1] Martin, III, 146–7, 168–9, 177–9, 190n.

he was her ally, she was unwilling to meet him;
but at last a visit of the Emperor and Empress
to England was arranged. Directly he appeared
at Windsor her heart began to soften. She found
that she was charmed by his quiet manners, his
low, soft voice, and by the soothing simplicity of
his conversation. The good-will of England was
essential to the Emperor's position in Europe,
and he had determined to fascinate the Queen.
He succeeded. There was something deep within
her which responded immediately and vehemently
to natures that offered a romantic contrast with
her own. Her adoration of Lord Melbourne was
intimately interwoven with her half-unconscious
appreciation of the exciting unlikeness between
herself and that sophisticated, subtle, aristocratical
old man. Very different was the quality of her
unlikeness to Napoleon; but its quantity was at
least as great. From behind the vast solidity of
her respectability, her conventionality, her established happiness, she peered out with a strange
delicious pleasure at that unfamiliar, darkly-glit-
tering foreign object, moving so meteorically before her, an ambiguous creature of wilfulness and
Destiny. And, to her surprise, where she had
dreaded antagonisms, she discovered only sympathies. He was, she said, " so quiet, so simple, *naïf*

even, so pleased to be informed about things he does not know, so gentle, so full of tact, dignity, and modesty, so full of kind attention towards us, never saying a word, or doing a thing, which could put me out . . . There is something fascinating, melancholy, and engaging, which draws you to him, in spite of any *prévention* you may have against him, and certainly without the assistance of any outward appearance, though I like his face." She observed that he rode " extremely well, and looks well on horseback, as he sits high." And he danced " with great dignity and spirit." Above all, he listened to Albert; listened with the most respectful attention; showed, in fact, how pleased he was " to be informed about things he did not know "; and afterwards was heard to declare that he had never met the Prince's equal. On one occasion, indeed—but only on one—he had seemed to grow slightly restive. In a diplomatic conversation, " I expatiated a little on the Holstein question," wrote the Prince in a memorandum, " which appeared to bore the Emperor as ' *très-compliquée.*' " [1]

Victoria, too, became much attached to the Empress, whose looks and graces she admired without a touch of jealousy. Eugénie, indeed, in the plen-

1 Martin, III, 242, 245, 351; IV, 111.

itude of her beauty, exquisitely dressed in wonderful Parisian crinolines which set off to perfection her tall and willowy figure, might well have caused some heartburning in the breast of her hostess, who, very short, rather stout, quite plain, in garish middle-class garments, could hardly be expected to feel at her best in such company. But Victoria had no misgivings. To her it mattered nothing that her face turned red in the heat and that her purple pork-pie hat was of last year's fashion, while Eugénie, cool and modish, floated in an infinitude of flounces by her side. She was Queen of England, and was not that enough? It certainly seemed to be; true majesty was hers, and she knew it. More than once, when the two were together in public, it was the woman to whom, as it seemed, nature and art had given so little, who, by the sheer force of an inherent grandeur, completely threw her adorned and beautiful companion into the shade.[1]

There were tears when the moment came for parting, and Victoria felt " quite *wehmüthig*," as her guests went away from Windsor. But before long she and Albert paid a return visit to France, where everything was very delightful, and she drove incognito through the streets of Paris

[1] *Quarterly Review*, cxciii, 313–4; *Spinster Lady*, 7.

in a "common bonnet," and saw a play in the theatre at St. Cloud, and, one evening, at a great party given by the Emperor in her honour at the Château of Versailles, talked a little to a distinguished-looking Prussian gentleman, whose name was Bismarck. Her rooms were furnished so much to her taste that she declared they gave her quite a home feeling—that, if her little dog were there, she should really imagine herself at home. Nothing was said, but three days later her little dog barked a welcome to her as she entered the apartments. The Emperor himself, sparing neither trouble nor expense, had personally arranged the charming surprise.[1] Such were his attentions. She returned to England more enchanted than ever. "Strange indeed," she exclaimed, " are the dispensations and ways of Providence!"[2]

The alliance prospered, and the war drew towards a conclusion. Both the Queen and the Prince, it is true, were most anxious that there should not be a premature peace. When Lord Aberdeen wished to open negotiations Albert attacked him in a "*geharnischten*" letter, while Victoria rode about on horseback reviewing the troops. At last, however, Sebastopol was cap-

1 Crawford, 311–2.   2 Martin, III, 350.

tured. The news reached Balmoral late at night, and " in a few minutes Albert and all the gentlemen in every species of attire sallied forth, followed by all the servants, and gradually by all the population of the village—keepers, gillies, workmen—up to the top of the cairn." A bonfire was lighted, the pipes were played, and guns were shot off. " About three-quarters of an hour after Albert came down and said the scene had been wild and exciting beyond everything. The people had been drinking healths in whisky and were in great ecstasy."[1] The " great ecstasy," perhaps, would be replaced by other feelings next morning; but at any rate the war was over—though, to be sure, its end seemed as difficult to account for as its beginning. The dispensations and ways of Providence continued to be strange.

IV

An unexpected consequence of the war was a complete change in the relations between the royal pair and Palmerston. The Prince and the Minister drew together over their hostility to Russia, and thus it came about that when Victoria found it necessary to summon her old enemy to form an administration she did so without reluctance. The

[1] *Leaves*, 105–6.

premiership, too, had a sobering effect upon Palmerston; he grew less impatient and dictatorial; considered with attention the suggestions of the Crown, and was, besides, genuinely impressed by the Prince's ability and knowledge.[1] Friction, no doubt, there still occasionally was, for, while the Queen and the Prince devoted themselves to foreign politics as much as ever, their views, when the war was over, became once more antagonistic to those of the Prime Minister. This was especially the case with regard to Italy. Albert, theoretically the friend of constitutional government, distrusted Cavour, was horrified by Garibaldi, and dreaded the danger of England being drawn into war with Austria. Palmerston, on the other hand, was eager for Italian independence; but he was no longer at the Foreign Office, and the brunt of the royal displeasure had now to be borne by Lord John Russell. In a few years the situation had curiously altered. It was Lord John who now filled the subordinate and the ungrateful rôle; but the Foreign Secretary, in his struggle with the Crown, was supported, instead of opposed, by the Prime Minister. Nevertheless the struggle was fierce, and the policy, by which the vigorous sympathy of England became one of the decisive fac-

[1] Martin, II, 429.

tors in the final achievement of Italian unity, was only carried through in face of the violent opposition of the Court.[1]

Towards the other European storm-centre, also, the Prince's attitude continued to be very different to that of Palmerston. Albert's great wish was for a united Germany under the leadership of a constitutional and virtuous Prussia; Palmerston did not think that there was much to be said for the scheme, but he took no particular interest in German politics, and was ready enough to agree to a proposal which was warmly supported by both the Prince and the Queen—that the royal Houses of England and Prussia should be united by the marriage of the Princess Royal with the Prussian Crown Prince. Accordingly, when the Princess was not yet fifteen, the Prince, a young man of twenty-four, came over on a visit to Balmoral, and the betrothal took place.[2] Two years later, in 1857, the marriage was celebrated. At the last moment, however, it seemed that there might be a hitch. It was pointed out in Prussia that it was customary for Princes of the blood royal to be married in Berlin, and it was suggested that there was no reason why the present case

1 *Letters*, III, especially July-December, 1859; Martin, IV, 488–91; V, 189.

2 *Leaves*, 107.

should be treated as an exception. When this
reached the ears of Victoria, she was speechless
with indignation. In a note, emphatic even for
Her Majesty, she instructed the Foreign Secretary
to tell the Prussian Ambassador " not to *entertain*
the *possibility* of such a question. . . . The Queen
never could consent to it, both for public and for
private reasons, and the assumption of its being
too much for a Prince Royal of Prussia to *come*
over to marry *the Princess Royal of Great Britain
in* England is too *absurd* to say the least. . . .
Whatever may be the usual practice of Prussian
princes, it is not *every* day that one marries the
eldest daughter of the Queen of England. The
question must therefore be considered as settled
and closed." [1] It was, and the wedding took place
in St. James's Chapel. There were great festivities—illuminations, state concerts, immense crowds,
and general rejoicings. At Windsor a magnificent banquet was given to the bride and bridegroom in the Waterloo room, at which, Victoria
noted in her diary, " everybody was most friendly
and kind about Vicky and full of the universal
enthusiasm, of which the Duke of Buccleuch gave
us most pleasing instances, he having been in the
very thick of the crowd and among the lowest of

[1] *Letters,* III, 253.

the low." Her feelings during several days had
been growing more and more emotional, and when
the time came for the young couple to depart she
very nearly broke down—but not quite. "Poor
dear child!" she wrote afterwards. "I clasped
her in my arms and blessed her, and knew not what
to say. I kissed good Fritz and pressed his hand
again and again. He was unable to speak and
the tears were in his eyes. I embraced them both
again at the carriage door, and Albert got into
the carriage, an open one, with them and Bertie.
. . . The band struck up. I wished good-bye to
the good Perponchers. General Schreckenstein
was much affected. I pressed his hand, and the
good Dean's, and then went quickly upstairs." [1]

Albert, as well as General Schreckenstein, was
much affected. He was losing his favourite child,
whose opening intelligence had already begun to
display a marked resemblance to his own—an
adoring pupil, who, in a few years, might have become an almost adequate companion. An ironic
fate had determined that the daughter who was
taken from him should be sympathetic, clever, interested in the arts and sciences, and endowed with
a strong taste for memoranda, while not a single
one of these qualities could be discovered in the

[1] Martin, IV, 160–9.

son who remained. For certainly the Prince of
Wales did not take after his father. Victoria's
prayer had been unanswered, and with each succeeding year it became more obvious that Bertie
was a true scion of the House of Brunswick. But
these evidences of innate characteristics only served
to redouble the efforts of his parents; it still might
not be too late to incline the young branch, by
ceaseless pressure and careful fastenings, to grow
in the proper direction. Everything was tried.
The boy was sent on a continental tour with a
picked body of tutors, but the results were unsatisfactory. At his father's request he kept a diary
which, on his return, was inspected by the Prince.
It was found to be distressingly meagre: what a
multitude of highly interesting reflections might
have been arranged under the heading: " The First
Prince of Wales visiting the Pope! " But there
was not a single one. " Le jeune prince plaisit à
tout le monde," old Metternich reported to Guizot,
" mais avait l'air embarrassé et très triste." On
his seventeenth birthday a memorandum was
drawn up over the names of the Queen and the
Prince informing their eldest son that he was
now entering upon the period of manhood, and
directing him henceforward to perform the duties
of a Christian gentleman. " Life is composed of

duties," said the memorandum, " and in the due, punctual and cheerful performance of them the true Christian, true soldier, and true gentleman is recognised. . . . A new sphere of life will open for you in which you will have to be taught what to do and what not to do, a subject requiring study more important than any in which you have hitherto been engaged." On receipt of the memorandum Bertie burst into tears. At the same time another memorandum was drawn up, headed " confidential: for the guidance of the gentlemen appointed to attend on the Prince of Wales." This long and elaborate document laid down " certain principles " by which the " conduct and demeanour " of the gentlemen were to be regulated " and which it is thought may conduce to the benefit of the Prince of Wales." " The qualities which distinguish a gentleman in society," continued this remarkable paper, " are:—

(1) His appearance, his deportment and dress.

(2) The character of his relations with, and treatment of, others.

(3) His desire and power to acquit himself creditably in conversation or whatever is the occupation of the society with which he mixes."

A minute and detailed analysis of these subheadings followed, filling several pages, and the memorandum ended with a final exhortation to the gentlemen: " If they will duly appreciate the responsibility of their position, and taking the points above laid down as the outline, will exercise their own good sense in acting *upon all occasions* upon these principles, thinking no point of detail too minute to be important, but maintaining one steady consistent line of conduct they may render essential service to the young Prince and justify the flattering selection made by the royal parents." A year later the young Prince was sent to Oxford, where the greatest care was taken that he should not mix with the undergraduates. Yes, everything had been tried—everything . . . with one single exception. The experiment had never been made of letting Bertie enjoy himself. But why should it have been? " Life is composed of duties." What possible place could there be for enjoyment in the existence of a Prince of Wales?[1]

The same year which deprived Albert of the Princess Royal brought him another and a still more serious loss. The Baron had paid his last visit to England. For twenty years, as he himself said in a letter to the King of the Belgians, he had performed " the laborious and exhausting office of

---

[1] *D.N.B.*, Second Supplement, 551; *Quarterly Review*, ccxiii, 9–20, 24; Greville, VIII, 217.

a paternal friend and trusted adviser" to the
Prince and the Queen. He was seventy; he was
tired, physically and mentally; it was time to go.
He returned to his home in Coburg, exchanging,
once for all, the momentous secrecies of European
statecraft for the tittle-tattle of a provincial capital and the gossip of family life. In his stiff chair
by the fire he nodded now over old stories—not of
emperors and generals—but of neighbours and
relatives and the domestic adventures of long ago
—the burning of his father's library—and the goat
that ran upstairs to his sister's room and ran twice
round the table and then ran down again. Dyspepsia and depression still attacked him; but, looking back over his life, he was not dissatisfied. His
conscience was clear. "I have worked as long as
I had strength to work," he said, "and for a purpose no one can impugn. The consciousness of
this is my reward—the only one which I desired
to earn." [1]

Apparently, indeed, his "purpose" had been
accomplished. By his wisdom, his patience, and
his example he had brought about, in the fullness
of time, the miraculous metamorphosis of which
he had dreamed. The Prince was his creation.
An indefatigable toiler, presiding, for the highest

[1] Stockmar, 4, 44.

ends, over a great nation—that was his achievement; and he looked upon his work and it was
good. But had the Baron no misgivings? Did
he never wonder whether, perhaps, he might have
accomplished not too little but too much? How
subtle and how dangerous are the snares which
fate lays for the wariest of men! Albert, certainly,
seemed to be everything that Stockmar could have
wished—virtuous, industrious, persevering, intelligent. And yet—why was it?—all was not well
with him. He was sick at heart.

For in spite of everything he had never reached
to happiness. His work, for which at last he came
to crave with an almost morbid appetite, was a
solace and not a cure; the dragon of his dissatis-
faction devoured with dark relish that ever-growing tribute of laborious days and nights; but it
was hungry still. The causes of his melancholy
were hidden, mysterious, unanalysable perhaps—
too deeply rooted in the innermost recesses of his
temperament for the eye of reason to apprehend.
There were contradictions in his nature, which, to
some of those who knew him best, made him seem
an inexplicable enigma: he was severe and gentle;
he was modest and scornful; he longed for affection and he was cold.[1] He was lonely, not merely

1 Ernest, I, 140–1.

with the loneliness of exile but with the loneliness
of conscious and unrecognised superiority. He
had the pride, at once resigned and overweening,
of a doctrinaire. And yet to say that he was simply a doctrinaire would be a false description; for
the pure doctrinaire rejoices always in an internal
contentment, and Albert was very far from doing
that. There was something that he wanted and
that he could never get. What was it? Some absolute, some ineffable sympathy? Some extraordinary, some sublime success? Possibly, it was a
mixture of both. To dominate and to be understood! To conquer, by the same triumphant influence, the submission and the appreciation of men—
that would be worth while indeed! But, to such
imaginations, he saw too clearly how faint were
the responses of his actual environment. Who
was there who appreciated him, really and truly?
Who *could* appreciate him in England? And, if
the gentle virtue of an inward excellence availed
so little, could he expect more from the hard ways
of skill and force? The terrible land of his exile
loomed before him a frigid, an impregnable mass.
Doubtless he had made some slight impression:
it was true that he had gained the respect of his
fellow workers, that his probity, his industry, his
exactitude, had been recognised, that he was a

highly influential, an extremely important man.
But how far, how very far, was all this from the
goal of his ambitions! How feeble and futile his
efforts seemed against the enormous coagulation
of dullness, of folly, of slackness, of ignorance, of
confusion that confronted him! He might have
the strength or the ingenuity to make some small
change for the better here or there—to rearrange
some detail, to abolish some anomaly, to insist
upon some obvious reform; but the heart of the
appalling organism remained untouched. England lumbered on, impervious and self-satisfied, in
her old intolerable course. He threw himself
across the path of the monster with rigid purpose
and set teeth, but he was brushed aside. Yes! even
Palmerston was still unconquered—was still there
to afflict him with his jauntiness, his muddle-head-
edness, his utter lack of principle. It was too
much. Neither nature nor the Baron had given
him a sanguine spirit; the seeds of pessimism,
once lodged within him, flourished in a propitious
soil. He

> " questioned things, and did not find
> One that would answer to his mind;
> And all the world appeared unkind."

He believed that he was a failure and he began
to despair.

Yet Stockmar had told him that he must "never relax," and he never would. He would go on, working to the utmost and striving for the highest, to the bitter end. His industry grew almost maniacal. Earlier and earlier was the green lamp lighted; more vast grew the correspondence; more searching the examination of the newspapers; the interminable memoranda more punctilious, analytical, and precise. His very recreations became duties. He enjoyed himself by time-table, went deer-stalking with meticulous gusto, and made puns at lunch—it was the right thing to do. The mechanism worked with astonishing efficiency, but it never rested and it was never oiled. In dry exactitude the innumerable cog-wheels perpetually revolved. No, whatever happened, the Prince would not relax; he had absorbed the doctrines of Stockmar too thoroughly. He knew what was right, and, at all costs, he would pursue it. That was certain. But alas! in this our life what are the certainties? "In nothing be over-zealous!" says an old Greek. "The due measure in all the works of man is best. For often one who zealously pushes towards some excellence, though he be pursuing a gain, is really being led utterly astray by the will of some Power, which makes those things that are evil seem to him good, and those things seem to him evil that are for his advantage." [1]   Surely, both the Prince and the Baron might have learnt something from the frigid wisdom of Theognis.

Victoria noticed that her husband sometimes seemed to be depressed and overworked. She tried to cheer him up. Realising uneasily that he was still regarded as a foreigner, she hoped that by conferring upon him the title of Prince Consort (1857) she would improve his position in the country. " The Queen has a right to claim that her husband should be an Englishman," she wrote. [2] But unfortunately, in spite of the Royal Letters Patent, Albert remained as foreign as before; and as the years passed his dejection deepened. She worked with him, she watched over him, she walked with him through the woods at Osborne, while he whistled to the nightingales, as he had whistled once at Rosenau so long ago. [3] When his birthday came round, she took the greatest pains to choose him presents that he would really like. In 1858, when he was thirty-nine, she gave him " a picture of Beatrice, life-size, in oil, by Horsley, a complete collection of photographic views of Gotha and the country round, which I had taken by Bedford, and a paper-weight of Balmoral granite and

1 *Theognis*, 401 ff.   2 *Letters*, III, 194.   3 Grey, 195*n*.

deers' teeth, designed by Vicky." [1] Albert was of course delighted, and his merriment at the family gathering was more pronounced than ever: and yet . . . what was there that was wrong?

No doubt it was his health. He was wearing himself out in the service of the country; and certainly his constitution, as Stockmar had perceived from the first, was ill-adapted to meet a serious strain. He was easily upset; he constantly suffered from minor ailments. His appearance in itself was enough to indicate the infirmity of his physical powers. The handsome youth of twenty years since with the flashing eyes and the soft complexion had grown into a sallow, tired-looking man, whose body, in its stoop and its loose fleshiness, betrayed the sedentary labourer, and whose head was quite bald on the top. Unkind critics, who had once compared Albert to an operatic tenor, might have remarked that there was something of the butler about him now. Beside Victoria, he presented a painful contrast. She, too, was stout, but it was with the plumpness of a vigorous matron; and an eager vitality was everywhere visible—in her energetic bearing, her protruding, enquiring glances, her small, fat, capable, and commanding hands. If only, by some sympa-

1 Martin, IV, 298.

thetic magic, she could have conveyed into that
portly, flabby figure, that desiccated and discour-
aged brain, a measure of the stamina and the self-
assurance which were so pre-eminently hers!

But suddenly she was reminded that there were
other perils besides those of ill-health. During a
visit to Coburg in 1860, the Prince was very nearly
killed in a carriage accident. He escaped with a
few cuts and bruises; but Victoria's alarm was
extreme, though she concealed it. " It is when the
Queen feels most deeply," she wrote afterwards,
" that she always appears calmest, and she could
not and dared not allow herself to speak of what
might have been, or even to admit to herself (and
she cannot and dare not now) the entire danger,
for her head would turn! " Her agitation, in fact,
was only surpassed by her thankfulness to God.
She felt, she said, that she could not rest " without
doing something to mark permanently her feelings," and she decided that she would endow a
charity in Coburg. " £1,000, or even £2,000,
given either at once, or in instalments yearly,
would not, in the Queen's opinion, be too much."
Eventually, the smaller sum having been fixed
upon, it was invested in a trust, called the " Vic-
toria-Stift," in the name of the Burgomaster and
chief clergyman of Coburg, who were directed to

distribute the interest yearly among a certain number of young men and women of exemplary character belonging to the humbler ranks of life.[1]

Shortly afterwards the Queen underwent, for the first time in her life, the actual experience of close personal loss. Early in 1861 the Duchess of Kent was taken seriously ill, and in March she died. The event overwhelmed Victoria. With a morbid intensity, she filled her diary for pages with minute descriptions of her mother's last hours, her dissolution, and her corpse, interspersed with vehement apostrophes, and the agitated outpourings of emotional reflection. In the grief of the present the disagreements of the past were totally forgotten. It was the horror and the mystery of Death—Death, present and actual—that seized upon the imagination of the Queen. Her whole being, so instinct with vitality, recoiled in agony from the grim spectacle of the triumph of that awful power. Her own mother, with whom she had lived so closely and so long that she had become a part almost of her existence, had fallen into nothingness before her very eyes! She tried to forget, but she could not. Her lamentations continued with a strange abundance, a strange persistency. It was almost as if, by some mysterious

[1] Martin, V, 202–4, 217–9.

and unconscious precognition, she realised that
for her, in an especial manner, that grisly Majesty
had a dreadful dart in store.

For indeed, before the year was out, a far more
terrible blow was to fall upon her. Albert, who
had for long been suffering from sleeplessness,
went, on a cold and drenching day towards the end
of November, to inspect the buildings for the new
Military Academy at Sandhurst. On his return,
it was clear that the fatigue and exposure to which
he had been subjected had seriously affected his
health. He was attacked by rheumatism, his sleeplessness continued, and he complained that he felt
thoroughly unwell. Three days later a painful
duty obliged him to visit Cambridge. The Prince
of Wales, who had been placed at that University
in the previous year, was behaving in such a manner that a parental visit and a parental admonition
had become necessary. The disappointed father,
suffering in mind and body, carried through his
task; but, on his return journey to Windsor, he
caught a fatal chill.[1] During the next week he
gradually grew weaker and more miserable. Yet,
depressed and enfeebled as he was, he continued
to work. It so happened that at that very moment a grave diplomatic crisis had arisen. Civil

[1] *D.N.B.*, Second Supplement, 557.

war had broken out in America, and it seemed as
if England, owing to a violent quarrel with the
Northern States, was upon the point of being
drawn into the conflict. A severe despatch by
Lord John Russell was submitted to the Queen;
and the Prince perceived that, if it was sent off
unaltered, war would be the almost inevitable consequence. At seven o'clock on the morning of
December 1, he rose from his bed, and with a
quavering hand wrote a series of suggestions for
the alteration of the draft, by which its language
might be softened, and a way left open for a
peaceful solution of the question. These changes
were accepted by the Government, and war was
averted. It was the Prince's last memorandum.[1]

He had always declared that he viewed the prospect of death with equanimity. "I do not cling
to life," he had once said to Victoria. "You do;
but I set no store by it." And then he had added:
"I am sure, if I had a severe illness, I should give
up at once, I should not struggle for life. I have
no tenacity of life."[2] He had judged correctly.
Before he had been ill many days, he told a friend
that he was convinced he would not recover.[3] He
sank and sank. Nevertheless, if his case had been

[1] Martin, V, 416–27.   [2] Martin, V, 415.
[3] Bloomfield, II, 155.

properly understood and skilfully treated from the
first, he might conceivably have been saved; but
the doctors failed to diagnose his symptoms; and
it is noteworthy that his principal physician was
Sir James Clark. When it was suggested that
other advice should be taken, Sir James pooh-
poohed the idea: " there was no cause for alarm,"
he said. But the strange illness grew worse. At
last, after a letter of fierce remonstrance from
Palmerston, Dr. Watson was sent for; and Dr.
Watson saw at once that he had come too late.
The Prince was in the grip of typhoid fever. " I
think that everything so far is satisfactory," said
Sir James Clark.[1]

The restlessness and the acute suffering of the
earlier days gave place to a settled torpor and an
ever-deepening gloom. Once the failing patient
asked for music—" a fine chorale at a distance ";
and a piano having been placed in the adjoining
room, Princess Alice played on it some of
Luther's hymns, after which the Prince repeated
" The Rock of Ages." Sometimes his mind wandered; sometimes the distant past came rushing

---

[1] Martin, V, 427–35; Clarendon, II, 253–4: " One cannot speak
with certainty; but it is horrible to think that such a life *may* have
been sacrificed to Sir J. Clark's selfish jealousy of every member
of his profession."—The Earl of Clarendon to the Duchess of
Manchester, December 17, 1861.

upon him; he heard the birds in the early morning, and was at Rosenau again, a boy. Or Victoria would come and read to him " Peveril of
the Peak," and he showed that he could follow
the story, and then she would bend over him, and
he would murmur " liebes Frauchen " and " gutes
Weibchen," stroking her cheek. Her distress and
her agitation were great, but she was not seriously
frightened. Buoyed up by her own abundant
energies, she would not believe that Albert's might
prove unequal to the strain. She refused to face
such a hideous possibility. She declined to see Dr.
Watson. Why should she? Had not Sir James
Clark assured her that all would be well? Only
two days before the end, which was seen now to
be almost inevitable by everyone about her, she
wrote, full of apparent confidence, to the King of
the Belgians: " I do not sit up with him at night,"
she said, " as I could be of no use; and there is
nothing to cause alarm." [1] The Princess Alice
tried to tell her the truth, but her hopefulness
would not be daunted. On the morning of December 14, Albert, just as she had expected,
seemed to be better; perhaps the crisis was
over. But in the course of the day there was
a serious relapse. Then at last she allowed her-

[1] *Letters*, III, 472–3.

self to see that she was standing on the edge of an appalling gulf. The whole family was summoned, and, one after another, the children took a silent farewell of their father. " It was a terrible moment," Victoria wrote in her diary, " but, thank God! I was able to command myself, and to be perfectly calm, and remained sitting by his side." He murmured something, but she could not hear what it was; she thought he was speaking in French. Then all at once he began to arrange his hair, " just as he used to do when well and he was dressing." " Es ist kleines Fräuchen," she whispered to him; and he seemed to understand. For a moment, towards the evening, she went into another room, but was immediately called back; she saw at a glance that a ghastly change had taken place. As she knelt by the bed, he breathed deeply, breathed gently, breathed at last no more. His features became perfectly rigid; she shrieked one long wild shriek that rang through the terror-stricken castle—and understood that she had lost him for ever.[1]

[1] Martin, V, 435–42; Hare, II, 286–8; *Spinster Lady*, 176–7.

CHAPTER VII

WIDOWHOOD

I

THE death of the Prince Consort was the central turning-point in the history of Queen Victoria. She herself felt that her true life had ceased with her husband's, and that the remainder of her days upon earth was of a twilight nature—an epilogue to a drama that was done. Nor is it possible that her biographer should escape a similar impression. For him, too, there is a darkness over the latter half of that long career. The first forty-two years of the Queen's life are illuminated by a great and varied quantity of authentic information. With Albert's death a veil descends. Only occasionally, at fitful and disconnected intervals, does it lift for a moment or two; a few main outlines, a few remarkable details may be discerned; the rest is all conjecture and ambiguity. Thus, though the Queen survived her great bereavement for almost as many years as she had lived before it, the chronicle of those years can bear no proportion to the tale of her earlier life. We must be content in our ignorance with a brief and summary relation.

The sudden removal of the Prince was not merely a matter of overwhelming personal concern to Victoria; it was an event of national, of European importance. He was only forty-two, and in the ordinary course of nature he might have been expected to live at least thirty years longer. Had he done so it can hardly be doubted that the whole development of the English polity would have been changed. Already at the time of his death he filled a unique place in English public life; already among the inner circle of politicians he was accepted as a necessary and useful part of the mechanism of the State. Lord Clarendon, for instance, spoke of his death as " a national calamity of far greater importance than the public dream of," and lamented the loss of his " sagacity and foresight," which, he declared, would have been " more than ever valuable " in the event of an American war.[1] And, as time went on, the Prince's influence must have enormously increased. For, in addition to his intellectual and moral qualities, he enjoyed, by virtue of his position, one supreme advantage which every other holder of high office in the country was without: he was permanent.

[1] Clarendon, II, 251.

Politicians came and went, but the Prince was perpetually installed at the centre of affairs. Who can doubt that, towards the end of the century, such a man, grown grey in the service of the nation, virtuous, intelligent, and with the unexampled experience of a whole life-time of government, would have acquired an extraordinary prestige? If, in his youth, he had been able to pit the Crown against the mighty Palmerston and to come off with equal honours from the contest, of what might he not have been capable in his old age? What Minister, however able, however popular, could have withstood the wisdom, the irreproachability, the vast prescriptive authority, of the venerable Prince? It is easy to imagine how, under such a ruler, an attempt might have been made to convert England into a State as exactly organised, as elaborately trained, as efficiently equipped, and as autocratically controlled, as Prussia herself. Then perhaps, eventually, under some powerful leader—a Gladstone or a Bright—the democratic forces in the country might have rallied together, and a struggle might have followed in which the Monarchy would have been shaken to its foundations. Or, on the other hand, Disraeli's hypothetical prophecy might have come true. "With Prince Albert," he said, "we have buried our sovereign. This German Prince has governed England for twenty-one years with a wisdom and energy such as none of our kings have ever shown. . . . If he had outlived some of our " old stagers " he would have given us the blessings of absolute government." [1]

The English Constitution—that indescribable entity—is a living thing, growing with the growth of men, and assuming ever-varying forms in accordance with the subtle and complex laws of human character. It is the child of wisdom and chance. The wise men of 1688 moulded it into the shape we know; but the chance that George I could not speak English gave it one of its essential peculiarities—the system of a Cabinet independent of the Crown and subordinate to the Prime Minister. The wisdom of Lord Grey saved it from petrifaction and destruction, and set it upon the path of Democracy. Then chance intervened once more; a female sovereign happened to marry an able and pertinacious man; and it seemed likely that an element which had been quiescent within it for years—the element of irresponsible administrative power—was about to become its predominant characteristic and to change completely the direction of its growth. But what

1 Vitzthum, II, 161.

chance gave chance took away. The Consort perished in his prime; and the English Constitution, dropping the dead limb with hardly a tremor, continued its mysterious life as if he had never been.

One human being, and one alone, felt the full force of what had happened. The Baron, by his fireside at Coburg, suddenly saw the tremendous fabric of his creation crash down into sheer and irremediable ruin. Albert was gone, and he had lived in vain. Even his blackest hypochondria had never envisioned quite so miserable a catastrophe. Victoria wrote to him, visited him, tried to console him by declaring with passionate conviction that she would carry on her husband's work. He smiled a sad smile and looked into the fire. Then he murmured that he was going where Albert was— that he would not be long.[1] He shrank into himself. His children clustered round him and did their best to comfort him, but it was useless: the Baron's heart was broken. He lingered for eighteen months, and then, with his pupil, explored the shadow and the dust.

II

With appalling suddenness Victoria had exchanged the serene radiance of happiness for the

[1] Stockmar, 49; Ernest, IV, 71.

utter darkness of woe. In the first dreadful moments those about her had feared that she might lose her reason, but the iron strain within her held firm, and in the intervals between the intense paroxysms of grief it was observed that the Queen was calm. She remembered, too, that Albert had always disapproved of exaggerated manifestations of feeling, and her one remaining desire was to do nothing but what he would have wished. Yet there were moments when her royal anguish would brook no restraints. One day she sent for the Duchess of Sutherland, and, leading her to the Prince's room, fell prostrate before his clothes in a flood of weeping, while she adjured the Duchess to tell her whether the beauty of Albert's character had ever been surpassed.[1] At other times a feeling akin to indignation swept over her. "The poor fatherless baby of eight months," she wrote to the King of the Belgians, "is now the utterly heartbroken and crushed widow of forty-two! My *life* as a *happy* one is *ended!* The world is gone for *me!* . . . Oh! to be cut off in the prime of life— to see our pure, happy, quiet, domestic life, which *alone* enabled me to bear my *much* disliked position, CUT OFF at forty-two—when I *had* hoped with such instinctive certainty that God never

[1] Clarendon, II, 251, 253.

would part us, and would let us grow old together
(though *he* always talked of the shortness of life)
—is *too awful,* too cruel! "[1] The tone of outraged
Majesty seems to be discernible. Did she wonder
in her heart of hearts how the Deity could have
dared?

But all other emotions gave way before her
overmastering determination to continue, absolutely unchanged, and for the rest of her life on
earth, her reverence, her obedience, her idolatry.
" I am anxious to repeat *one* thing," she told her
uncle, " and *that one* is *my firm* resolve, my *irrevocable decision,* viz., that *his* wishes—*his* plans—
about everything, *his* views about *every* thing
are to be *my law!* And *no human power* will
make me swerve from *what he* decided and
wished." She grew fierce, she grew furious, at the
thought of any possible intrusion between her and
her desire. Her uncle was coming to visit her,
and it flashed upon her that *he* might try to interfere with her and seek to " rule the roast " as of
old. She would give him a hint. " I am *also
determined,*" she wrote, " that *no one* person—
may *he* be ever so good, ever so devoted among
my servants—is to lead or guide or dictate *to me*.
I know *how he* would disapprove it . . . Though

[1] *Letters,* III, 474–5.

miserably weak and utterly shattered, my spirit rises when I think *any* wish or plan of his is to be touched or changed, or I am to be *made to do* anything." She ended her letter in grief and affection. She was, she said, his "ever wretched but devoted child, Victoria R." And then she looked at the date: it was the 24th of December. An agonising pang assailed her, and she dashed down a postcript.—"What a Xmas! I won't think of it."[1]

At first, in the tumult of her distresses, she declared that she could not see her Ministers, and the Princess Alice, assisted by Sir Charles Phipps, the keeper of the Privy Purse, performed, to the best of her ability, the functions of an intermediary. After a few weeks, however, the Cabinet, through Lord John Russell, ventured to warn the Queen that this could not continue.[2] She realised that they were right: Albert would have agreed with them; and so she sent for the Prime Minister. But when Lord Palmerston arrived at Osborne, in the pink of health, brisk, with his whiskers freshly dyed, and dressed in a brown overcoat, light grey trousers, green gloves, and blue studs, he did not create a very good impression.[3]

---

[1] *Letters*, III, 476.   [2] Lee, 322–3; Crawford, 368.
[3] Clarendon, II, 257.

Nevertheless, she had grown attached to her old enemy, and the thought of a political change filled her with agitated apprehensions. The Government, she knew, might fall at any moment; she felt she could not face such an eventuality; and therefore, six months after the death of the Prince, she took the unprecedented step of sending a private message to Lord Derby, the leader of the Opposition, to tell him that she was not in a fit state of mind or body to undergo the anxiety of a change of Government, and that if he turned the present Ministers out of office it would be at the risk of sacrificing her life—or her reason. When this message reached Lord Derby he was considerably surprised. "Dear me!" was his cynical comment. "I didn't think she was so fond of them as *that*." [1]

Though the violence of her perturbations gradually subsided, her cheerfulness did not return. For months, for years, she continued in settled gloom. Her life became one of almost complete seclusion. Arrayed in thickest *crêpe,* she passed dolefully from Windsor to Osborne, from Osborne to Balmoral. Rarely visiting the capital, refusing to take any part in the ceremonies of state, shutting herself off from the slightest intercourse with

1 Clarendon, II, 261–2.

society, she became almost as unknown to her
subjects as some potentate of the East. They
might murmur, but they did not understand. What
had she to do with empty shows and vain enjoyments? No! She was absorbed by very different
preoccupations. She was the devoted guardian
of a sacred trust. Her place was in the inmost
shrine of the house of mourning—where she alone
had the right to enter, where she could feel the
effluence of a mysterious presence, and interpret,
however faintly and feebly, the promptings of a
still living soul. That, and that only was her
glorious, her terrible duty. For terrible indeed
it was. As the years passed her depression seemed
to deepen and her loneliness to grow more intense.
"I am on a dreary sad pinnacle of solitary grandeur," she said.[1] Again and again she felt that she
could bear her situation no longer—that she would
sink under the strain. And then, instantly, that
Voice spoke: and she braced herself once more to
perform, with minute conscientiousness, her grim
and holy task.

Above all else, what she had to do was to make
her own the master-impulse of Albert's life—she
must work, as he had worked, in the service of
the country. That vast burden of toil which he

[1] Martin, *Queen Victoria*, 155.

had taken upon his shoulders it was now for her
to bear. She assumed the gigantic load; and naturally she staggered under it. While he had lived,
she had worked, indeed, with regularity and conscientiousness; but it was work made easy, made
delicious, by his care, his forethought, his advice,
and his infallibility. The mere sound of his voice,
asking her to sign a paper, had thrilled her; in
such a presence she could have laboured gladly for
ever. But now there was a hideous change. Now
there were no neat piles and docketings under the
green lamp; now there were no simple explanations of difficult matters; now there was nobody
to tell her what was right and what was wrong.
She had her secretaries, no doubt: there were Sir
Charles Phipps, and General Grey, and Sir
Thomas Biddulph; and they did their best. But
they were mere subordinates: the whole weight of
initiative and responsibility rested upon her alone.
For so it had to be. "I am *determined*"—had
she not declared it?—"that *no one* person is to
lead or guide or dictate to *me*"; anything else
would be a betrayal of her trust. She would follow the Prince in all things. He had refused to
delegate authority; he had examined into every
detail with his own eyes; he had made it a rule
never to sign a paper without having first, not

merely read it, but made notes on it too. She
would do the same. She sat from morning till
night surrounded by huge heaps of despatch-
boxes, reading and writing at her desk—at her
desk, alas! which stood alone now in the room.[1]

Within two years of Albert's death a violent
disturbance in foreign politics put Victoria's faith-
fulness to a crucial test. The fearful Schleswig-
Holstein dispute, which had been smouldering for
more than a decade, showed signs of bursting out
into conflagration. The complexity of the questions at issue was indescribable. " Only three people," said Palmerston, " have ever really understood the Schleswig-Holstein business—the Prince
Consort, who is dead—a German professor, who
has gone mad—and I, who have forgotten all
about it." [2] But, though the Prince might be dead,
had he not left a vicegerent behind him? Victoria
threw herself into the seething embroilment with
the vigour of inspiration. She devoted hours daily
to the study of the affair in all its windings; but
she had a clue through the labyrinth: whenever the
question had been discussed, Albert, she recollected
it perfectly, had always taken the side of Prussia.
Her course was clear. She became an ardent cham-

---

[1] Clarendon, II, 261; Lee, 327; Martin, *Queen Victoria*, 30.
[2] Grant Robertson, *Bismarck*, 156.

QUEEN VICTORIA IN 1863.

QUEEN VICTORIA AND THE PRINCE CONSORT IN 1860.

Copyright of H.M. The King.

QUEEN VICTORIA, PRINCE ALBERT AND THE ROYAL FAMILY.

From the Picture by F. Winterhalter.

pion of the Prussian point of view. It was a legacy from the Prince, she said.[1] She did not realise
that the Prussia of the Prince's day was dead, and
that a new Prussia, the Prussia of Bismarck, was
born. Perhaps Palmerston, with his queer pre-
science, instinctively apprehended the new danger;
at any rate, he and Lord John were agreed upon
the necessity of supporting Denmark against Prussia's claims. But opinion was sharply divided, not
only in the country but in the Cabinet. For eighteen months the controversy raged; while the
Queen, with persistent vehemence, opposed the
Prime Minister and the Foreign Secretary. When
at last the final crisis arose—when it seemed possible that England would join forces with Denmark in a war against Prussia—Victoria's agitation grew febrile in its intensity. Towards her
German relatives she preserved a discreet appearance of impartiality; but she poured out upon her
Ministers a flood of appeals, protests, and expos-
tulations. She invoked the sacred cause of Peace.
" The only chance of preserving peace for Europe," she wrote, " is by not assisting Denmark,
who has brought this entirely upon herself. . . .

[1] Morley, II, 102; Ernest, IV, 133: " I know that our dear angel
Albert, always regarded a strong Prussia as a necessity, for which,
therefore, it is a sacred duty for *me* to work."—Queen Victoria
to the Duke of Saxe-Coburg-Gotha, August 29, 1863.

The Queen suffers much, and her nerves are more and more totally shattered. . . . But though all this anxiety is wearing her out, it will not shake her firm purpose of resisting any attempt to involve this country in a mad and useless combat." She was, she declared, " prepared to make a stand," even if the resignation of the Foreign Secretary should follow.[1]   " The Queen," she told Lord Granville, " is completely exhausted by the anxiety and suspense, and misses her beloved husband's help, advice, support, and love in an overwhelming manner."   She was so worn out by her efforts for peace that she could " hardly hold up her head or hold her pen." [2]   England did not go to war, and Denmark was left to her fate; but how far the attitude of the Queen contributed to this result it is impossible, with our present knowledge, to say.   On the whole, however, it seems probable that the determining factor in the situation was the powerful peace party in the Cabinet rather than the imperious and pathetic pressure of Victoria.

It is, at any rate, certain that the Queen's enthusiasm for the sacred cause of peace was short-lived.   Within a few months her mind had completely altered.   Her eyes were opened to the true

[1] Fitzmaurice, I, 459, 460.'   [2] Ibid., I, 472-3.

nature of Prussia, whose designs upon Austria
were about to culminate in the Seven Weeks' War.
Veering precipitately from one extreme to the
other, she now urged her Ministers to interfere by
force of arms in support of Austria. But she
urged in vain.[1]

Her political activity, no more than her social
seclusion, was approved by the public. As the
years passed, and the royal mourning remained as
unrelieved as ever, the animadversions grew more
general and more severe. It was observed that
the Queen's protracted privacy not only cast a
gloom over high society, not only deprived the
populace of its pageantry, but also exercised a
highly deleterious effect upon the dressmaking,
millinery, and hosiery trades. This latter consideration carried great weight. At last, early in
1864, the rumour spread that Her Majesty was
about to go out of mourning, and there was much
rejoicing in the newspapers; but unfortunately it
turned out that the rumour was quite without
foundation. Victoria, with her own hand, wrote a
letter to *The Times* to say so. " This idea," she
declared, " cannot be too explicitly contradicted.
" The Queen," the letter continued, " heartily ap-
preciates the desire of her subjects to see her, and

[1] Clarendon, II, 310–1.

whatever she *can* do to gratify them in this loyal
and affectionate wish, she *will* do. . . . But there
are other and higher duties than those of mere
representation which are now thrown upon the
Queen, alone and unassisted—duties which she
cannot neglect without injury to the public service, which weigh unceasingly upon her, overwhelming her with work and anxiety." [1] The justifica-
tion might have been considered more cogent had
it not been known that those " other and higher
duties " emphasised by the Queen consisted for the
most part of an attempt to counteract the foreign
policy of Lord Palmerston and Lord John Russell. A large section—perhaps a majority—of the
nation were violent partisans of Denmark in the
Schleswig-Holstein quarrel; and Victoria's support of Prussia was widely denounced. A wave of
unpopularity, which reminded old observers of the
period preceding the Queen's marriage more than
twenty-five years before, was beginning to rise.
The press was rude; Lord Ellenborough attacked
the Queen in the House of Lords; there were
curious whispers in high quarters that she had had
thoughts of abdicating—whispers followed by regrets that she had not done so. [2] Victoria, out-

[1] *The Times,* April 6, 1864; Clarendon, II, 290.
[2] Clarendon, II, 292–3.

raged and injured, felt that she was misunderstood. She was profoundly unhappy. After Lord
Ellenborough's speech, General Grey declared
that he " had never seen the Queen so completely
upset." " Oh, how fearful it is," she herself wrote
to Lord Granville, " to be suspected—uncheered—
unguided and unadvised—and how alone the poor
Queen feels! " [1] Nevertheless, suffer as she might,
she was as resolute as ever; she would not move by
a hair's breadth from the course that a supreme
obligation marked out for her; she would be faithful to the end.

And so, when Schleswig-Holstein was forgotten, and even the image of the Prince had begun
to grow dim in the fickle memories of men, the
solitary watcher remained immutably concentrated
at her peculiar task. The world's hostility, steadily
increasing, was confronted and outfaced by the impenetrable weeds of Victoria. Would the world
never understand? It was not mere sorrow that
kept her so strangely sequestered; it was devotion,
it was self-immolation; it was the laborious legacy
of love. Unceasingly the pen moved over the
black-edged paper. The flesh might be weak, but
that vast burden must be borne. And fortunately,
if the world would not understand, there were

1 Fitzmaurice, I, 466, 469.

faithful friends who did.   There was Lord Granville, and there was kind Mr. Theodore Martin.
Perhaps Mr. Martin, who was so clever, would
find means to make people realise the facts.   She
would send him a letter, pointing out her arduous
labours and the difficulties under which she struggled, and then he might write an article for one
of the magazines.   It is not, she told him in 1863,
"the Queen's *sorrow* that keeps her secluded.
. . . It is her *overwhelming work* and her health,
which is greatly shaken by her sorrow, and the totally overwhelming amount of work and responsibility—work which she feels really wears her out.
Alice Helps was wonderfully struck at the Queen's
room; and if Mrs. Martin will look at it, she can
tell Mr. Martin what surrounds her.   From the
hour she gets out of bed till she gets into it again
there is work, work, work,—letter-boxes, questions, &c., which are dreadfully exhausting—and
if she had not comparative rest and quiet in the
evening she would most likely not be *alive*.   Her
brain is constantly overtaxed." [1]   It was too true.

III

To carry on Albert's work—that was her first
duty; but there was another, second only to that,

---

[1] Martin, *Queen Victoria*, 28–9.

and yet nearer, if possible, to her heart—to impress
the true nature of his genius and character upon
the minds of her subjects. She realised that during his life he had not been properly appreciated;
the full extent of his powers, the supreme quality
of his goodness, had been necessarily concealed;
but death had removed the need of barriers, and
now her husband, in his magnificent entirety,
should stand revealed to all. She set to work
methodically. She directed Sir Arthur Helps to
bring out a collection of the Prince's speeches and
addresses, and the weighty tome appeared in 1862.
Then she commanded General Grey to write an
account of the Prince's early years—from his birth
to his marriage; she herself laid down the design
of the book, contributed a number of confidential
documents, and added numerous notes; General
Grey obeyed, and the work was completed in 1866.
But the principal part of the story was still untold,
and Mr. Martin was forthwith instructed to write
a complete biography of the Prince Consort. Mr.
Martin laboured for fourteen years. The mass
of material with which he had to deal was almost
incredible, but he was extremely industrious, and
he enjoyed throughout the gracious assistance of
Her Majesty. The first bulky volume was published in 1874; four others slowly followed; so

that it was not until 1880 that the monumental work was finished.[1]

Mr. Martin was rewarded by a knighthood; and yet it was sadly evident that neither Sir Theodore nor his predecessors had achieved the purpose which the Queen had in view. Perhaps she was unfortunate in her coadjutors, but, in reality, the responsibility for the failure must lie with Victoria herself. Sir Theodore and the others faithfully carried out the task which she had set them—faithfully put before the public the very image of Albert that filled her own mind. The fatal drawback was that the public did not find that image attractive. Victoria's emotional nature, far more remarkable for vigour than for subtlety, rejecting utterly the qualifications which perspicuity, or humour, might suggest, could be satisfied with nothing but the absolute and the categorical. When she disliked she did so with an unequivocal emphasis which swept the object of her repugnance at once and finally outside the pale of consideration; and her feelings of affection were equally unmitigated. In the case of Albert her passion for superlatives reached its height. To have conceived of him as anything short of perfect—perfect in virtue, in wisdom, in beauty, in all the glories and

[1] Martin, *Queen Victoria*, 97–106.

graces of man—would have been an unthinkable
blasphemy: perfect he was, and perfect he must be
shown to have been. And so, Sir Arthur, Sir
Theodore, and the General painted him. In the
circumstances, and under such supervision, to have
done anything else would have required talents
considerably more distinguished than any that
those gentlemen possessed. But that was not all.
By a curious mischance Victoria was also able to
press into her service another writer, the distinction of whose talents was this time beyond a doubt.
The Poet Laureate, adopting, either from com-
plaisance or conviction, the tone of his sovereign,
joined in the chorus, and endowed the royal formula with the magical resonance of verse. This
settled the matter. Henceforward it was impossible to forget that Albert had worn the white
flower of a blameless life.

The result was doubly unfortunate. Victoria,
disappointed and chagrined, bore a grudge against
her people for their refusal, in spite of all her
efforts, to rate her husband at his true worth. She
did not understand that the picture of an embodied
perfection is distasteful to the majority of mankind. The cause of this is not so much an envy
of the perfect being as a suspicion that he must be
inhuman; and thus it happened that the public,

when it saw displayed for its admiration a figure
resembling the sugary hero of a moral story-book
rather than a fellow man of flesh and blood, turned
away with a shrug, a smile, and a flippant ejacula-
tion. But in this the public was the loser as well
as Victoria. For in truth Albert was a far more
interesting personage than the public dreamed.
By a curious irony an impeccable waxwork had
been fixed by the Queen's love in the popular
imagination, while the creature whom it represented—the real creature, so full of energy and
stress and torment, so mysterious and so unhappy,
and so fallible and so very human—had altogether
disappeared.

IV

Words and books may be ambiguous memorials;
but who can misinterpret the visible solidity of
bronze and stone? At Frogmore, near Windsor,
where her mother was buried, Victoria constructed,
at the cost of £200,000, a vast and elaborate
mausoleum for herself and her husband.[1] But
that was a private and domestic monument, and
the Queen desired that wherever her subjects
might be gathered together they should be reminded of the Prince. Her desire was gratified;

[1] Lee, 390.

all over the country—at Aberdeen, at Perth, and
at Wolverhampton—statues of the Prince were
erected; and the Queen, making an exception to
her rule of retirement, unveiled them herself. Nor
did the capital lag behind. A month after the
Prince's death a meeting was called together at
the Mansion House to discuss schemes for honour-
ing his memory. Opinions, however, were divided
upon the subject. Was a statue or an institution
to be preferred? Meanwhile a subscription was
opened; an influential committee was appointed,
and the Queen was consulted as to her wishes in
the matter. Her Majesty replied that she would
prefer a granite obelisk, with sculptures at the
base, to an institution. But the committee hesi-
tated: an obelisk, to be worthy of the name, must
clearly be a monolith; and where was the quarry
in England capable of furnishing a granite block
of the required size? It was true that there was
granite in Russian Finland; but the committee
were advised that it was not adapted to resist exposure to the open air. On the whole, therefore,
they suggested that a Memorial Hall should be
erected, together with a statue of the Prince. Her
Majesty assented; but then another difficulty arose.
It was found that not more than £60,000 had been
subscribed—a sum insufficient to defray the dou-

ble expense. The Hall, therefore, was abandoned; a statue alone was to be erected; and certain eminent architects were asked to prepare designs. Eventually the committee had at their disposal a total sum of £120,000, since the public subscribed another £10,000, while £50,000 was voted by Parliament. Some years later a joint stock company was formed and built, as a private speculation, the Albert Hall.[1]

The architect whose design was selected, both by the committee and by the Queen, was Mr. Gilbert Scott, whose industry, conscientiousness, and genuine piety had brought him to the head of his profession. His lifelong zeal for the Gothic style having given him a special prominence, his handiwork was strikingly visible, not only in a multitude of original buildings, but in most of the cathedrals of England. Protests, indeed, were occasionally raised against his renovations; but Mr. Scott replied with such vigour and unction in articles and pamphlets that not a Dean was unconvinced, and he was permitted to continue his labours without interruption. On one occasion, however, his devotion to Gothic had placed him in an unpleasant situation. The Government offices in Whitehall were to be rebuilt; Mr. Scott com-

[1] *National Memorial.*

peted, and his designs were successful. Naturally, they were in the Gothic style, combining " a certain squareness and horizontality of outline " with pillar-mullions, gables, high-pitched roofs, and dormers; and the drawings, as Mr. Scott himself observed, " were, perhaps, the best ever sent in to a competition, or nearly so." After the usual difficulties and delays the work was at last to be put in hand, when there was a change of Government and Lord Palmerston became Prime Minister. Lord Palmerston at once sent for Mr. Scott. " Well, Mr. Scott," he said, in his jaunty way, " I can't have anything to do with this Gothic style. I must insist on your making a design in the Italian manner, which I am sure you can do very cleverly." Mr. Scott was appalled; the style of the Italian renaissance was not only unsightly, it was positively immoral, and he sternly refused to have anything to do with it. Thereupon Lord Palmerston assumed a fatherly tone. " Quite true; a Gothic architect can't be expected to put up a Classical building; I must find someone else." This was intolerable, and Mr. Scott, on his return home, addressed to the Prime Minister a strongly-worded letter, in which he dwelt upon his position as an architect, upon his having won two European competitions, his being an A.R.A., a gold

medallist of the Institute, and a lecturer on archi-
tecture at the Royal Academy; but it was useless
—Lord Palmerston did not even reply. It then
occurred to Mr. Scott that, by a judicious mixture, he might, while preserving the essential character of the Gothic, produce a design which would
give a superficial impression of the Classical style.
He did so, but no effect was produced upon Lord
Palmerston. The new design, he said, was " neither
one thing nor 'tother—a regular mongrel affair—
and he would have nothing to do with it either."
After that Mr. Scott found it necessary to recruit
for two months at Scarborough, " with a course of
quinine." He recovered his tone at last, but only
at the cost of his convictions. For the sake of his
family he felt that it was his unfortunate duty to
obey the Prime Minister; and, shuddering with
horror, he constructed the Government offices in
a strictly Renaissance style.

Shortly afterwards Mr. Scott found some consolation in building the St. Pancras Hotel in a
style of his own.[1]

And now another and yet more satisfactory task
was his. " My idea in designing the Memorial,"
he wrote, " was to erect a kind of ciborium to pro-
tect a statue of the Prince; and its special charac-

[1] Scott, 177–201, 271.

teristic was that the ciborium was designed in some degree on the principles of the ancient shrines. These shrines were models of imaginary buildings, such as had never in reality been erected; and my idea was to realise one of these imaginary structures with its precious materials, its inlaying, its enamels, &c. &c." [1] His idea was particularly appropriate since it chanced that a similar conception, though in the reverse order of magnitude, had occurred to the Prince himself, who had designed and executed several silver cruet-stands upon the same model. At the Queen's request a site was chosen in Kensington Gardens as near as possible to that of the Great Exhibition; and in May, 1864, the first sod was turned. The work was long, complicated, and difficult; a great number of workmen were employed, besides several subsidiary sculptors and metal-workers under Mr. Scott's direction, while at every stage sketches and models were submitted to Her Majesty, who criticised all the details with minute care, and constantly suggested improvements. The frieze, which encircled the base of the monument, was in itself a very serious piece of work. "This," said Mr. Scott, "taken as a whole, is perhaps one of the most laborious works of sculpture ever under-

[1] Scott, 225.

taken, consisting, as it does, of a continuous range of figure-sculpture of the most elaborate description, in the highest *alto-relievo* of life-size, of more than 200 feet in length, containing about 170 figures, and executed in the hardest marble which could be procured." After three years of toil the memorial was still far from completion, and Mr. Scott thought it advisable to give a dinner to the workmen, " as a substantial recognition of his appreciation of their skill and energy." " Two long tables," we are told, " constructed of scaffold planks, were arranged in the workshops, and covered with newspapers, for want of table-cloths. Upwards of eighty men sat down. Beef and mutton, plum pudding and cheese were supplied in abundance, and each man who desired it had three pints of beer, gingerbeer and lemonade being provided for the teetotalers, who formed a very considerable proportion. . . . Several toasts were given and many of the workmen spoke, almost all of them commencing by " Thanking God that they enjoyed good health "; some alluded to the temperance that prevailed amongst them, others observed how little swearing was ever heard, whilst all said how pleased and proud they were to be engaged on so great a work."

Gradually the edifice approached completion.

The one hundred and seventieth life-size figure in the frieze was chiselled, the granite pillars arose, the mosaics were inserted in the allegorical pediments, the four colossal statues representing the greater Christian virtues, the four other colossal statues representing the greater moral virtues, were hoisted into their positions, the eight bronzes representing the greater sciences—Astronomy, Chemistry, Geology, Geometry, Rhetoric, Medicine, Philosophy, and Physiology—were fixed on their glittering pinnacles, high in air. The statue of Physiology was particularly admired. " On her left arm," the official description informs us, " she bears a new-born infant, as a representation of the development of the highest and most perfect of physiological forms; her hand points towards a microscope, the instrument which lends its assistance for the investigation of the minuter forms of animal and vegetable organisms." At last the gilded cross crowned the dwindling galaxies of superimposed angels, the four continents in white marble stood at the four corners of the base, and, seven years after its inception, in July, 1872, the monument was thrown open to the public.

But four more years were to elapse before the central figure was ready to be placed under its starry canopy. It was designed by Mr. Foley, though in one particular the sculptor's freedom was restricted by Mr. Scott. " I have chosen the sitting posture," Mr. Scott said, " as best conveying the idea of dignity befitting a royal personage." Mr. Foley ably carried out the conception of his principal. " In the attitude and expression," he said, " the aim has been, with the individuality of portraiture, to embody rank, character, and enlightenment, and to convey a sense of that responsive intelligence indicating an active, rather than a passive, interest in those pursuits of civilisation illustrated in the surrounding figures, groups, and relievos. . . . To identify the figure with one of the most memorable undertakings of the public life of the Prince—the International Exhibition of 1851—a catalogue of the works collected in that first gathering of the industry of all nations, is placed in the right hand." The statue was of bronze gilt and weighed nearly ten tons. It was rightly supposed that the simple word " Albert," cast on the base, would be a sufficient means of identification.[1]

[1] *National Memorial;* Dafforne, 43–4.

CHAPTER VIII

MR. GLADSTONE AND LORD BEA-CONSFIELD

I

LORD PALMERSTON's laugh—a queer metallic
" Ha! ha! ha!" with reverberations in it from the
days of Pitt and the Congress of Vienna—was
heard no more in Piccadilly;[1] Lord John Russell
dwindled into senility; Lord Derby tottered from
the stage. A new scene opened; and new pro-
tagonists—Mr. Gladstone and Mr. Disraeli—
struggled together in the limelight. Victoria, from
her post of vantage, watched these developments
with that passionate and personal interest which
she invariably imported into politics. Her prepossessions were of an unexpected kind. Mr.
Gladstone had been the disciple of her revered
Peel, and had won the approval of Albert; Mr.
Disraeli had hounded Sir Robert to his fall with
hideous virulence, and the Prince had pronounced
that he " had not one single element of a gentleman in his composition." [2] Yet she regarded Mr.
Gladstone with a distrust and dislike which

[1] Adams, 135. [2] Clarendon, II, 342.

327

steadily deepened, while upon his rival she lavished an abundance of confidence, esteem, and
affection such as Lord Melbourne himself had
hardly known.

Her attitude towards the Tory Minister had
suddenly changed when she found that he alone
among public men had divined her feelings at Albert's death. Of the others she might have said
" they pity me and not my grief "; but Mr. Disraeli had understood; and all his condolences had
taken the form of reverential eulogies of the departed. The Queen declared that he was " the
only person who appreciated the Prince." [1] She
began to show him special favour; gave him and
his wife two of the coveted seats in St. George's
Chapel at the Prince of Wales's wedding, and invited him to stay a night at Windsor. When the
grant for the Albert Memorial came before the
House of Commons, Disraeli, as leader of the
Opposition, eloquently supported the project. He
was rewarded by a copy of the Prince's speeches,
bound in white morocco, with an inscription in the
royal hand. In his letter of thanks he " ventured
to touch upon a sacred theme," and, in a strain
which re-echoed with masterly fidelity the sentiments of his correspondent, dwelt at length upon

[1] Buckle, IV, 385.

the absolute perfection of Albert. " The Prince,"
he said, " is the only person whom Mr. Disraeli
has ever known who realised the Ideal. None with
whom he is acquainted have ever approached it.
There was in him an union of the manly grace and
sublime simplicity, of chivalry with the intellectual
splendour of the Attic Academe. The only character in English history that would, in some respects, draw near to him is Sir Philip Sidney: the
same high tone, the same universal accomplishments, the same blended tenderness and vigour,
the same rare combination of romantic energy
and classic repose." As for his own acquaintance
with the Prince, it had been, he said, " one of the
most satisfactory incidents of his life: full of re-
fined and beautiful memories, and exercising, as he
hopes, over his remaining existence, a soothing and
exalting influence." Victoria was much affected
by " the depth and delicacy of these touches," and
henceforward Disraeli's place in her affections
was assured.[1] When, in 1866, the Conservatives
came into office, Disraeli's position as Chancellor
of the Exchequer and leader of the House necessarily brought him into a closer relation with the
Sovereign. Two years later Lord Derby resigned,
and Victoria, with intense delight and peculiar

[1] Buckle, IV, 382-95.

graciousness, welcomed Disraeli as her First Minister.[1]

But only for nine agitated months did he remain in power. The Ministry, in a minority in the Commons, was swept out of existence by a general election. Yet by the end of that short period the ties which bound together the Queen and her Premier had grown far stronger than ever before; the relationship between them was now no longer merely that between a grateful mistress and a devoted servant: they were friends. His official letters, in which the personal element had always been perceptible, developed into racy records of political news and social gossip, written, as Lord Clarendon said, " in his best novel style." Victoria was delighted; she had never, she declared, had such letters in her life, and had never before known *everything*.[2] In return, she sent him, when the spring came, several bunches of flowers, picked by her own hands. He despatched to her a set of his novels, for which, she said, she was " most grateful, and which she values much." She herself had lately published her " Leaves from the Journal of our Life in the Highlands," and it was observed that the Prime Minister, in conversing with Her Majesty at this period, constantly used

the words " we authors, ma'am." [1] Upon political
questions, she was his staunch supporter. " Really
there never was such conduct as that of the Opposition," she wrote. And when the Government
was defeated in the House she was " really shocked
at the way in which the House of Commons go
on; they really bring discredit on Constitutional
Government." [2] She dreaded the prospect of a
change; she feared that if the Liberals insisted
upon disestablishing the Irish Church, her Coronation Oath might stand in the way.[1] But a
change there had to be, and Victoria vainly tried
to console herself for the loss of her favourite
Minister by bestowing a peerage upon Mrs.
Disraeli.

Mr. Gladstone was in his shirt-sleeves at Ha-
warden, cutting down a tree, when the royal message was brought to him. " Very significant,"
he remarked, when he had read the letter, and
went on cutting down his tree. His secret thoughts
on the occasion were more explicit, and were committed to his diary. " The Almighty," he wrote,
" seems to sustain and spare me for some purpose
of His own, deeply unworthy as I know myself
to be. Glory be to His name." [4]

[1] Buckle, V, 49.
[2] *Ibid.*, V, 48.
[3] *Ibid.*, V, 28.
[4] Morley, II, 252, 256.

The Queen, however, did not share her new Minister's view of the Almighty's intentions. She could not believe that there was any divine purpose to be detected in the programme of sweeping changes which Mr. Gladstone was determined to carry out. But what could she do? Mr. Gladstone, with his daemonic energy and his powerful majority in the House of Commons, was irresistible; and for five years (1869-74) Victoria found herself condemned to live in an agitating atmosphere of interminable reform—reform in the Irish Church and the Irish land system, reform in education, reform in parliamentary elections, reform in the organisation of the Army and the Navy, reform in the administration of justice. She disapproved, she struggled, she grew very angry; she felt that if Albert had been living things would never have happened so; but her protests and her complaints were alike unavailing. The mere effort of grappling with the mass of documents which poured in upon her in an ever-growing flood was terribly exhausting. When the draft of the lengthy and intricate Irish Church Bill came before her, accompanied by an explanatory letter from Mr. Gladstone covering a dozen closely-written quarto pages, she almost despaired. She turned from the Bill to the explanation, and from the explanation back again to the Bill, and she could not decide which was the most confusing. But she had to do her duty: she had not only to read, but to make notes. At last she handed the whole heap of papers to Mr. Martin, who happened to be staying at Osborne, and requested him to make a précis of them.[1] When he had done so, her disapproval of the measure became more marked than ever; but, such was the strength of the Government, she actually found herself obliged to urge moderation upon the Opposition, lest worse should ensue.[2]

In the midst of this crisis, when the future of the Irish Church was hanging in the balance, Victoria's attention was drawn to another proposed reform. It was suggested that the sailors in the Navy should henceforward be allowed to wear beards. "Has Mr. Childers ascertained anything on the subject of the beards?" the Queen wrote anxiously to the First Lord of the Admiralty. On the whole, Her Majesty was in favour of the change. "Her own personal feeling," she wrote, "would be for the beards without the moustaches, as the latter have rather a soldierlike appearance; but then the object in view would not be obtained, viz. to prevent the necessity of shav-

<hr>

[1] Martin, *Queen Victoria*, 50–1.　　　　[2] Tait, II, chap. i.

ing. Therefore it had better be as proposed, the entire beard, only it should be kept short and very clean." After thinking over the question for another week, the Queen wrote a final letter. She wished, she said, " to make one additional observation respecting the beards, viz. that on no account should moustaches be allowed without beards. That must be clearly understood." [1]

Changes in the Navy might be tolerated; to lay hands upon the Army was a more serious matter. From time immemorial there had been a particularly close connection between the Army and the Crown; and Albert had devoted even more time and attention to the details of military business than to the processes of fresco-painting or the planning of sanitary cottages for the deserving poor. But now there was to be a great alteration: Mr. Gladstone's fiat had gone forth, and the Commander-in-Chief was to be removed from his direct dependence upon the Sovereign, and made subordinate to Parliament and the Secretary of State for War. Of all the liberal reforms this was the one which aroused the bitterest resentment in Victoria. She considered that the change was an attack upon her personal position—almost an attack upon the personal position of Albert. But

[1] Childers, I, 175–7.

she was helpless, and the Prime Minister had his way. When she heard that the dreadful man had yet another reform in contemplation—that he was about to abolish the purchase of military commissions—she could only feel that it was just what might have been expected. For a moment she hoped that the House of Lords would come to the rescue; the Peers opposed the change with unexpected vigour; but Mr. Gladstone, more conscious than ever of the support of the Almighty, was ready with an ingenious device. The purchase of commissions had been originally allowed by Royal Warrant; it should now be disallowed by the same agency. Victoria was faced by a curious dilemma: she abominated the abolition of purchase; but she was asked to abolish it by an exercise of sovereign power which was very much to her taste. She did not hesitate for long; and when the Cabinet, in a formal minute, advised her to sign the Warrant, she did so with a good grace.[1]

Unacceptable as Mr. Gladstone's policy was, there was something else about him which was even more displeasing to Victoria. She disliked his personal demeanour towards herself. It was not that Mr. Gladstone, in his intercourse with her, was in any degree lacking in courtesy or respect.

[1] Morley, II, 360-5.

On the contrary, an extraordinary reverence impregnated his manner, both in his conversation and his correspondence with the Sovereign. Indeed, with that deep and passionate conservatism which, to the very end of his incredible career, gave such an unexpected colouring to his inexplicable character, Mr. Gladstone viewed Victoria through a haze of awe which was almost religious—as a sacrosanct embodiment of venerable traditions—a vital element in the British Constitution—a Queen by Act of Parliament. But unfortunately the lady did not appreciate the compliment. The well-known complaint—" He speaks to me as if I were a public meeting "—whether authentic or no—and the turn of the sentence is surely a little too epigrammatic to be genuinely Victorian—undoubtedly expresses the essential element of her antipathy. She had no objection to being considered as an institution; she was one, and she knew it. But she was a woman too, and to be considered *only* as an institution—that was unbearable. And thus all Mr. Gladstone's zeal and devotion, his ceremonious phrases, his low bows, his punctilious correctitudes, were utterly wasted; and when, in the excess of his loyalty, he went further, and imputed to the object of his veneration, with obsequious blindness, the subtlety of intellect, the wide reading, the grave enthusiasm, which he himself possessed, the misunderstanding became complete. The discordance between the actual Victoria and this strange Divinity made in Mr. Gladstone's image produced disastrous results. Her discomfort and dislike turned at last into positive animosity, and, though her manners continued to be perfect, she never for a moment unbent; while he on his side was overcome with disappointment, perplexity, and mortification.[1]

Yet his fidelity remained unshaken. When the Cabinet met, the Prime Minister, filled with his beatific vision, would open the proceedings by reading aloud the letters which he had received from the Queen upon the questions of the hour. The assembly sat in absolute silence while, one after another, the royal missives, with their emphases, their ejaculations, and their grammatical peculiarities, boomed forth in all the deep solemnity of Mr. Gladstone's utterance. Not a single comment, of any kind, was ever hazarded; and, after a fitting pause, the Cabinet proceeded with the business of the day.[2]

[1] Morley, II, 423–8; Crawford, 356, 370–1.
[2] Private information.

II

Little as Victoria appreciated her Prime Minister's attitude towards her, she found that it had its uses. The popular discontent at her uninterrupted seclusion had been gathering force for many years, and now burst out in a new and alarming shape. Republicanism was in the air. Radical opinion in England, stimulated by the fall of Napoleon III and the establishment of a republican government in France, suddenly grew more extreme than it ever had been since 1848. It also became for the first time almost respectable. Chartism had been entirely an affair of the lower classes; but now Members of Parliament, learned professors, and ladies of title openly avowed the most subversive views. The monarchy was attacked both in theory and in practice. And it was attacked at a vital point: it was declared to be too expensive. What benefits, it was asked, did the nation reap to counterbalance the enormous sums which were expended upon the Sovereign? Victoria's retirement gave an unpleasant handle to the argument. It was pointed out that the ceremonial functions of the Crown had virtually lapsed; and the awkward question remained whether any of the other functions which it did continue to perform were really worth £385,000 per annum. The royal balance-

sheet was curiously examined. An anonymous
pamphlet entitled " What does she do with it? "
appeared, setting forth the financial position with
malicious clarity. The Queen, it stated, was granted
by the Civil List £60,000 a year for her private
use; but the rest of her vast annuity was given, as
the Act declared, to enable her " to defray the expenses of her royal household and to support the
honour and dignity of the Crown." Now it was
obvious that, since the death of the Prince, the
expenditure for both these purposes must have
been very considerably diminished, and it was
difficult to resist the conclusion that a large sum
of money was diverted annually from the uses
for which it had been designed by Parliament, to
swell the private fortune of Victoria. The precise
amount of that private fortune it was impossible
to discover; but there was reason to suppose that
it was gigantic; perhaps it reached a total of five
million pounds. The pamphlet protested against
such a state of affairs, and its protests were repeated vigorously in newspapers and at public
meetings. Though it is certain that the estimate
of Victoria's riches was much exaggerated, it is
equally certain that she was an exceedingly wealthy
woman. She probably saved £20,000 a year from
the Civil List, the revenues of the Duchy of Lan-

caster were steadily increasing, she had inherited
a considerable property from the Prince Consort,
and she had been left, in 1852, an estate of half a
million by Mr. John Neild, an eccentric miser.
In these circumstances it was not surprising that
when, in 1871, Parliament was asked to vote a
dowry of £30,000 to the Princess Louise on her
marriage with the eldest son of the Duke of
Argyle, together with an annuity of £6,000, there
should have been a serious outcry.[1]

In order to conciliate public opinion, the Queen
opened Parliament in person, and the vote was
passed almost unanimously. But a few months
later another demand was made: the Prince
Arthur had come of age, and the nation was asked
to grant him an annuity of £15,000. The outcry
was redoubled. The newspapers were filled
with angry articles; Bradlaugh thundered against
"princely paupers" to one of the largest crowds
that had ever been seen in Trafalgar Square; and
Sir Charles Dilke expounded the case for a re-

---

[1] In 1889 it was officially stated that the Queen's total savings
from the Civil List amounted to £824,025, but that out of this sum
much had been spent on special entertainments to foreign visitors
(Lee, 499). Taking into consideration the proceeds from the Duchy
of Lancaster, which were more than £60,000 a year (Lee, 79),
the savings of the Prince Consort, and Mr. Neild's legacy, it
seems probable that, at the time of her death, Victoria's private
fortune approached two million pounds.

QUEEN VICTORIA IN 1876.

From the Portrait by Von Angeli.

QUEEN VICTORIA IN 1897.

public in a speech to his constituents at Newcastle. The Prince's annuity was ultimately sanctioned in the House of Commons by a large majority; but a minority of fifty members voted in favour of reducing the sum to £10,000.

Towards every aspect of this distasteful question, Mr. Gladstone presented an iron front. He absolutely discountenanced the extreme section of his followers. He declared that the whole of the Queen's income was justly at her personal disposal, argued that to complain of royal savings was merely to encourage royal extravagance, and successfully convoyed through Parliament the unpopular annuities, which, he pointed out, were strictly in accordance with precedent. When, in 1872, Sir Charles Dilke once more returned to the charge in the House of Commons, introducing a motion for a full enquiry into the Queen's expenditure with a view to a root and branch reform of the Civil List, the Prime Minister brought all the resources of his powerful and ingenious eloquence to the support of the Crown. He was completely successful; and amid a scene of great disorder the motion was ignominiously dismissed. Victoria was relieved; but she grew no fonder of Mr. Gladstone.[1]

[1] Morley, II, 425-6; Lee, 410-2, 415-8; Jerrold, *Widowhood*, 153-7, 162-3, 169-71.

It was perhaps the most miserable moment of her life. The Ministers, the press, the public, all conspired to vex her, to blame her, to misinterpret her actions, to be unsympathetic and disrespectful in every way. She was "a cruelly misunderstood woman," she told Mr. Martin, complaining to him bitterly of the unjust attacks which were made upon her, and declaring that "the great worry and anxiety and hard work for ten years, alone, un-aided, with increasing age and never very strong health" were breaking her down, and "almost drove her to despair."[1] The situation was indeed deplorable. It seemed as if her whole existence had gone awry; as if an irremediable antagonism had grown up between the Queen and the nation. If Victoria had died in the early seventies, there can be little doubt that the voice of the world would have pronounced her a failure.

III

But she was reserved for a very different fate. The outburst of republicanism had been in fact the last flicker of an expiring cause. The liberal tide, which had been flowing steadily ever since the Reform Bill, reached its height with Mr. Glad-stone's first administration; and towards the end

[1] Martin, *Queen Victoria,* 41–2.

of that administration the inevitable ebb began. The reaction, when it came, was sudden and complete. The General Election of 1874 changed the whole face of politics. Mr. Gladstone and the Liberals were routed; and the Tory party, for the first time for over forty years, attained an unquestioned supremacy in England. It was obvious that their surprising triumph was pre-eminently due to the skill and vigour of Disraeli. He returned to office, no longer the dubious commander of an insufficient host, but with drums beating and flags flying, a conquering hero. And as a conquering hero Victoria welcomed her new Prime Minister.

Then there followed six years of excitement, of enchantment, of felicity, of glory, of romance. The amazing being, who now at last, at the age of seventy, after a lifetime of extraordinary struggles, had turned into reality the absurdest of his boyhood's dreams, knew well enough how to make his own, with absolute completeness, the heart of the Sovereign Lady whose servant, and whose master, he had so miraculously become. In women's hearts he had always read as in an open book. His whole career had turned upon those curious entities; and the more curious they were, the more intimately at home with them he seemed to be.

But Lady Beaconsfield, with her cracked idolatry, and Mrs. Brydges-Williams, with her clogs, her corpulence, and her legacy, were gone: an even more remarkable phenomenon stood in their place. He surveyed what was before him with the eye of a past-master; and he was not for a moment at a loss. He realised everything—the interacting complexities of circumstance and character, the pride of place mingled so inextricably with personal arrogance, the superabundant emotionalism, the ingenuousness of outlook, the solid, the laborious respectability, shot through so incongruously by temperamental cravings for the coloured and the strange, the singular intellectual limitations, and the mysteriously essential female elements impregnating every particle of the whole. A smile hovered over his impassive features, and he dubbed Victoria " the Faery." The name delighted him, for, with that epigrammatic ambiguity so dear to his heart, it precisely expressed his vision of the Queen. The Spenserian allusion was very pleasant—the elegant evocations of Gloriana; but there was more in it than that: there was the suggestion of a diminutive creature, endowed with magical—and mythical—properties, and a portentousness almost ridiculously out of keeping with the rest of her make-up. The Faery, he determined, should

henceforward wave her wand for him alone. Detachment is always a rare quality, and rarest of all,
perhaps, among politicians; but that veteran egotist possessed it in a supreme degree. Not only
did he know what he had to do, not only did he do
it; he was in the audience as well as on the stage;
and he took in with the rich relish of a connoisseur
every feature of the entertaining situation, every
phase of the delicate drama, and every detail of
his own consummate performance.

The smile hovered and vanished, and, bowing
low with Oriental gravity and Oriental submis-
siveness, he set himself to his task. He had understood from the first that in dealing with the Faery
the appropriate method of approach was the very
antithesis of the Gladstonian; and such a method
was naturally his. It was not his habit to harangue
and exhort and expatiate in official conscientiousness; he liked to scatter flowers along the path of
business, to compress a weighty argument into a
happy phrase, to insinuate what was in his mind
with an air of friendship and confidential courtesy.
He was nothing if not personal; and he had perceived that personality was the key that opened
the Faery's heart. Accordingly, he never for a
moment allowed his intercourse with her to lose
the personal tone; he invested all the transactions

of State with the charms of familiar conversation;
she was always the royal lady, the adored and
revered mistress, he the devoted and respectful
friend. When once the personal relation was
firmly established, every difficulty disappeared.
But to maintain that relation uninterruptedly in
a smooth and even course a particular care was
necessary: the bearings had to be most assiduously
oiled. Nor was Disraeli in any doubt as to the
nature of the lubricant. "You have heard me
called a flatterer," he said to Matthew Arnold,
"and it is true. Everyone likes flattery; and when
you come to royalty you should lay it on with a
trowel." [1] He practised what he preached. His
adulation was incessant, and he applied it in the
very thickest slabs. "There is no honor and no
reward," he declared, "that with him can ever
equal the possession of your Majesty's kind
thoughts. All his own thoughts and feelings and
duties and affections are now concentrated in your
Majesty, and he desires nothing more for his remaining years than to serve your Majesty, or, if
that service ceases, to live still on its memory as
a period of his existence most interesting and fascinating." [2] "In life," he told her, "one must
have for one's thoughts a sacred depository, and

1 Buckle, VI, 463.　　　　　　　2 *Ibid.*, VI, 226.

Lord Beaconsfield ever presumes to seek that in his Sovereign Mistress." [1] She was not only his own solitary support; she was the one prop of the State. " If your Majesty is ill," he wrote during a grave political crisis, " he is sure he will himself break down. All, really, depends upon your Majesty." "He lives only for Her," he asseverated, " and works only for Her, and without Her all is lost." [2] When her birthday came he produced an elaborate confection of hyperbolic compliment. " To-day Lord Beaconsfield ought fitly, perhaps, to congratulate a powerful Sovereign on her imperial sway, the vastness of her Empire, and the success and strength of her fleets and armies. But he cannot, his mind is in another mood. He can only think of the strangeness of his destiny that it has come to pass that he should be the servant of one so great, and whose infinite kindness, the brightness of whose intelligence and the firmness of whose will, have enabled him to undertake labours to which he otherwise would be quite unequal, and supported him in all things by a condescending sympathy, which in the hour of difficulty alike charms and inspires. Upon the Sovereign of many lands and many hearts may an omnipotent Providence shed every blessing that the wise can

[1] Buckle, VI, 445m.   [2] *Ibid.*, VI, 254-5.

desire and the virtuous deserve!"[1] In those expert hands the trowel seemed to assume the qualities of some lofty masonic symbol—to be the
ornate and glittering vehicle of verities unrealised
by the profane.

Such tributes were delightful, but they remained
in the nebulous region of words, and Disraeli had
determined to give his blandishments a more significant solidity. He deliberately encouraged
those high views of her own position which had
always been native to Victoria's mind and had
been reinforced by the principles of Albert and
the doctrines of Stockmar. He professed to a
belief in a theory of the Constitution which gave
the Sovereign a leading place in the councils of
government; but his pronouncements upon the
subject were indistinct; and when he emphatically
declared that there ought to be " a real Throne,"
it was probably with the mental addition that that
throne would be a very unreal one indeed whose
occupant was unamenable to his cajoleries. But
the vagueness of his language was in itself an
added stimulant to Victoria. Skilfully confusing
the woman and the Queen, he threw, with a gran-
diose gesture, the government of England at her
feet, as if in doing so he were performing an act

[1] Buckle, VI, 430.

of personal homage. In his first audience after returning to power, he assured her that " whatever she wished should be done." [1] When the intricate Public Worship Regulation Bill was being discussed by the Cabinet, he told the Faery that his " only object " was " to further your Majesty's wishes in this matter." [2] When he brought off his great *coup* over the Suez Canal, he used expressions which implied that the only gainer by the transaction was Victoria. " It is just settled," he wrote in triumph; " you have it, Madam . . . Four millions sterling! and almost immediately. There was only one firm that could do it—Rothschilds. They behaved admirably; advanced the money at a low rate, and the entire interest of the Khedive is now yours, Madam." [3] Nor did he limit himself to highly-spiced insinuations. Writing with all the authority of his office, he advised the Queen that she had the constitutional right to dismiss a Ministry which was supported by a large majority in the House of Commons; he even urged her to do so, if, in her opinion, " your Majesty's Government have from wilfulness, or even from weakness, deceived your Majesty." [4] To the horror of Mr. Gladstone, he not only kept the Queen in-

[1] Buckle, V, 286.
[2] *Ibid.*, V, 321.

[3] *Ibid.*, V, 448–9.
[4] *Ibid.*, II, 246.

formed as to the general course of business in the Cabinet, but revealed to her the part taken in its discussions by individual members of it.[1] Lord Derby, the son of the late Prime Minister and Disraeli's Foreign Secretary, viewed these developments with grave mistrust. " Is there not," he ventured to write to his Chief, " just a risk of encouraging her in too large ideas of her personal power, and too great indifference to what the public expects? I only ask; it is for you to judge."[2]

As for Victoria, she accepted everything—compliments, flatteries, Elizabethan prerogatives—without a single qualm. After the long gloom of her bereavement, after the chill of the Gladstonian discipline, she expanded to the rays of Disraeli's devotion like a flower in the sun. The change in her situation was indeed miraculous. No longer was she obliged to puzzle for hours over the complicated details of business, for now she had only to ask Mr. Disraeli for an explanation, and he would give it her in the most concise, in the most amusing, way. No longer was she worried by alarming novelties; no longer was she put out at finding herself treated, by a reverential gentleman in high collars, as if she were some em-

1 Morley, II, 574–5.   2 Buckle, V, 414.

bodied precedent, with a recondite knowledge of
Greek. And her deliverer was surely the most fascinating of men. The strain of charlatanism,
which had unconsciously captivated her in Napoleon III, exercised the same enchanting effect in
the case of Disraeli. Like a dram-drinker, whose
ordinary life is passed in dull sobriety, her unso-
phisticated intelligence gulped down his rococo
allurements with peculiar zest. She became intox-
icated, entranced. Believing all that he told her
of herself, she completely regained the self-confi-
dence which had been slipping away from her
throughout the dark period that followed Albert's
death. She swelled with a new elation, while he,
conjuring up before her wonderful Oriental visions, dazzled her eyes with an imperial grandeur
of which she had only dimly dreamed. Under the
compelling influence, her very demeanour altered.
Her short, stout figure, with its folds of black velvet, its muslin streamers, its heavy pearls at the
heavy neck, assumed an almost menacing air. In
her countenance, from which the charm of youth
had long since vanished, and which had not yet
been softened by age, the traces of grief, of disappointment, and of displeasure were still visible, but
they were overlaid by looks of arrogance and sharp
lines of peremptory hauteur. Only, when Mr.

Disraeli appeared, the expression changed in an
instant, and the forbidding visage became charged
with smiles.[1] For him she would do anything.
Yielding to his encouragements, she began to
emerge from her seclusion; she appeared in London in semi-state, at hospitals and concerts; she
opened Parliament; she reviewed troops and dis-
tributed medals at Aldershot.[2] But such public
signs of favour were trivial in comparison with her
private attentions. During his hours of audience,
she could hardly restrain her excitement and delight. "I can only describe my reception," he
wrote to a friend on one occasion, "by telling you
that I really thought she was going to embrace me.
She was wreathed with smiles, and, as she tattled,
glided about the room like a bird."[3] In his absence, she talked of him perpetually, and there was
a note of unusual vehemence in her solicitude for
his health. "John Manners," Disraeli told Lady
Bradford, "who has just come from Osborne, says
that the Faery only talked of one subject, and
that was her Primo. According to him, it was her
gracious opinion that the Government should make
my health a Cabinet question. Dear John seemed
quite surprised at what she said; but you are more

used to these ebullitions." [1] She often sent him
presents; an illustrated album arrived for him
regularly from Windsor on Christmas Day. [2] But
her most valued gifts were the bunches of spring
flowers which, gathered by herself and her ladies
in the woods at Osborne, marked in an especial
manner the warmth and tenderness of her sentiments. Among these it was, he declared, the primroses that he loved the best. They were, he said,
" the ambassadors of Spring," " the gems and
jewels of Nature." He liked them, he assured
her, " so much better for their being wild; they
seem an offering from the Fauns and Dryads of
Osborne." " They show," he told her, " that your
Majesty's sceptre has touched the enchanted Isle."
He sat at dinner with heaped-up bowls of them on
every side, and told his guests that " they were all
sent to me this morning by the Queen from Osborne, as she knows it is my favorite flower." [3]

As time went on, and as it became clearer and
clearer that the Faery's thraldom was complete,
his protestations grew steadily more highly-coloured and more unabashed. At last he ventured
to import into his blandishments a strain of adoration that was almost avowedly romantic. In
phrases of baroque convolution, he conveyed the

---

1 Buckle, V, 384.   2 *Ibid.*, VI, 468.   3 *Ibid.*, VI, 629.

message of his heart. The pressure of business,
he wrote, had " so absorbed and exhausted him,
that towards the hour of post he has not had clear-
ness of mind, and vigour of pen, adequate to convey his thoughts and facts to the most loved and
illustrious being, who deigns to consider them." [1]
She sent him some primroses, and he replied that
he could " truly say they are ' more precious than
rubies,' coming, as they do, and at such a moment,
from a Sovereign whom he adores." [2] She sent
him snowdrops, and his sentiment overflowed into
poetry. " Yesterday eve," he wrote, " there appeared, in Whitehall Gardens, a delicate-looking
case, with a royal superscription, which, when he
opened, he thought, at first, that your Majesty
had graciously bestowed upon him the stars of
your Majesty's principal orders. And, indeed, he
was so impressed with this graceful illusion, that,
having a banquet, where there were many stars
and ribbons, he could not resist the temptation,
by placing some snowdrops on his heart, of showing that, he, too, was decorated by a gracious Sovereign.

" Then, in the middle of the night, it occurred
to him, that it might all be an enchantment, and
that, perhaps, it was a Faery gift and came from

[1] Buckle, VI, 248.   [2] *Ibid.*, VI, 246-7.

another monarch: Queen Titania, gathering flowers, with her Court, in a soft and sea-girt isle, and sending magic blossoms, which, they say, turn the heads of those who receive them." [1]

A Faery gift! Did he smile as he wrote the words? Perhaps; and yet it would be rash to conclude that his perfervid declarations were altogether without sincerity. Actor and spectator both, the two characters were so intimately blended together in that odd composition that they formed an inseparable unity, and it was impossible to say that one of them was less genuine than the other. With one element, he could coldly appraise the Faery's intellectual capacity, note with some surprise that she could be on occasion " most interesting and amusing," and then continue his use of the trowel with an ironical solemnity; while, with the other, he could be overwhelmed by the immemorial panoply of royalty, and, thrilling with the sense of his own strange elevation, dream himself into a gorgeous phantasy of crowns and powers and chivalric love. When he told Victoria that " during a somewhat romantic and imaginative life, nothing has ever occurred to him so interesting as this confidential correspondence with one so exalted and so inspiring," [2] was he not in earnest

1 Buckle, VI, 464–7.   2 Buckle, VI, 238.

after all? When he wrote to a lady about the Court, " I love the Queen—perhaps the only person in this world left to me that I do love," [1] was he not creating for himself an enchanted palace out of the Arabian Nights, full of melancholy and spangles, in which he actually believed? Victoria's state of mind was far more simple; untroubled by imaginative yearnings, she never lost herself in that nebulous region of the spirit where feeling and fancy grow confused. Her emotions, with all their intensity and all their exaggeration, retained the plain prosaic texture of everyday life. And it was fitting that her expression of them should be equally commonplace. She was, she told her Prime Minister, at the end of an official letter, " yours aff'ly V. R. and I." In such a phrase the deep reality of her feeling is instantly manifest. The Faery's feet were on the solid earth; it was the *rusé* cynic who was in the air.

He had taught her, however, a lesson, which she had learnt with alarming rapidity. A second Gloriana, did he call her? Very well, then, she would show that she deserved the compliment. Disquieting symptoms followed fast. In May, 1874, the Tsar, whose daughter had just been married to Victoria's second son, the Duke of

[1] Buckle, VI, 462.

Edinburgh, was in London, and, by an unfortunate error, it had been arranged that his departure should not take place until two days after the date on which his royal hostess had previously decided to go to Balmoral. Her Majesty refused to modify her plans. It was pointed out to her that the Tsar would certainly be offended, that the most serious consequences might follow; Lord Derby protested; Lord Salisbury, the Secretary of State for India, was much perturbed. But the Faery was unconcerned; she had settled to go to Balmoral on the 18th, and on the 18th she would go. At last Disraeli, exercising all his influence, induced her to agree to stay in London for two days more. " My head is still on my shoulders," he told Lady Bradford. " The great lady has absolutely postponed her departure! Everybody had failed, even the Prince of Wales; . . . and I have no doubt I am not in favour. I can't help it. Salisbury says I have saved an Afghan War, and Derby compliments me on my unrivalled triumph." [1] But before very long, on another issue, the triumph was the Faery's. Disraeli, who had suddenly veered towards a new Imperialism, had thrown out the suggestion that the Queen of England ought to become the Empress of India. Vic-

[1] Buckle, V, 414–5.

toria seized upon the idea with avidity, and, in season and out of season, pressed upon her Prime Minister the desirability of putting his proposal into practice. He demurred; but she was not to be baulked; and in 1876, in spite of his own unwillingness and that of his entire Cabinet, he found himself obliged to add to the troubles of a stormy session by introducing a bill for the alteration of the Royal Title.[1] His compliance, however, finally conquered the Faery's heart. The measure was angrily attacked in both Houses, and Victoria was deeply touched by the untiring energy with which Disraeli defended it. She was, she said, much grieved by " the worry and annoyance " to which he was subjected; she feared she was the cause of it; and she would never forget what she owed to " her kind, good, and considerate friend." At the same time, her wrath fell on the Opposition. Their conduct, she declared, was " extraordinary, incomprehensible, and mistaken," and, in an emphatic sentence which seemed to contradict both itself and all her former proceedings, she protested that she " would be glad if it were more generally known that it was *her* wish, as people *will* have it, that it has been *forced upon her!* "[2] When the affair was successfully over, the imperial triumph was

1 Buckle, V, 456–8; VI, 457–8.   2 *Ibid.*, V, 468–9, 473.

celebrated in a suitable manner. On the day of
the Delhi Proclamation, the new Earl of Beaconsfield went to Windsor to dine with the new Empress of India. That night the Faery, usually so
homely in her attire, appeared in a glittering
panoply of enormous uncut jewels, which had been
presented to her by the reigning Princes of her
Raj. At the end of the meal the Prime Minister,
breaking through the rules of etiquette, arose, and
in a flowery oration proposed the health of the
Queen-Empress. His audacity was well received,
and his speech was rewarded by a smiling
curtsey.[1]

These were significant episodes; but a still more
serious manifestation of Victoria's temper occurred in the following year, during the crowning
crisis of Beaconsfield's life. His growing imperialism, his desire to magnify the power and prestige
of England, his insistence upon a "spirited foreign policy," had brought him into collision with
Russia; the terrible Eastern Question loomed up;
and when war broke out between Russia and Tur-
key, the gravity of the situation became extreme.
The Prime Minister's policy was fraught with difficulty and danger. Realising perfectly the appalling implications of an Anglo-Russian war, he was

[1] Hamilton, 120; *Quarterly Review*, cxxxix, 334.

yet prepared to face even that eventuality if he could obtain his ends by no other method; but he believed that Russia in reality was still less desirous of a rupture, and that, if he played his game with sufficient boldness and adroitness, she would yield, when it came to the point, all that he required without a blow. It was clear that the course he had marked out for himself was full of hazard, and demanded an extraordinary nerve; a single false step, and either himself, or England, might be plunged in disaster. But nerve he had never lacked; he began his diplomatic egg-dance with high assurance; and then he discovered that, besides the Russian Government, besides the Liberals and Mr. Gladstone, there were two additional sources of perilous embarrassment with which he would have to reckon. In the first place there was a strong party in the Cabinet, headed by Lord Derby, the Foreign Secretary, which was unwilling to take the risk of war; but his culminating anxiety was the Faery.

From the first, her attitude was uncompromising. The old hatred of Russia, which had been engendered by the Crimean War, surged up again within her; she remembered Albert's prolonged animosity; she felt the prickings of her own greatness; and she flung herself into the turmoil with passionate heat. Her indignation with the Opposition—with anyone who ventured to sympathise with the Russians in their quarrel with the Turks —was unbounded. When anti-Turkish meetings were held in London, presided over by the Duke of Westminster and Lord Shaftesbury, and attended by Mr. Gladstone and other prominent Radicals, she considered that " the Attorney-General ought to be set at these men "; " it can't," she exclaimed, " be constitutional." [1] Never in her life, not even in the crisis over the Ladies of the Bedchamber, did she show herself a more furious partisan. But her displeasure was not reserved for the Radicals; the backsliding Conservatives equally felt its force. She was even discontented with Lord Beaconsfield himself. Failing entirely to appreciate the delicate complexity of his policy, she constantly assailed him with demands for vigorous action, interpreted each finesse as a sign of weakness, and was ready at every juncture to let slip the dogs of war. As the situation developed, her anxiety grew feverish. " The Queen," she wrote, " is feeling terribly anxious lest delay should cause us to be too late and lose our prestige for ever! It worries her night and day." [2] " The Faery," Beaconsfield told Lady Bradford,

[1] Buckle, VI, 106–7.   [2] *Ibid.*, VI, 144.

" writes every day and telegraphs every hour; this
is almost literally the case." [1]   She raged loudly
against the Russians. " And the language," she
cried, " the insulting language—used by the Russians against us! It makes the Queen's blood
boil! " [2] " Oh," she wrote a little later, " if the
Queen were a man, she would like to go and give
those Russians, whose word one cannot believe,
such a beating! We shall never be friends again
till we have it out. This the Queen feels sure of." [3]

The unfortunate Prime Minister, urged on to
violence by Victoria on one side, had to deal, on
the other, with a Foreign Secretary who was fun-
damentally opposed to any policy of active inter-
ference at all. Between the Queen and Lord
Derby he held a harassed course. He gained, indeed, some slight satisfaction in playing off the
one against the other—in stimulating Lord Derby
with the Queen's missives, and in appeasing the
Queen by repudiating Lord Derby's opinions; on
one occasion he actually went so far as to com-
pose, at Victoria's request, a letter bitterly attacking his colleague, which Her Majesty forthwith
signed, and sent, without alteration, to the Foreign
Secretary. [4] But such devices only gave a tem-

1 Buckle, VI, 150.   3 Ibid., VI, 217.
2 Ibid., VI, 154.   4 Ibid., VI, 157–9.

porary relief; and it soon became evident that Victoria's martial ardour was not to be side-tracked by hostilities against Lord Derby; hostilities against Russia were what she wanted, what she would, what she must, have. For now, casting aside the last relics of moderation, she began to attack her friend with a series of extraordinary threats. Not once, not twice, but many times she held over his head the formidable menace of her imminent abdication. "If England," she wrote to Beaconsfield, " is to kiss Russia's feet, she will not be a party to the humiliation of England and would lay down her crown," and she added that the Prime Minister might, if he thought fit, repeat her words to the Cabinet.[1] " This delay," she ejaculated, "this uncertainty by which, abroad, we are losing our prestige and our position, while Russia is advancing and will be before Constantinople in no time! Then the Government will be fearfully blamed and the Queen so humiliated that she thinks she would abdicate at once. Be bold!"[2] " She feels," she reiterated, " she cannot, as she before said, remain the Sovereign of a country that is letting itself down to kiss the feet of the great barbarians, the retarders of all liberty and civilisation that exists."[3] When the Russians ad-

[1] Buckle, VI, 132. [2] *Ibid.*, VI, 148. [3] *Ibid.*, VI, 217.

vanced to the outskirts of Constantinople she fired
off three letters in a day demanding war; and
when she learnt that the Cabinet had only decided
to send the Fleet to Gallipoli she declared that
" her first impulse " was " to lay down the thorny
crown, which she feels little satisfaction in retaining if the position of this country is to remain as it
is now." [1] It is easy to imagine the agitating effect
of such a correspondence upon Beaconsfield. This
was no longer the Faery; it was a genie whom he
had rashly called out of her bottle, and who was
now intent upon showing her supernal power.
More than once, perplexed, dispirited, shattered
by illness, he had thoughts of withdrawing altogether from the game. One thing alone, he told
Lady Bradford, with a wry smile, prevented him.
" If I could only," he wrote, " face the scene which
would occur at headquarters if I resigned, I would
do so at once." [2]

He held on, however, to emerge victorious at
last. The Queen was pacified; Lord Derby was
replaced by Lord Salisbury; and at the Congress
of Berlin *der alte Jude* carried all before him.
He returned to England in triumph, and assured
the delighted Victoria that she would very soon be,

---

[1] Buckle, VI, 243-5.   [2] *Ibid.,* VI, 190.

if she was not already, the " Dictatress of Europe." [1]

But soon there was an unexpected reverse. At the General Election of 1880 the country, mistrustful of the forward policy of the Conservatives, and carried away by Mr. Gladstone's oratory, returned the Liberals to power. Victoria was horrified, but within a year she was to be yet more nearly hit. The grand romance had come to its conclusion. Lord Beaconsfield, worn out with age and maladies, but moving still, an assiduous mummy, from dinner-party to dinner-party, suddenly moved no longer. When she knew that the end was inevitable, she seemed, by a pathetic instinct, to divest herself of her royalty, and to shrink, with hushed gentleness, beside him, a woman and nothing more. " I send some Osborne primroses," she wrote to him with touching simplicity, " and I meant to pay you a little visit this week, but I thought it better you should be quite quiet and not speak. And I beg you will be very good and obey the doctors." She would see him, she said, " when we come back from Osborne, which won't be long." " Everyone is so distressed at your not being well," she added; and she was, " Ever yours very aff'ly, V.R.I." When the royal

[1] Lee, 445-6.

letter was given him, the strange old comedian, stretched on his bed of death, poised it in his hand, appeared to consider deeply, and then whispered to those about him, " This ought to be read to me by a Privy Councillor." [1]

[1] Buckle, VI, 613–4.

CHAPTER IX

OLD AGE

I

MEANWHILE in Victoria's private life many changes and developments had taken place. With the marriages of her elder children her family circle widened; grandchildren appeared; and a multitude of new domestic interests sprang up. The death of King Leopold in 1865 had removed the predominant figure of the older generation, and the functions he had performed as the centre and adviser of a large group of relatives in Germany and in England devolved upon Victoria. These functions she discharged with unremitting industry, carrying on an enormous correspondence, and following with absorbed interest every detail in the lives of the ever-ramifying cousinhood. And she tasted to the full both the joys and the pains of family affection. She took a particular delight in her grandchildren, to whom she showed an indulgence which their parents had not always enjoyed, though, even to her grandchildren, she could be, when the occasion demanded it, severe.

The eldest of them, the little Prince Wilhelm of
Prussia, was a remarkably headstrong child; he
dared to be impertinent even to his grandmother;
and once, when she told him to bow to a visitor at
Osborne, he disobeyed her outright. This would
not do: the order was sternly repeated, and the
naughty boy, noticing that his kind grandmama
had suddenly turned into a most terrifying lady,
submitted his will to hers, and bowed very low
indeed.[1]

It would have been well if all the Queen's
domestic troubles could have been got over as
easily. Among her more serious distresses was the
conduct of the Prince of Wales. The young man
was now independent and married; he had shaken
the parental yoke from his shoulders; he was positively beginning to do as he liked. Victoria was
much perturbed, and her worst fears seemed to
be justified when in 1870 he appeared as a witness
in a society divorce case. It was clear that the
heir to the throne had been mixing with people
of whom she did not at all approve. What was
to be done? She saw that it was not only her son
that was to blame—that it was the whole system
of society; and so she despatched a letter to Mr.
Delane, the editor of *The Times,* asking him if

1 Hallé, 296.

he would " frequently *write* articles pointing out the *immense* danger and evil of the wretched frivolity and levity of the views and lives of the Higher Classes." And five years later Mr. Delane did write an article upon that very subject.[1] Yet it seemed to have very little effect.

Ah! if only the Higher Classes would learn to live as she lived in the domestic sobriety of her sanctuary at Balmoral! For more and more did she find solace and refreshment in her Highland domain; and twice yearly, in the spring and in the autumn, with a sigh of relief, she set her face northwards, in spite of the humble protests of Ministers, who murmured vainly in the royal ears that to transact the affairs of State over an interval of six hundred miles added considerably to the cares of government. Her ladies, too, felt occasionally a slight reluctance to set out, for, especially in the early days, the long pilgrimage was not without its drawbacks. For many years the Queen's conservatism forbade the continuation of the railway up Deeside, so that the last stages of the journey had to be accomplished in carriages. But, after all, carriages had their good points; they were easy, for instance, to get in and out of, which was an important consideration, for the

[1] *Notes and Queries*, May 20, 1920.

royal train remained for long immune from modern conveniences, and when it drew up, on some border moorland, far from any platform, the high-bred dames were obliged to descend to earth by the perilous foot-board, the only pair of folding steps being reserved for Her Majesty's saloon. In the days of crinolines such moments were sometimes awkward; and it was occasionally necessary to summon Mr. Johnstone, the short and sturdy Manager of the Caledonian Railway, who, more than once, in a high gale and drenching rain with great difficulty " pushed up "—as he himself described it—some unlucky Lady Blanche or Lady Agatha into her compartment.[1] But Victoria cared for none of these things. She was only intent upon regaining, with the utmost swiftness, her enchanted Castle, where every spot was charged with memories, where every memory was sacred, and where life was passed in an incessant and delightful round of absolutely trivial events.

And it was not only the place that she loved; she was equally attached to " the simple mountaineers," from whom, she said, " she learnt many a lesson of resignation and faith." [2] Smith and Grant and Ross and Thompson—she was devoted

---

[1] Neele, 476-8, 487.   [2] *More Leaves, v.*

to them all; but, beyond the rest, she was devoted to John Brown. The Prince's gillie had now become the Queen's personal attendant—a body servant from whom she was never parted, who accompanied her on her drives, waited on her during the day, and slept in a neighbouring chamber at night. She liked his strength, his solidity, the sense he gave her of physical security; she even liked his rugged manners and his rough unaccommodating speech. She allowed him to take liberties with her which would have been unthinkable from anybody else. To bully the Queen, to order her about, to reprimand her—who could dream of venturing upon such audacities? And yet, when she received such treatment from John Brown, she positively seemed to enjoy it. The eccentricity appeared to be extraordinary; but, after all, it is no uncommon thing for an autocratic dowager to allow some trusted indispensable servant to adopt towards her an attitude of authority which is jealously forbidden to relatives or friends: the power of a dependant still remains, by a psychological sleight-of-hand, one's own power, even when it is exercised over oneself. When Victoria meekly obeyed the abrupt commands of her henchman to get off her pony or put on her shawl, was she not displaying, and in the highest degree, the force of her volition? People might wonder; she could not help that; this was the manner in which it pleased her to act, and there was an end of it. To have submitted her judgment to a son or a Minister might have seemed wiser or more natural; but if she had done so, she instinctively felt, she would indeed have lost her independence. And yet upon somebody she longed to depend. Her days were heavy with the long process of domination. As she drove in silence over the moors she leaned back in the carriage, oppressed and weary; but what a relief!—John Brown was behind on the rumble, and his strong arm would be there for her to lean upon when she got out.

He had, too, in her mind, a special connection with Albert. In their expeditions the Prince had always trusted him more than anyone; the gruff, kind, hairy Scotsman was, she felt, in some mysterious way, a legacy from the dead. She came to believe at last—or so it appeared—that the spirit of Albert was nearer when Brown was near. Often, when seeking inspiration over some complicated question of political or domestic import, she would gaze with deep concentration at her late husband's bust. But it was also noticed that sometimes in such moments of doubt and hesitation Her Majesty's looks would fix themselves upon John Brown.

Eventually, the "simple mountaineer" became almost a state personage. The influence which he wielded was not to be overlooked. Lord Beaconsfield was careful, from time to time, to send courteous messages to "Mr. Brown" in his letters to the Queen, and the French Government took particular pains to provide for his comfort during the visits of the English Sovereign to France. It was only natural that among the elder members of the royal family he should not have been popular, and that his failings—for failings he had, though Victoria would never notice his too acute appreciation of Scotch whisky—should have been the subject of acrimonious comment at Court. But he served his mistress faithfully, and to ignore him would be a sign of disrespect in her biographer. For the Queen, far from making a secret of her affectionate friendship, took care to publish it to the world. By her orders two gold medals were struck in his honour; on his death, in 1883, a long and eulogistic obituary notice of him appeared in the *Court Circular;* and a Brown memorial brooch—of gold, with the late gillie's head on one side and the royal monogram on the other—was designed by Her Majesty for presen-

tation to her Highland servants and cottagers, to
be worn by them on the anniversary of his death,
with a mourning scarf and pins. In the second
series of extracts from the Queen's Highland
Journal, published in 1884, her " devoted personal attendant and faithful friend " appears upon
almost every page, and is in effect the hero of the
book. With an absence of reticence remarkable
in royal persons, Victoria seemed to demand, in
this private and delicate matter, the sympathy of
the whole nation; and yet—such is the world!—
there were those who actually treated the relations
between their Sovereign and her servant as a
theme for ribald jests.[1]

II

The busy years hastened away; the traces of
Time's unimaginable touch grew manifest; and
old age, approaching, laid a gentle hold upon Victoria. The grey hair whitened; the mature features
mellowed; the short firm figure amplified and
moved more slowly, supported by a stick. And,
simultaneously, in the whole tenour of the Queen's
existence an extraordinary transformation came
to pass. The nation's attitude towards her, critical and even hostile as it had been for so many

[1] More Leaves, passim; Crawford, 326-31; private information

years, altogether changed; while there was a corresponding alteration in the temper of Victoria's
own mind.

Many causes led to this result. Among them
were the repeated strokes of personal misfortune
which befell the Queen during a cruelly short
space of years. In 1878 the Princess Alice, who
had married in 1862 the Prince Louis of Hesse-
Darmstadt, died in tragic circumstances. In the
following year the Prince Imperial, the only son
of the Empress Eugénie, to whom Victoria, since
the catastrophe of 1870, had become devotedly attached, was killed in the Zulu War. Two years
later, in 1881, the Queen lost Lord Beaconsfield,
and, in 1883, John Brown. In 1884 the Prince
Leopold, Duke of Albany, who had been an invalid from birth, died prematurely, shortly after
his marriage. Victoria's cup of sorrows was indeed overflowing; and the public, as it watched the
widowed mother weeping for her children and her
friends, displayed a constantly increasing sympathy.

An event which occurred in 1882 revealed and
accentuated the feelings of the nation. As the
Queen, at Windsor, was walking from the train to
her carriage, a youth named Roderick Maclean
fired a pistol at her from a distance of a few

yards. An Eton boy struck up Maclean's arm
with an umbrella before the pistol went off; no
damage was done, and the culprit was at once
arrested. This was the last of a series of seven
attempts upon the Queen—attempts which, taking
place at sporadic intervals over a period of forty
years, resembled one another in a curious manner.
All, with a single exception, were perpetrated by
adolescents, whose motives were apparently not
murderous, since, save in the case of Maclean,
none of their pistols was loaded. These unhappy
youths, who, after buying their cheap weapons,
stuffed them with gunpowder and paper, and then
went off, with the certainty of immediate detection,
to click them in the face of royalty, present a
strange problem to the psychologist. But, though
in each case their actions and their purposes
seemed to be so similar, their fates were remarkably varied. The first of them, Edward Oxford,
who fired at Victoria within a few months of her
marriage, was tried for high treason, declared to
be insane, and sent to an asylum for life. It
appears, however, that this sentence did not commend itself to Albert, for when, two years later,
John Francis committed the same offence, and
was tried upon the same charge, the Prince pronounced that there was no insanity in the matter.

" The wretched creature," he told his father, was
" not out of his mind, but a thorough scamp."
" I hope," he added, " his trial will be conducted
with the greatest strictness." Apparently it was;
at any rate, the jury shared the view of the
Prince, the plea of insanity was set aside, and
Francis was found guilty of high treason and condemned to death; but, as there was no proof of
an intent to kill or even to wound, this sentence,
after a lengthened deliberation between the Home
Secretary and the Judges, was commuted for one
of transportation for life. As the law stood, these
assaults, futile as they were, could only be treated
as high treason; the discrepancy between the
actual deed and the tremendous penalties involved was obviously grotesque; and it was, besides, clear that a jury, knowing that a verdict of
guilty implied a sentence of death, would tend to
the alternative course, and find the prisoner not
guilty but insane—a conclusion which, on the face
of it, would have appeared to be the more reasonable. In 1842, therefore, an Act was passed
making any attempt to hurt the Queen a mis-
demeanour, punishable by transportation for seven
years, or imprisonment, with or without hard
labour, for a term not exceeding three years—the
misdemeanant, at the discretion of the Court, " to

be publicly or privately whipped, as often, and in
such manner and form, as the Court shall direct,
not exceeding thrice." [1] The four subsequent attempts were all dealt with under this new law;
William Bean, in 1842, was sentenced to eighteen
months' imprisonment; William Hamilton, in
1849, was transported for seven years; and, in
1850, the same sentence was passed upon Lieu-
tenant Robert Pate, who struck the Queen on the
head with his cane in Piccadilly. Pate, alone
among these delinquents, was of mature years; he
had held a commission in the Army, dressed himself as a dandy, and was, the Prince declared,
" manifestly deranged." [2] In 1872 Arthur O'Con-
nor, a youth of seventeen, fired an unloaded pistol
at the Queen outside Buckingham Palace; he was
immediately seized by John Brown, and sentenced
to one year's imprisonment and twenty strokes of
the birch rod. It was for his bravery upon this
occasion that Brown was presented with one of his
gold medals. In all these cases the jury had refused to allow the plea of insanity; but Roderick
Maclean's attempt in 1882 had a different issue.
On this occasion the pistol was found to have
been loaded, and the public indignation, emphasised as it was by Victoria's growing popularity,

[1] Martin, I, 88, 137–43.   [2] *Ibid.,* II, 285.

was particularly great. Either for this or for some other reason the procedure of the last forty years was abandoned, and Maclean was tried for high treason. The result was what might have been expected: the jury brought in a verdict of " not guilty, but insane "; and the prisoner was sent to an asylum during Her Majesty's pleasure.[1] Their verdict, however, produced a remarkable consequence. Victoria, who doubtless carried in her mind some memory of Albert's disapproval of a similar verdict in the case of Oxford, was very much annoyed. What did the jury mean, she asked, by saying that Maclean was not guilty? It was perfectly clear that he was guilty—she had seen him fire off the pistol herself. It was in vain that Her Majesty's constitutional advisers reminded her of the principle of English law which lays down that no man can be found guilty of a crime unless he be proved to have had a criminal intention. Victoria was quite unconvinced. " If that is the law," she said, " the law must be altered ": and altered it was. In 1883 an Act was passed changing the form of the verdict in cases of insanity, and the confusing anomaly remains upon the Statute Book to this day.[2]

[1] *The Times*, April 20, 1882.
[2] Letter from Sir Herbert Stephen to *The Times*, December 15, 1920.

But it was not only through the feelings—commiserating or indignant—of personal sympathy that the Queen and her people were being drawn more nearly together; they were beginning, at last, to come to a close and permanent agreement upon the conduct of public affairs. Mr. Gladstone's second administration (1880-85) was a succession of failures, ending in disaster and disgrace; liberalism fell into discredit with the country, and Victoria perceived with joy that her distrust of her Ministers was shared by an ever-increasing number of her subjects. During the crisis in the Sudan, the popular temper was her own. She had been among the first to urge the necessity of an expedition to Khartoum, and, when the news came of the catastrophic death of General Gordon, her voice led the chorus of denunciation which raved against the Government. In her rage, she despatched a fulminating telegram to Mr. Gladstone, not in the usual cypher, but open; [1] and her letter of condolence to Miss Gordon, in which she attacked her Ministers for breach of faith, was widely published. It was rumoured that she had sent for Lord Hartington, the Secretary of State for War, and vehemently upbraided him. " She

[1] Morley, III, 167.

rated me," he was reported to have told a friend, " as if I'd been a footman." " Why didn't she send for the butler? " asked his friend. " Oh," was the reply, " the butler generally manages to keep out of the way on such occasions." [1]

But the day came when it was impossible to keep out of the way any longer. Mr. Gladstone was defeated, and resigned. Victoria, at a final interview, received him with her usual amenity, but, besides the formalities demanded by the occasion, the only remark which she made to him of a personal nature was to the effect that she supposed Mr. Gladstone would now require some rest. He remembered with regret how, at a similar audience in 1874, she had expressed her trust in him as a supporter of the throne; but he noted the change without surprise. " Her mind and opinions," he wrote in his diary afterwards, " have since that day been seriously warped." [2]

Such was Mr. Gladstone's view; but the majority of the nation by no means agreed with him; and, in the General Election of 1886, they showed decisively that Victoria's politics were identical with theirs by casting forth the contrivers of Home Rule—that abomination of desolation—into

[1] Private information.   [2] Morley, III, 347–8.

outer darkness, and placing Lord Salisbury in power. Victoria's satisfaction was profound. A flood of new unwonted hopefulness swept over her, stimulating her vital spirits with a surprising force. Her habit of life was suddenly altered; abandoning the long seclusion which Disraeli's persuasions had only momentarily interrupted, she threw herself vigorously into a multitude of public activities. She appeared at drawing-rooms, at concerts, at reviews; she laid foundation-stones; she went to Liverpool to open an international exhibition, driving through the streets in her open carriage in heavy rain amid vast applauding crowds. Delighted by the welcome which met her everywhere, she warmed to her work. She visited Edinburgh, where the ovation of Liverpool was repeated and surpassed. In London, she opened in high state the Colonial and Indian Exhibition at South Kensington. On this occasion the ceremonial was particularly magnificent; a blare of trumpets announced the approach of Her Majesty; the "National Anthem" followed; and the Queen, seated on a gorgeous throne of hammered gold, replied with her own lips to the address that was presented to her. Then she rose, and, advancing upon the platform with regal port, acknowledged the acclamations of the great assembly by a succession of curtseys, of elaborate and commanding grace.[1]

Next year was the fiftieth of her reign, and in June the splendid anniversary was celebrated in solemn pomp. Victoria, surrounded by the highest dignitaries of her realm, escorted by a glittering galaxy of kings and princes, drove through the crowded enthusiasm of the capital to render thanks to God in Westminster Abbey. In that triumphant hour the last remaining traces of past antipathies and past disagreements were altogether swept away. The Queen was hailed at once as the mother of her people and as the embodied symbol of their imperial greatness; and she responded to the double sentiment with all the ardour of her spirit. England and the people of England, she knew it, she felt it, were, in some wonderful and yet quite simple manner, *hers*. Exultation, affection, gratitude, a profound sense of obligation, an unbounded pride—such were her emotions; and, colouring and intensifying the rest, there was something else. At last, after so long, happiness—fragmentary, perhaps, and charged with gravity, but true and unmistakable none the less—had returned to her. The unaccustomed feeling filled and warmed her consciousness.

[1] Jerrold, *Widowhood*, 344; private information.

When, at Buckingham Palace again, the long
ceremony over, she was asked how she was, " I
am very tired, but very happy," she said.[1]

III

And so, after the toils and tempests of the day,
a long evening followed—mild, serene, and lighted
with a golden glory. For an unexampled atmosphere of success and adoration invested the
last period of Victoria's life. Her triumph was
the summary, the crown, of a greater triumph—
the culminating prosperity of a nation. The
solid splendour of the decade between Victoria's two jubilees can hardly be paralleled in
the annals of England. The sage counsels of
Lord Salisbury seemed to bring with them not
only wealth and power, but security; and the
country settled down, with calm assurance, to the
enjoyment of an established grandeur. And—it
was only natural—Victoria settled down too. For
she was a part of the establishment—an essential
part as it seemed—a fixture—a magnificent, im-
movable sideboard in the huge saloon of state.
Without her the heaped-up banquet of 1890 would
have lost its distinctive quality—the comfortable

[1] Lee, 487.

order of the substantial unambiguous dishes, with their background of weighty glamour, half out of sight.

Her own existence came to harmonise more and more with what was around her. Gradually, imperceptibly, Albert receded. It was not that he was forgotten—that would have been impossible— but that the void created by his absence grew less agonising, and even, at last, less obvious. At last Victoria found it possible to regret the bad weather without immediately reflecting that her " dear Albert always said we could not alter it, but must leave it as it was "; she could even enjoy a good breakfast without considering how " dear Albert " would have liked the buttered eggs.[1] And, as that figure slowly faded, its place was taken, inevitably, by Victoria's own. Her being, revolving for so many years round an external object, now changed its motion and found its centre in itself. It had to be so: her domestic position, the pressure of her public work, her indomitable sense of duty, made anything else impossible. Her egotism proclaimed its rights. Her age increased still further the surrounding deference; and her force of character, emerging at length in all its plenitude, imposed itself abso-

[1] *More Leaves*, 23, 29.

lutely upon its environment by the conscious effort of an imperious will.

Little by little it was noticed that the outward vestiges of Albert's posthumous domination grew less complete. At Court the stringency of mourning was relaxed. As the Queen drove through the Park in her open carriage with her Highlanders behind her, nursery-maids canvassed eagerly the growing patch of violet velvet in the bonnet with its jet appurtenances on the small bowing head.

It was in her family that Victoria's ascendency reached its highest point. All her offspring were married; the number of her descendants rapidly increased; there were many marriages in the third generation; and no fewer than thirty-seven of her great-grandchildren were living at the time of her death. A picture of the period displays the royal family collected together in one of the great rooms at Windsor—a crowded company of more than fifty persons, with the imperial matriarch in their midst. Over them all she ruled with a most potent sway. The small concerns of the youngest aroused her passionate interest; and the oldest she treated as if they were children still. The Prince of Wales, in particular, stood in tremendous awe of his mother. She had steadily refused to allow him the slightest participation in the business of government; and he had occupied himself in other ways. Nor could it be denied that he enjoyed himself—out of her sight; but, in that redoubtable presence, his abounding manhood suffered a miserable eclipse. Once, at Osborne, when, owing to no fault of his, he was too late for a dinner party, he was observed standing behind a pillar and, wiping the sweat from his forehead, trying to nerve himself to go up to the Queen. When at last he did so, she gave him a stiff nod, whereupon he vanished immediately behind another pillar, and remained there until the party broke up. At the time of this incident the Prince of Wales was over fifty years of age.[1]

It was inevitable that the Queen's domestic activities should occasionally trench upon the domain of high diplomacy; and this was especially the case when the interests of her eldest daughter, the Crown Princess of Prussia, were at stake. The Crown Prince held liberal opinions; he was much influenced by his wife; and both were detested by Bismarck, who declared with scurrilous emphasis that the Englishwoman and her mother were a menace to the Prussian State. The feud was still further intensified when, on the death of

[1] Eckardstein, I, 184–7.

the old Emperor (1888), the Crown Prince succeeded to the throne. A family entanglement
brought on a violent crisis. One of the daughters
of the new Empress had become betrothed to
Prince Alexander of Battenberg, who had lately
been ejected from the throne of Bulgaria owing
to the hostility of the Tsar. Victoria, as well as
the Empress, highly approved of the match. Of
the two brothers of Prince Alexander, the elder
had married another of her grand-daughters, and
the younger was the husband of her daughter, the
Princess Beatrice; she was devoted to the handsome young man; and she was delighted by the
prospect of the third brother—on the whole the
handsomest, she thought, of the three—also becoming a member of her family. Unfortunately,
however, Bismarck was opposed to the scheme.
He perceived that the marriage would endanger
the friendship between Germany and Russia,
which was vital to his foreign policy, and he announced that it must not take place. A fierce
struggle between the Empress and the Chancellor
followed. Victoria, whose hatred of her daughter's enemy was unbounded, came over to Char-
lottenburg to join in the fray. Bismarck, over
his pipe and lager, snorted out his alarm. The
Queen of England's object, he said, was clearly

political—she wished to estrange Germany and
Russia—and very likely she would have her way.
"In family matters," he added, "she is not used
to contradiction"; she would "bring the parson
with her in her travelling bag and the bridegroom
in her trunk, and the marriage would come off on
the spot." But the man of blood and iron was not
to be thwarted so easily, and he asked for a private
interview with the Queen. The details of their
conversation are unknown; but it is certain that
in the course of it Victoria was forced to realise
the meaning of resistance to that formidable personage, and that she promised to use all her influence to prevent the marriage. The engagement
was broken off; and in the following year Prince
Alexander of Battenberg united himself to Fräulein Loisinger, an actress at the court theatre of
Darmstadt.[1]

But such painful incidents were rare. Victoria
was growing very old; with no Albert to guide
her, with no Beaconsfield to enflame her, she was
willing enough to abandon the dangerous questions of diplomacy to the wisdom of Lord Salisbury, and to concentrate her energies upon objects
which touched her more nearly and over which she
could exercise an undisputed control. Her home

[1] Grant Robertson, 458–9; Busch, III, 174–88; Lee, 490–2.

—her court—the monuments at Balmoral—the livestock at Windsor—the organisation of her engagements—the supervision of the multitudinous details of her daily routine—such matters played now an even greater part in her existence than before. Her life passed in an extraordinary exactitude. Every moment of her day was mapped out beforehand; the succession of her engagements was immutably fixed; the dates of her journeys— to Osborne, to Balmoral, to the South of France, to Windsor, to London—were hardly altered from year to year. She demanded from those who surrounded her a rigid precision in details, and she was preternaturally quick in detecting the slightest deviation from the rules which she had laid down. Such was the irresistible potency of her personality, that anything but the most implicit obedience to her wishes was felt to be impossible; but sometimes somebody was unpunctual; and unpunctuality was one of the most heinous of sins. Then her displeasure—her dreadful displeasure— became all too visible. At such moments there seemed nothing surprising in her having been the daughter of a martinet.[1]

But these storms, unnerving as they were while they lasted, were quickly over, and they grew

[1] *Quarterly Review*, cxciii, 305–6; 308–10.

more and more exceptional. With the return of
happiness a gentle benignity flowed from the aged
Queen. Her smile, once so rare a visitant to those
saddened features, flitted over them with an easy
alacrity; the blue eyes beamed; the whole face,
starting suddenly from its pendulous expression-
lessness, brightened and softened and cast over
those who watched it an unforgettable charm.
For in her last years there was a fascination in
Victoria's amiability which had been lacking even
from the vivid impulse of her youth. Over all
who approached her—or very nearly all—she
threw a peculiar spell. Her grandchildren adored
her; her ladies waited upon her with a reverential
love. The honour of serving her obliterated a
thousand inconveniences—the monotony of a court
existence, the fatigue of standing, the necessity for
a superhuman attentiveness to the minutiæ of time
and space. As one did one's wonderful duty one
could forget that one's legs were aching from the
infinitude of the passages at Windsor, or that
one's bare arms were turning blue in the Balmoral
cold.

What, above all, seemed to make such service
delightful was the detailed interest which the
Queen took in the circumstances of those around
her. Her absorbing passion for the comfortable

commonplaces, the small crises, the recurrent sen-
timentalities, of domestic life constantly demanded
wider fields for its activity; the sphere of her own
family, vast as it was, was not enough; she became the eager confidante of the household affairs
of her ladies; her sympathies reached out to the
palace domestics; even the housemaids and scul-
lions—so it appeared—were the objects of her
searching inquiries, and of her heartfelt solicitude
when their lovers were ordered to a foreign station, or their aunts suffered from an attack of
rheumatism which was more than usually acute.[1]

Nevertheless the due distinctions of rank were
immaculately preserved. The Queen's mere presence was enough to ensure that; but, in addition,
the dominion of court etiquette was paramount.
For that elaborate code, which had kept Lord
Melbourne stiff upon the sofa and ranged the
other guests in silence about the round table according to the order of precedence, was as punctiliously enforced as ever. Every evening after
dinner, the hearth-rug, sacred to royalty, loomed
before the profane in inaccessible glory, or, on
one or two terrific occasions, actually lured them
magnetically forward to the very edge of the

---

[1] *Quarterly Review*, cxciii, 315–6; Miss Ethel Smyth, *London
Mercury*. November, 1920; private information.

abyss. The Queen, at the fitting moment, moved towards her guests; one after the other they were led up to her; and, while dualogue followed dualogue in constraint and embarrassment, the rest of the assembly stood still, without a word.[1] Only in one particular was the severity of the etiquette allowed to lapse. Throughout the greater part of the reign the rule that ministers must stand during their audiences with the Queen had been absolute. When Lord Derby, the Prime Minister, had an audience of Her Majesty after a serious illness, he mentioned it afterwards, as a proof of the royal favour, that the Queen had remarked " How sorry she was she could not ask him to be seated." Subsequently, Disraeli, after an attack of gout and in a moment of extreme expansion on the part of Victoria, had been offered a chair; but he had thought it wise humbly to decline the privilege. In her later years, however, the Queen invariably asked Mr. Gladstone and Lord Salisbury to sit down.[2]

Sometimes the solemnity of the evening was diversified by a concert, an opera, or even a play. One of the most marked indications of Victoria's enfranchisement from the thraldom of widowhood

[1] *Quarterly Review,* cxciii, 325; Miss Ethel Smyth, *London Mercury,* November, 1920.

[2] Buckle, V, 339; Morley, III, 347, 514.

had been her resumption—after an interval of
thirty years—of the custom of commanding dra-
matic companies from London to perform before
the Court at Windsor. On such occasions her
spirits rose high. She loved acting; she loved a
good plot; above all, she loved a farce. Engrossed
by everything that passed upon the stage she
would follow, with childlike innocence, the un-
winding of the story; or she would assume an
air of knowing superiority and exclaim in triumph,
"There! You didn't expect *that,* did you?"
when the *dénouement* came. Her sense of humour was of a vigorous though primitive kind.
She had been one of the very few persons who
had always been able to appreciate the Prince
Consort's jokes; and, when those were cracked
no more, she could still roar with laughter, in
the privacy of her household, over some small
piece of fun—some oddity of an ambassador, or
some ignorant Minister's *faux pas.* When the
jest grew subtle she was less pleased; but, if it
approached the confines of the indecorous, the danger was serious. To take a liberty called down
at once Her Majesty's most crushing disapproba-
tion; and to say something improper was to take
the greatest liberty of all. Then the royal lips
sank down at the corners, the royal eyes stared

in astonished protrusion, and in fact the royal
countenance became inauspicious in the highest
degree. The transgressor shuddered into silence,
while the awful " We are not amused " annihilated
the dinner table. Afterwards, in her private en-
tourage, the Queen would observe that the person
in question was, she very much feared, " not discreet "; it was a verdict from which there was no
appeal.[1]

In general, her æsthetic tastes had remained
unchanged since the days of Mendelssohn, Landseer, and Lablache. She still delighted in the
roulades of Italian opera; she still demanded a
high standard in the execution of a pianoforte
duet. Her views on painting were decided; Sir
Edwin, she declared, was perfect; she was much
impressed by Lord Leighton's manners; and she
profoundly distrusted Mr. Watts. From time
to time she ordered engraved portraits to be taken
of members of the royal family; on these occasions she would have the first proofs submitted to
her, and, having inspected them with minute par-
ticularity, she would point out their mistakes to
the artists, indicating at the same time how they
might be corrected. The artists invariably dis-

---

[1] *Quarterly Review*, vol. 193, pp. 315, 316-7, 324-5, 326; *Spinster
Lady*, 268-9; Lee, 504-5.

covered that Her Majesty's suggestions were of
the highest value. In literature her interests were
more restricted. She was devoted to Lord Tennyson; and, as the Prince Consort had admired
George Eliot, she perused "Middlemarch": she
was disappointed. There is reason to believe,
however, that the romances of another female
writer, whose popularity among the humbler
classes of Her Majesty's subjects was at one
time enormous, secured, no less, the approval of
Her Majesty. Otherwise she did not read very
much.[1]

Once, however, the Queen's attention was drawn
to a publication which it was impossible for her
to ignore. "The Greville Memoirs," filled with a
mass of historical information of extraordinary
importance, but filled also with descriptions, which
were by no means flattering, of George IV,
William IV, and other royal persons, was brought
out by Mr. Reeve. Victoria read the book, and
was appalled. It was, she declared, a "dreadful
and really scandalous book," and she could not
say "how *horrified* and *indignant*" she was at
Greville's "indiscretion, indelicacy, ingratitude
towards friends, betrayal of confidence and shame-

[1] *Quarterly Review,* vol. 193, pp. 322–4; Martin, *Queen Victoria,*
46–9; private information.

ful disloyalty towards his Sovereign." She wrote
to Disraeli to tell him that in her opinion it was
"*very important* that the book should be severely
censured and discredited." " The tone in which
he speaks of royalty," she added, " is unlike anything one sees in history even, and is most repre-
hensible." Her anger was directed with almost
equal vehemence against Mr. Reeve for his having published " such an abominable book," and
she charged Sir Arthur Helps to convey to him
her deep displeasure. Mr. Reeve, however, was
impenitent. When Sir Arthur told him that, in
the Queen's opinion, " the book degraded royalty,"
he replied: " Not at all; it elevates it by the contrast it offers between the present and the defunct
state of affairs." But this adroit defence failed
to make any impression upon Victoria; and Mr.
Reeve, when he retired from the public service,
did not receive the knighthood which custom entitled him to expect.[1] Perhaps if the Queen had
known how many caustic comments upon herself
Mr. Reeve had quietly suppressed in the published
Memoirs, she would have been almost grateful to
him; but, in that case, what would she have said
of Greville? Imagination boggles at the thought.
As for more modern essays upon the same topic,

[1] Buckle, V, 349–51; Laughton, II, 226.

Her Majesty, it is to be feared, would have characterised them as " not discreet."

But as a rule the leisure hours of that active life were occupied with recreations of a less intangible quality than the study of literature or the appreciation of art. Victoria was a woman not only of vast property but of innumerable possessions. She had inherited an immense quantity of furniture, of ornaments, of china, of plate, of valuable objects of every kind; her purchases, throughout a long life, made a formidable addition to these stores; and there flowed in upon her, besides, from every quarter of the globe, a constant stream of gifts. Over this enormous mass she exercised an unceasing and minute supervision, and the arrangement and the contemplation of it, in all its details, filled her with an intimate satisfaction. The collecting instinct has its roots in the very depths of human nature; and, in the case of Victoria, it seemed to owe its force to two of her dominating impulses—the intense sense, which had always been hers, of her own personality, and the craving which, growing with the years, had become in her old age almost an obsession, for fixity, for solidity, for the setting up of palpable barriers against the outrages of change and time. When she considered the multitudinous objects which belonged to her, or, better still, when, choosing out some section of them as the fancy took her, she actually savoured the vivid richness of their individual qualities, she saw herself deliciously reflected from a million facets, felt herself magnified miraculously over a boundless area, and was well pleased. That was just as it should be; but then came the dismaying thought—everything slips away, crumbles, vanishes; Sèvres dinner-services get broken; even golden basins go unaccountably astray; even one's self, with all the recollections and experiences that make up one's being, fluctuates, perishes, dissolves . . . But no! It could not, should not be so! There should be no changes and no losses! Nothing should ever move—neither the past nor the present—and she herself least of all! And so the tenacious woman, hoarding her valuables, decreed their immortality with all the resolution of her soul. She would not lose one memory or one pin.

She gave orders that nothing should be thrown away—and nothing was. There, in drawer after drawer, in wardrobe after wardrobe, reposed the dresses of seventy years. But not only the dresses —the furs and the mantles and subsidiary frills and the muffs and the parasols and the bonnets—

all were ranged in chronological order, dated and complete. A great cupboard was devoted to the dolls; in the china room at Windsor a special table held the mugs of her childhood, and her children's mugs as well. Mementoes of the past surrounded her in serried accumulations. In every room the tables were powdered thick with the photographs of relatives; their portraits, revealing them at all ages, covered the walls; their figures, in solid marble, rose up from pedestals, or gleamed from brackets in the form of gold and silver statuettes. The dead, in every shape—in miniatures, in porcelain, in enormous life-size oil-paintings—were perpetually about her. John Brown stood upon her writing-table in solid gold. Her favourite horses and dogs, endowed with a new durability, crowded round her footsteps. Sharp, in silver gilt, dominated the dinner table; Boy and Boz lay together among unfading flowers, in bronze. And it was not enough that each particle of the past should be given the stability of metal or of marble: the whole collection, in its arrangement, no less than its entity, should be immutably fixed. There might be additions, but there might never be alterations. No chintz might change, no carpet, no curtain, be replaced by another; or, if long use at last made it necessary,

the stuffs and the patterns must be so identically
reproduced that the keenest eye might not detect
the difference.   No new picture could be hung
upon the walls at Windsor, for those already there
had been put in their places by Albert, whose decisions were eternal.   So, indeed, were Victoria's.
To ensure that they should be the aid of the
camera was called in.   Every single article in the
Queen's possession was photographed from several
points of view.   These photographs were submitted to Her Majesty, and when, after careful
inspection, she had approved of them, they were
placed in a series of albums, richly bound.   Then,
opposite each photograph, an entry was made, indicating the number of the article, the number of
the room in which it was kept, its exact position
in the room and all its principal characteristics.
The fate of every object which had undergone
this process was henceforth irrevocably sealed.
The whole multitude, once and for all, took up
its steadfast station.   And Victoria, with a gigantic volume or two of the endless catalogue always
beside her, to look through, to ponder upon, to
expatiate over, could feel, with a double contentment, that the transitoriness of this world had
been arrested by the amplitude of her might.[1]

[1] *Private Life*, 13, 66, 69, 70–1, 151, 182.

Thus the collection, ever multiplying, ever en-
croaching upon new fields of consciousness, ever
rooting itself more firmly in the depths of instinct,
became one of the dominating influences of that
strange existence. It was a collection not merely
of things and of thoughts, but of states of mind
and ways of living as well. The celebration of
anniversaries grew to be an important branch of
it—of birthdays and marriage days and death
days, each of which demanded its appropriate
feeling, which, in its turn, must be itself expressed
in an appropriate outward form. And the form,
of course—the ceremony of rejoicing or lamenta-
tion—was stereotyped with the rest: it was part
of the collection. On a certain day, for instance,
flowers must be strewn on John Brown's monument at Balmoral; and the date of the yearly
departure for Scotland was fixed by that fact.
Inevitably it was around the central circumstance
of death—death, the final witness to human muta-
bility—that these commemorative cravings clustered most thickly. Might not even death itself
be humbled, if one could recall enough?—if one
asserted, with a sufficiently passionate and reiterated emphasis, the eternity of love? Accordingly,
every bed in which Victoria slept had attached to
it, at the back, on the right-hand side, above the

pillow, a photograph of the head and shoulders of Albert as he lay dead, surmounted by a wreath of immortelles.[1] At Balmoral, where memories came crowding so closely, the solid signs of memory appeared in surprising profusion. Obelisks, pyramids, tombs, statues, cairns, and seats of inscribed granite, proclaimed Victoria's dedication to the dead. There, twice a year, on the days that followed her arrival, a solemn pilgrimage of inspection and meditation was performed. There, on August 26—Albert's birthday—at the foot of the bronze statue of him in Highland dress, the Queen, her family, her Court, her servants, and her tenantry, met together and in silence drank to the memory of the dead. In England the tokens of remembrance pullulated hardly less. Not a day passed without some addition to the multifold assemblage—a gold statuette of Ross, the piper—a life-sized marble group of Victoria and Albert, in medieval costume, inscribed upon the base with the words: " Allured to brighter worlds and led the way "—a granite slab in the shrubbery at Osborne, informing the visitor of " Waldmann: the very favourite little dachshund of Queen Victoria; who brought him from Baden, April 1872; died, July 11, 1881." [2]

[1] *Private Life*, 19.   [2] *Ibid.*, 207, 212.

At Frogmore, the great mausoleum, perpetually enriched, was visited almost daily by the Queen when the Court was at Windsor.[1] But there was another, a more secret and a hardly less holy shrine. The suite of rooms which Albert had occupied in the Castle was kept for ever shut away from the eyes of any save the most privileged. Within those precincts everything remained as it had been at the Prince's death; but the mysterious preoccupation of Victoria had commanded that her husband's clothing should be laid afresh, each evening, upon the bed, and that, each evening, the water should be set ready in the basin, as if he were still alive; and this incredible rite was performed with scrupulous regularity for nearly forty years.[2]

Such was the inner worship; and still the flesh obeyed the spirit; still the daily hours of labour proclaimed Victoria's consecration to duty and to the ideal of the dead. Yet, with the years, the sense of self-sacrifice faded; the natural energies of that ardent being discharged themselves with satisfaction into the channel of public work; the love of business which, from her girlhood, had been strong within her, reasserted itself in all its vigour, and, in her old age, to have been cut off from her

[1] *Private Life*, 233.   [2] Private information.

papers and her boxes would have been, not a relief, but an agony to Victoria. Thus, though
toiling Ministers might sigh and suffer, the whole
process of government continued, till the very end,
to pass before her. Nor was that all; ancient
precedent had made the validity of an enormous
number of official transactions dependent upon the
application of the royal sign-manual; and a great
proportion of the Queen's working hours was
spent in this mechanical task. Nor did she show
any desire to diminish it. On the contrary, she
voluntarily resumed the duty of signing commissions in the army, from which she had been set
free by Act of Parliament, and from which, during the years of middle life, she had abstained. In
no case would she countenance the proposal that
she should use a stamp. But, at last, when the
increasing pressure of business made the delays of
the antiquated system intolerable, she consented
that, for certain classes of documents, her oral
sanction should be sufficient. Each paper was
read aloud to her, and she said at the end " Approved." Often, for hours at a time, she would
sit, with Albert's bust in front of her, while the
word " Approved " issued at intervals from her
lips. The word came forth with a majestic sono-
rity; for her voice now—how changed from the

silvery treble of her girlhood!—was a contralto, full and strong.[1]

IV

The final years were years of apotheosis. In the dazzled imagination of her subjects Victoria soared aloft towards the regions of divinity through a nimbus of purest glory. Criticism fell dumb; deficiencies which, twenty years earlier, would have been universally admitted, were now as universally ignored. That the nation's idol was a very incomplete representative of the nation was a circumstance that was hardly noticed, and yet it was conspicuously true. For the vast changes which, out of the England of 1837, had produced the England of 1897, seemed scarcely to have touched the Queen. The immense industrial development of the period, the significance of which had been so thoroughly understood by Albert, meant little indeed to Victoria. The amazing scientific movement, which Albert had appreciated no less, left Victoria perfectly cold. Her conception of the universe, and of man's place in it, and of the stupendous problems of nature and philosophy remained, throughout her life, entirely unchanged. Her religion was the religion which she had learnt

[1] Lee, 514–5; Crawford, 362–3.

from the Baroness Lehzen and the Duchess of
Kent. Here, too, it might have been supposed
that Albert's views might have influenced her.
For Albert, in matters of religion, was advanced.
Disbelieving altogether in evil spirits, he had had
his doubts about the miracle of the Gaderene
Swine.[1] Stockmar, even, had thrown out, in a
remarkable memorandum on the education of the
Prince of Wales, the suggestion that while the
child " must unquestionably be brought up in the
creed of the Church of England," it might nevertheless be in accordance with the spirit of the
times to exclude from his religious training the
inculcation of a belief in " the supernatural doctrines of Christianity." [2] This, however, would
have been going too far; and all the royal children
were brought up in complete orthodoxy. Anything else would have grieved Victoria, though her
own conceptions of the orthodox were not very
precise. But her nature, in which imagination
and subtlety held so small a place, made her in-
stinctively recoil from the intricate ecstasies of
High Anglicanism; and she seemed to feel most at
home in the simple faith of the Presbyterian
Church of Scotland.[3] This was what might have

[1] Wilberforce, Samuel, II, 275.
[2] Martin, II, 185–7.
[3] *Quarterly Review,* vol. 193, pp. 319–20.

been expected; for Lehzen was the daughter of a
Lutheran pastor, and the Lutherans and the Pres-
byterians have much in common.   For many years
Dr. Norman Macleod, an innocent Scotch minister, was her principal spiritual adviser; and,
when he was taken from her, she drew much comfort from quiet chats about life and death with the
cottagers at Balmoral.[1] Her piety, absolutely
genuine, found what it wanted in the sober ex-
hortations of old John Grant and the devout saws
of Mrs. P. Farquharson.   They possessed the
qualities, which, as a child of fourteen, she had so
sincerely admired in the Bishop of Chester's " Exposition of the Gospel of St. Matthew "; they
were " just plain and comprehensible and full of
truth and good feeling."   The Queen, who gave
her name to the Age of Mill and of Darwin,
never got any further than that.

From the social movements of her time Victoria
was equally remote.   Towards the smallest no less
than towards the greatest changes she remained
inflexible.   During her youth and middle age
smoking had been forbidden in polite society, and
so long as she lived she would not withdraw her
anathema against it.   Kings might protest; bishops
and ambassadors, invited to Windsor, might be re-

[1] Crawford, 349.

duced, in the privacy of their bedrooms, to lie full-length upon the floor and smoke up the chimney—the interdict continued.[1] It might have been supposed that a female sovereign would have lent her countenance to one of the most vital of all the reforms to which her epoch gave birth—the emancipation of women—but, on the contrary, the mere mention of such a proposal sent the blood rushing to her head. In 1870, her eye having fallen upon the report of a meeting in favour of Women's Suffrage, she wrote to Mr. Martin in royal rage—" The Queen is most anxious to enlist everyone who can speak or write to join in checking this mad, wicked folly of ' Woman's Rights,' with all its attendant horrors, on which her poor feeble sex is bent, forgetting every sense of womanly feeling and propriety. Lady —— ought to get a *good whipping*. It is a subject which makes the Queen so furious that she cannot contain herself. God created men and women different—then let them remain each in their own position. Tennyson has some beautiful lines on the difference of men and women in ' The Princess.' Woman would become the most hateful, heartless, and disgusting of human beings were she allowed to unsex herself; and where would be the

[1] Eckardstein, I, 177.

protection which man was intended to give the weaker sex? The Queen is sure that Mrs. Martin agrees with her." [1] The argument was irrefutable; Mrs. Martin agreed; and yet the canker spread.

In another direction Victoria's comprehension of the spirit of her age has been constantly asserted. It was for long the custom for courtly historians and polite politicians to compliment the Queen upon the correctness of her attitude towards the Constitution. But such praises seem hardly to be justified by the facts. In her later years Victoria more than once alluded with regret to her conduct during the Bedchamber crisis, and let it be understood that she had grown wiser since.[2] Yet in truth it is difficult to trace any fundamental change either in her theory or her practice in constitutional matters throughout her life. The same despotic and personal spirit which led her to break off the negotiations with Peel is equally visible in her animosity towards Palmerston, in her threats of abdication to Disraeli, and in her desire to prosecute the Duke of Westminster for attending a meeting upon Bulgarian atrocities. The complex and delicate principles of the Constitution cannot be said to have come within the

[1] Martin, *Queen Victoria*, 69–70.
[2] *Girlhood*, II, 142.

compass of her mental faculties; and in the actual
developments which it underwent during her reign
she played a passive part. From 1840 to 1861
the power of the Crown steadily increased in England; from 1861 to 1901 it steadily declined. The
first process was due to the influence of the Prince
Consort, the second to that of a series of great
Ministers. During the first Victoria was in effect
a mere accessory; during the second the threads
of power, which Albert had so laboriously collected,
inevitably fell from her hands into the vigorous grasp of Mr. Gladstone, Lord Beaconsfield,
and Lord Salisbury. Perhaps, absorbed as she
was in routine, and difficult as she found it to distinguish at all clearly between the trivial and the
essential, she was only dimly aware of what was
happening. Yet, at the end of her reign, the
Crown was weaker than at any other time in English history. Paradoxically enough, Victoria received the highest eulogiums for assenting to a
political evolution, which, had she completely realised its import, would have filled her with supreme
displeasure.

Nevertheless it must not be supposed that she
was a second George III. Her desire to impose
her will, vehement as it was, and unlimited by any
principle, was yet checked by a certain shrewd-

ness. She might oppose her Ministers with extraordinary violence; she might remain utterly impervious to arguments and supplications; the pertinacity of her resolution might seem to be unconquerable; but, at the very last moment of all, her obstinacy would give way. Her innate respect and capacity for business, and perhaps, too, the memory of Albert's scrupulous avoidance of extreme courses, prevented her from ever entering an *impasse*. By instinct she understood when the facts were too much for her, and to them she invariably yielded. After all, what else could she do?

But if, in all these ways, the Queen and her epoch were profoundly separated, the points of contact between them also were not few. Victoria understood very well the meaning and the attractions of power and property, and in such learning the English nation, too, had grown to be more and more proficient. During the last fifteen years of the reign—for the short Liberal Administration of 1892 was a mere interlude—imperialism was the dominant creed of the country. It was Victoria's as well. In this direction, if in no other, she had allowed her mind to develop. Under Disraeli's tutelage the British Dominions over the seas had come to mean much more to her than ever before, and, in particular, she had grown enamoured of the East. The thought of India fascinated her; she set to, and learnt a little Hindustani; she engaged some Indian servants, who became her inseparable attendants, and one of whom, Munshi Abdul Karim, eventually almost succeeded to the position which had once been John Brown's.[1] At the same time, the imperialist temper of the nation invested her office with a new significance exactly harmonising with her own inmost proclivities. The English polity was in the main a common-sense structure; but there was always a corner in it where common-sense could not enter—where, somehow or other, the ordinary measurements were not applicable and the ordinary rules did not apply. So our ancestors had laid it down, giving scope, in their wisdom, to that mystical element which, as it seems, can never quite be eradicated from the affairs of men. Naturally it was in the Crown that the mysticism of the English polity was concentrated—the Crown, with its venerable antiquity, its sacred associations, its imposing spectacular array. But, for nearly two centuries, common-sense had been predominant in the great building, and the little, unexplored, inexplicable corner had attracted small attention.

[1] Lee, 485; private information.

Then, with the rise of imperialism, there was a change. For imperialism is a faith as well as a business; as it grew, the mysticism in English public life grew with it; and simultaneously a new importance began to attach to the Crown. The need for a symbol—a symbol of England's might, of England's worth, of England's extraordinary and mysterious destiny—became felt more urgently than ever before. The Crown was that symbol: and the Crown rested upon the head of Victoria. Thus it happened that while by the end of the reign the power of the sovereign had appreciably diminished, the prestige of the sovereign had enormously grown.

Yet this prestige was not merely the outcome of public changes; it was an intensely personal matter, too. Victoria was the Queen of England, the Empress of India, the quintessential pivot round which the whole magnificent machine was revolving—but how much more besides! For one thing, she was of a great age—an almost indispensable qualification for popularity in England. She had given proof of one of the most admired characteristics of the race—persistent vitality. She had reigned for sixty years, and she was not out. And then, she was a character. The outlines of her nature were firmly drawn, and, even

through the mists which envelop royalty, clearly
visible. In the popular imagination her familiar
figure filled, with satisfying ease, a distinct and
memorable place. It was, besides, the kind of
figure which naturally called forth the admiring
sympathy of the great majority of the nation.
Goodness they prized above every other human
quality; and Victoria, who had said that she
would be good at the age of twelve, had kept
her word. Duty, conscience, morality—yes! in the
light of those high beacons the Queen had always
lived. She had passed her days in work and not
in pleasure—in public responsibilities and family
cares. The standard of solid virtue which had
been set up so long ago amid the domestic happiness of Osborne had never been lowered for an
instant. For more than half a century no divorced lady had approached the precincts of the
Court. Victoria, indeed, in her enthusiasm for
wifely fidelity, had laid down a still stricter ordi-
nance: she frowned severely upon any widow
who married again.[1] Considering that she herself
was the offspring of a widow's second marriage,
this prohibition might be regarded as an eccentricity; but, no doubt, it was an eccentricity on
the right side. The middle classes, firm in the

[1] Lee, 555.

triple brass of their respectability, rejoiced with a special joy over the most respectable of Queens. They almost claimed her, indeed, as one of themselves; but this would have been an exaggeration. For, though many of her characteristics were most often found among the middle classes, in other respects—in her manners, for instance—Victoria was decidedly aristocratic. And, in one important particular, she was neither aristocratic nor middle-class: her attitude toward herself was simply regal.

Such qualities were obvious and important; but, in the impact of a personality, it is something deeper, something fundamental and common to all its qualities, that really tells. In Victoria, it is easy to discern the nature of this underlying element: it was a peculiar sincerity. Her truthfulness, her single-mindedness, the vividness of her emotions and her unrestrained expression of them, were the varied forms which this central characteristic assumed. It was her sincerity which gave her at once her impressiveness, her charm, and her absurdity. She moved through life with the imposing certitude of one to whom concealment was impossible—either towards her surroundings or towards herself. There she was, all of her—the Queen of England, complete and ob-

vious; the world might take her or leave her; she
had nothing more to show, or to explain, or to
modify; and, with her peerless carriage, she swept
along her path. And not only was concealment
out of the question; reticence, reserve, even dignity itself, as it sometimes seemed, might be very
well dispensed with. As Lady Lyttelton said:
" There is a transparency in her truth that is
very striking—not a shade of exaggeration in describing feelings or facts; like very few other
people I ever knew. Many may be as true, but I
think it goes often along with some reserve. She
talks all out; just as it is, no more and no less." [1]
She talked all out; and she wrote all out, too.
Her letters, in the surprising jet of their expression, remind one of a turned-on tap. What is
within pours forth in an immediate, spontaneous
rush. Her utterly unliterary style has at least the
merit of being a vehicle exactly suited to her
thoughts and feelings; and even the platitude of
her phraseology carries with it a curiously personal flavour. Undoubtedly it was through her
writings that she touched the heart of the public.
Not only in her " Highland Journals," where
the mild chronicle of her private proceedings was
laid bare without a trace either of affectation or

[1] Lyttelton, 331.

of embarrassment, but also in those remarkable messages to the nation which, from time to time, she published in the newspapers, her people found her very close to them indeed. They felt in-stinctively Victoria's irresistible sincerity, and they responded. And in truth it was an endearing trait.

The personality and the position, too—the won-derful combination of them—that, perhaps, was what was finally fascinating in the case. The little old lady, with her white hair and her plain mourn-ing clothes, in her wheeled chair or her donkey-carriage—one saw her so; and then—close be-hind—with their immediate suggestion of singu-larity, of mystery, and of power—the Indian servants. That was the familiar vision, and it was admirable; but, at chosen moments, it was right that the widow of Windsor should step forth apparent Queen. The last and the most glorious of such occasions was the Jubilee of 1897. Then, as the splendid procession passed along, escorting Victoria through the thronged re-echoing streets of London on her progress of thanksgiving to St. Paul's Cathedral, the greatness of her realm and the adoration of her subjects blazed out together. The tears welled to her eyes, and, while the multi-tude roared round her, "How kind they are to me! How kind they are!" she repeated over and over again.[1] That night her message flew over the Empire: "From my heart I thank my beloved people. May God bless them!" The long journey was nearly done. But the traveller, who had come so far, and through such strange experiences, moved on with the old unfaltering step. The girl, the wife, the aged woman, were the same: vitality, conscientiousness, pride, and simplicity were hers to the latest hour.

[1] *Quarterly Review,* vol. 193, p. 310.

CHAPTER X

THE END

THE evening had been golden; but, after all, the day was to close in cloud and tempest. Imperial needs, imperial ambitions, involved the country in the South African War. There were checks, reverses, bloody disasters; for a moment the nation was shaken, and the public distresses were felt with intimate solicitude by the Queen. But her spirit was high, and neither her courage nor her confidence wavered for a moment. Throwing herself heart and soul into the struggle, she laboured with redoubled vigour, interested herself in every detail of the hostilities, and sought by every means in her power to render service to the national cause. In April 1900, when she was in her eighty-first year, she made the extraordinary decision to abandon her annual visit to the South of France, and to go instead to Ireland, which had provided a particularly large number of recruits to the armies in the field. She stayed for three weeks in Dublin, driving through the streets, in spite of the warnings of her advisers, without an armed escort:

and the visit was a complete success But, in the course of it, she began, for the first time, to show signs of the fatigue of age.[1]

For the long strain and the unceasing anxiety, brought by the war, made themselves felt at last. Endowed by nature with a robust constitution, Victoria, though in periods of depression she had sometimes supposed herself an invalid, had in reality throughout her life enjoyed remarkably good health. In her old age, she had suffered from a rheumatic stiffness of the joints, which had necessitated the use of a stick, and, eventually, a wheeled chair; but no other ailments attacked her, until, in 1898, her eyesight began to be affected by incipient cataract. After that, she found reading more and more difficult, though she could still sign her name, and even, with some difficulty, write letters. In the summer of 1900, however, more serious symptoms appeared. Her memory, in whose strength and precision she had so long prided herself, now sometimes deserted her; there was a tendency towards aphasia; and, while no specific disease declared itself, by the autumn there were unmistakable signs of a general physical decay. Yet, even in these last months, the strain of iron held firm. The daily work continued;

[1] *Quarterly Review*, vol. 193, pp. 318, 336-7.

nay, it actually increased; for the Queen, with an astonishing pertinacity, insisted upon communicating personally with an ever-growing multitude of men and women who had suffered through the war.[1]

By the end of the year the last remains of her ebbing strength had almost deserted her; and through the early days of the opening century it was clear that her dwindling forces were only kept together by an effort of will. On January 14, she had at Osborne an hour's interview with Lord Roberts, who had returned victorious from South Africa a few days before. She inquired with acute anxiety into all the details of the war; she appeared to sustain the exertion successfully; but, when the audience was over, there was a collapse. On the following day her medical attendants recognised that her state was hopeless; and yet, for two days more, the indomitable spirit fought on; for two days more she discharged the duties of a Queen of England. But after that there was an end of working; and then, and not till then, did the last optimism of those about her break down. The brain was failing, and life was gently slipping away. Her family gathered round her; for a little more she lingered, speechless and ap-

[1] Lee. 536–7; private information.

parently insensible; and, on January 22, 1901, she died.[1]

When, two days previously, the news of the approaching end had been made public, astonished grief had swept over the country. It appeared as if some monstrous reversal of the course of nature was about to take place. The vast majority of her subjects had never known a time when Queen Victoria had not been reigning over them. She had become an indissoluble part of their whole scheme of things, and that they were about to lose her appeared a scarcely possible thought. She herself, as she lay blind and silent, seemed to those who watched her to be divested of all thinking—to have glided already, unawares, into oblivion. Yet, perhaps, in the secret chambers of consciousness, she had her thoughts, too. Perhaps her fading mind called up once more the shadows of the past to float before it, and retraced, for the last time, the vanished visions of that long history—passing back and back, through the cloud of years, to older and ever older memories—to the spring woods at Osborne, so full of primroses for Lord Beaconsfield—to Lord Palmerston's queer clothes and high demeanour, and Albert's face under the green lamp, and

[1] Lee, 537-9; *Quarterly Review*, cxciii, 309.

Albert's first stag at Balmoral, and Albert in his blue and silver uniform, and the Baron coming in through a doorway, and Lord M. dreaming at Windsor with the rooks cawing in the elm-trees, and the Archbishop of Canterbury on his knees in the dawn, and the old King's turkey-cock ejaculations, and Uncle Leopold's soft voice at Claremont, and Lehzen with the globes, and her mother's feathers sweeping down towards her, and a great old repeater-watch of her father's in its tortoise-shell case, and a yellow rug, and some friendly flounces of sprigged muslin, and the trees and the grass at Kensington.

BIBLIOGRAPHY

AND

LIST OF REFERENCES IN THE NOTES, ARRANGED
ALPHABETICALLY.

ADAMS. *The Education of Henry Adams: an autobiography.*
1918.

ASHLEY. *The Life and Correspondence of H. J. Temple,
Viscount Palmerston.* By A. E. M. Ashley. 2 vols.
1879.

BLOOMFIELD. *Reminiscences of Court and Diplomatic Life.*
By Georgiana, Lady Bloomfield. 2 vols. 1883.

BROUGHTON. *Recollections of a Long Life.* By Lord Broughton. Edited by Lady Dorchester. 6 vols. 1909-11.

BUCKLE. *The Life of Benjamin Disraeli, Earl of Beaconsfield.* By W. F. Monypenny and G. E. Buckle. 6 vols.
1910-20.

BULOW. *Gabriele von Bülow, 1791-1887.* Berlin. 1893.

BUNSEN. *A Memoir of Baron Bunsen.* By his widow,
Frances, Baroness Bunsen. 2 vols. 1868.

BUSCH. *Bismarck: some secret pages of hi. history.* By
Dr. Moritz Busch. (English translation.) 3 vols. 1898.

CHILDERS. *The Life and Correspondence of the Rt. Hon.
Hugh C. E. Childers.* 2 vols. 1901.

CLARENDON. *The Life and Letters of the Fourth Earl of
Clarendon.* By Sir Herbert Maxwell. 2 vols. 1913.

Cornhill Magazine, vol. 75.

CRAWFORD. *Victoria, Queen and Ruler.* By Emily Crawford.
1903.

CREEVEY. *The Creevey Papers.* Edited by Sir Herbert Maxwell. 2 vols. 1904.

CROKER. *The Croker Papers.* Edited by L. J. Jennings. 3
vols. 1884.

DAFFORNE. *The Albert Memorial: its history and description.*
By J. Dafforne. 1877.

DALLING. *The Life of H. J. Temple, Viscount Palmerston.*
By Lord Dalling. 3 vols. 1871-84.

Dictionary of National Biography.

DISRAELI. *Lord George Bentinck: a political biography.* By
B. Disraeli. 1852.

ECKARDSTEIN. *Lebens-Erinnerungen u. Politische Denkwürdigkeiten.* Von Freiherrn v. Eckardstein. 2 vols. Leip-
zig. 1919.

ERNEST. *Memoirs of Ernest II, Duke of Saxe-Coburg-Gotha.*
4 vols. 1888. (English translation.)

FITZMAURICE. *The Life of Earl Granville.* By Lord Fitzmaurice. 2 vols. 1905.

GASKELL. *The Life of Charlotte Brontë.* By Mrs. Gaskell,
2 vols. 1857.

GIRLHOOD. *The Girlhood of Queen Victoria.* Edited by Viscount Esher. 2 vols. 1912.

GOSSART. *Adolphe Quetelet et le Prince Albert de Saxe-
Cobourg.* Academie Royale de Belgique, Bruxelles.
1919.

GRANVILLE. *Letters of Harriet, Countess Granville.* 2 vols.
1894.

GREVILLE. *The Greville Memoirs.* 8 vols. (Silver Library
Edition.) 1896.

GREY. *Early Years of the Prince Consort.* By General
Charles Grey. 1867.

HALLE. *Life and Letters of Sir Charles Hallé.* Edited by
his Son. 1896.

HAMILTON. *Parliamentary Reminiscences and Reflections.*
By Lord George Hamilton. 1917.

HARE. *The Story of My Life.* By Augustus J. C. Hare. 6
vols. 1896-1900.

HAYDON. *Autobiography of Benjamin Robert Haydon.* 3
vols. 1853.

HAYWARD. *Sketches of Eminent Statesmen and Writers.* By A. Hayward. 2 vols. 1880.

HUISH. *The History of the Life and Reign of William the Fourth.* By Robert Huish. 1837.

HUNT. *The Old Court Suburb: or Memorials of Kensington, regal, critical, and anecdotal.* 2 vols. 1855.

JERROLD, EARLY COURT. *The Early Court of Queen Victoria.* By Clare Jerrold. 1912.

JERROLD, MARRIED LIFE. *The Married Life of Queen Victoria.* By Clare Jerrold. 1913.

JERROLD, WIDOWHOOD. *The Widowhood of Queen Victoria.* By Clare Jerrold. 1916.

KINGLAKE. *The Invasion of the Crimea.* By A. W. Kinglake. 9 vols. (Cabinet Edition.) 1877-88.

KNIGHT. *The Autobiography of Miss Cornelia Knight.* 2 vols. 1861.

LAUGHTON. *Memoirs of the Life and Correspondence of Henry Reeve.* By Sir John Laughton. 2 vols. 1898.

LEAVES. *Leaves from the Journal of our Life in the Highlands, from 1848 to 1861.* By Queen Victoria. Edited by A. Helps. 1868.

LEE. *Queen Victoria: a biography.* By Sidney Lee. 1902.

LESLIE. *Autobiographical Recollections by the late Charles Robert Leslie, R.A.* Edited by Tom Taylor. 2 vols. 1860.

LETTERS. *The Letters of Queen Victoria.* 3 vols. 1908.

LIEVEN. *Letters of Dorothea, Princess Lieven, during her residence in London, 1812-1834.* Edited by Lionel G. Robinson. 1902.

The London Mercury.

Lovely Albert! A Broadside.

LYTTELTON. *Correspondence of Sarah Spencer, Lady Lyttelton, 1787-1870.* Edited by Mrs. Hugh Wyndham. 1912.

MARTIN. *The Life of His Royal Highness the Prince Consort.* By Theodore Martin. 5 vols. 1875-80.

MARTIN, QUEEN VICTORIA. *Queen Victoria as I knew her.* By Sir Theodore Martin. 1908.

MARTINEAU. *The Autobiography of Harriet Martineau.* 3 vols. 1877.

MAXWELL. *The Hon. Sir Charles Murray, K.C.B.: a memoir.* By Sir Herbert Maxwell. 1898.

MORE LEAVES. *More Leaves from the Journal of a Life in the Highlands, from 1862 to 1882.* By Queen Victoria. 1884.

MORLEY. *The Life of William Ewart Gladstone.* By John Morley. 3 vols. 1903.

MURRAY. *Recollections from 1803 to 1837.* By the Hon. Amelia Murray. 1868.

NATIONAL MEMORIAL. *The National Memorial to H.R.H. the Prince Consort.* 1873.

NEELE. *Railway Reminiscences.* By George P. Neele. 1904.

OWEN. *The Life of Robert Owen,* written by himself. 1857.

OWEN, JOURNAL. *Owen's Rational Quarterly Review and Journal.*

PANAM. *A German Prince and his Victim.* Taken from the Memoirs of Madame Pauline Panam. 1915.

PRIVATE LIFE. *The Private Life of the Queen.* By One of Her Majesty's Servants. 1897.

The Quarterly Review, vols. 193 and 213.

ROBERTSON. *Bismarck.* By C. Grant Robertson 1918.

SCOTT. *Personal and Professional Recollections.* By Sir George Gilbert Scott. 1879.

SMITH. *Life of Her Majesty Queen Victoria.* Compiled from all available sources. By G. Barnett Smith. 1887.

SPINSTER LADY. *The Notebooks of a Spinster Lady.* 1919.

STEIN. *Denkschriften über Deutsche Verfassungen.* Herausgegeben von G. H. Pertz. 6 vols. 1848.

STOCKMAR. *Denkwürdigkeiten aus den Papieren des Freiherrn Christian Friedrich v. Stockmar,* zusammengestellt von Ernst Freiherr v. Stockmar. Braunschweig. 1872.

TAIT. *The Life of Archibald Campbell Tait, Archbishop of Canterbury.* 2 vols. 1891.

The London Times.

The Times LIFE. *The Life of Queen Victoria,* reproduced from *The London Times.* 1901.

TORRENS. *Memoirs of William Lamb, second Viscount Melbourne.* By W. M. Torrens. (Minerva Library Edition.) 1890.

VITZTHUM. *St. Petersburg und London in den Jahren* 1852-1864. Carl Friedrich Graf Vitzthum von Eckstädt. Stuttgart. 1886.

WALPOLE. *The Life of Lord John Russell.* By Sir Spencer Walpole. 2 vols. 1889.

WILBERFORCE, SAMUEL. *Life of Samuel Wilberforce, Bishop of Oxford.* By his son, R. G. Wilberforce. 3 vols. 1881.

WILBERFORCE, WILLIAM. *The Life of William Wilberforce.* 5 vols. 1838.

WYNN. *Diaries of a Lady of Quality.* By Miss Frances Williams Wynn. 1864.

INDEX

Aberdeen, Lord, Prime Minister, 240, 245, 276.

Adelaide, Queen, 69, 147.

Albert, Prince of Saxe-Coburg-Gotha, 51-53, 129 *et seq.;* appointed Regent, 161; biographies of, 313-318; birth and parentage, 134; growing power and influence, 167 *et seq.;* ignored by Palmerston, 207-208; last illness and death, 292-296; last years of, 253 *et seq.;* marriage to Queen Victoria, 152; memorials and monuments, 318-326; opposes Palmerston's policy, 220-235; plans " Great Exhibition," 196 *et seq.;* Private Secretary to the Queen, 187-188; references to, 385, 386, 402-406; remarkable triumph of, 202; reorganization of Royal household, 181-187; restored to popular favor, 252; tributes by British statesmen, 298-300; unpopular with upper classes, 204-206; violent outburst against, 241 *et seq;* visits to London, 51-53; 132-134.

Albert dock, opening of, 196.

Albert Memorial Hall, 320, 328.

Aldershot, 270, 352.

Alexander, Prince, 49.

Alexander, Prince of Battenberg, 383-389.

America, civil war in, 292-293.

Amorbach, 23, 30.

Anglo-Russian War, 359.

Anson, George, 148, 155, 166.

Arnold, Dr., 40.

Augustus, Prince, 1, 2, 50, 51.

Austria, 235-237, 311.

Balmoral Castle, 264-265, 277, 305, 357, 369, 390-391, 408;

life of Royal family at described, 265-268.

Balmoral House, 262.

Beaconsfield, Earl, *see Disraeli.*

Beaconsfield, Lady, 344.

Beards for British sailors, 333-334.

Bedford, Duke of, (footnote) 96.

Belgium, 21, 46, 106, 108.

Bismarck, 274, 309, 387, 388.

Brandon, Lady, 89.

Bronte, Charlotte, quoted, 176.

Brown, John, 371-375, 413.

Brougham, 2, 32-33.

Buckingham Palace, 75, 77, 79, 111, 173, 181-185, 378, 383.

Buggins, Lady Cecilia, 9.

Cadiz, Duke of, 213, 217.

Cambridge, Duke of, 8-9.

Canada, 10, 94-95, 226.

Canterbury, Archbishop of, 41, 67, 68, 100, 201.

Carleton House, 35.

Caroline, Lady, 84-85, 89.

Cavour, 276.

Charlotte, Princess, 1-6, 12, 21, 77, 176.

Chartism, 338.

Chester, Dean of, 44.

Claremont, 4, 5, 7, 45, 67.

Clarence, Duchess of, 25, 30, 31.

Clarence, Duke of, 8-9, 13, 15, 16; accession to the throne, 38; marriage of, 18.

Clarendon, Lord, 228, 240, 245, 298, 330.

Clarke, Sir James, 112, 113, 149, 151, 294.

" Coburg Trust," 214.

Colonial and Indian Exposition, 382.

Congress of Berlin, 364.

Congress of Vienna, 3, 327.